'A timely and fascinating exploration of how new virtual worlds expand, speed up and transform the wide range of cross-class, interlingual and inter-regional networks and relationships among queer men in India.'

Ruth Vanita, Professor, Liberal Studies and Humanities, University of Montana, USA, and author of *Love's Rite: Same-Sex Marriage in India and the West*

'In *Digital Queer Cultures in India*, Rohit Dasgupta examines the formation of contemporary middle-class Indian male queer subjectivities through language, class, intimacy and activism in both physical and virtual space. He combines his study of queer websites with fieldwork, employing the delightfully named methodology of "lurking", mostly in Kolkata. This study is important also for its reconsideration of the concept of a "queer community" in India, contextualising it among other social changes post-liberalisation. It will be of great interest to students of media and queer studies as well as to those involved in the wider study of sexuality and identity in today's India.'

Rachel Dwyer, Professor of Indian Cultures and Cinema, SOAS University of London, UK, and author of *Bollywood's India: Hindi Cinema as a Guide to Contemporary India*

'Dasgupta's groundbreaking interrogation of digital media usage in queer India identifies how and why the themes of nationality, class, gender and sexuality must always be central to the analysis of media engagement.'

Sharif Mowlabocus, Senior Lecturer of Media and Digital Media, University of Sussex, UK, and author of *Gaydar Culture: Gay Men, Technology and Embodiment in the Digital Age*

'This work by Rohit Dasgupta is very timely and necessary. It is a must-read for anyone in South Asian studies, digital culture studies, internet research, media studies, queer studies and many other interdisciplinary areas of research. The background and historical context for digital queer India are mapped in detail and clearly take us through the main theoretical frameworks, the media and social policy histories and the engagement of issues to do with LGBTQ populations in India.'

Radhika Gajjala, Professor of Media and Communication, Bowling Green State University, USA, and author of *Cyberselves: Feminist Ethnographies of South Asian Women*

T0383582

# Digital Queer Cultures in India

Sexuality in India offers an expression of nationalist anxieties and is a significant marker of modernity through which subjectivities are formed among the middle class. This book investigates the everyday experience of queer Indian men on digital spaces. It explores how queer identities are formed in virtual spaces and how the existence of such spaces challenge and critique 'Indian'-ness. It also looks at the role of class and intimacy within the discourse. This work argues that new media, social networking sites (SNSs), both web and mobile, and related technologies do not exist in isolation; rather they are critically embedded within other social spaces. Similarly, online queer spaces exist parallel to and in conjunction with the larger queer movement in the country.

This book will be of great interest to scholars and researchers of gender studies, especially men's and masculinity studies, queer and LGBT studies, media and cultural studies, particularly new media and digital culture, sexuality and identity, politics, sociology and social anthropology, and South Asian studies.

**Rohit K. Dasgupta** is Lecturer in Media and Creative Industries at Loughborough University, UK. He has previously lectured at the University of Southampton and University of the Arts, London. He is the co-editor of *Masculinity and Its Challenges in India* (2014) and *Rituparno Ghosh: Cinema, Gender and Art* (2015), and has published essays in journals such as *Convergence: International Journal of New Media Technologies*, *Digital Culture and Education*; *Economic and Political Weekly*, *Film Quarterly*, *International Journal of Fashion Studies*, *Theory, Culture and Society*, *South Asian History and Culture*; and *South Asian Review*.

# Digital Queer Cultures in India

Politics, Intimacies and Belonging

Rohit K. Dasgupta

Routledge
Taylor & Francis Group

LONDON AND NEW YORK

First published 2017 by Routledge

2 Park Square, Milton Park, Abingdon, Oxfordshire OX14 4RN
52 Vanderbilt Avenue, New York, NY 10017

*Routledge is an imprint of the Taylor & Francis Group, an informa business*

First issued in paperback 2019

*British Library Cataloguing-in-Publication Data*
A catalogue record for this book is available from the British Library

*Library of Congress Cataloging-in-Publication Data*
A catalog record for this book has been requested

ISBN: 978-1-138-22034-8 (hbk)
ISBN: 978-0-367-27988-2 (pbk)

Typeset in Galliard
by Apex CoVantage, LLC

# Contents

# Figures

# Acknowledgements

This book would not have been possible without the help and support of my research participants, who spent hours with me during my fieldwork in West Bengal and New Delhi. My main acknowledgement is to them.

I am thankful to the University of the Arts, London, for providing me with three years of funding for pursuing this research. I would also like to thank the Royal Society for Asian Affairs for awarding me the Sir Peter Holmes Memorial grant that helped fund a further field trip to India. Parts of this book have been presented as individual papers at several conferences: BSSN Conference at University of Sussex, 2012; MeCCSA Conference in 2013; QPPL2 Conference at Ohio State University, 2014 (OSU also awarded me a travel grant); IASSCS Conference, 2014, in Dublin; Queering Paradigms Conference at Canterbury Christ Church University, 2015; European Geographies of Sexualities Conference, 2015, in Rome; and the AAA Conference in Denver, 2015. Funding for the last four conferences was made available by Winchester School of Art, University of Southampton. Some chapters of this book have appeared in a different form in the following publications: 'Queer Sexuality: A Cultural Narrative of India's Historical Archive', *Rupkatha Journal of Interdisciplinary Studies in Humanities,* 3(4): 651–70, 2011; 'Parties, Advocacy and Activism: Interrogating Community and Class in Digital Queer India', in Christopher Pullen (ed.), *Queer Youth and Media*, 265–77 (Basingstoke: Palgrave Macmillan, 2014); 'Dissident Citizenship: Articulating Belonging, Dissidence and Queerness on Cyberspace', *South Asian Review*, 35(3): 203–23, 2015; and 'Intimate Subjects and Virtual Spaces: Rethinking Sexuality as a Category for Intimate Ethnographies', *Sexualities* (2016).

I would like to thank the numerous friends, colleagues and teachers who have been a part of this writing journey, commenting on drafts, providing support and keeping me sane through this process: my supervisors – Dr Sara Davidmann, Dr Sharif Mowlabocus, Professor William Raban and Sunil Gupta; my examiners – Professor Oriana Baddeley and Dr Christopher

Pullen; and my friends and well-wishers scattered across the globe – Kaustav Bakshi, Dr Lipi Begum, Abhimanyu Bose, Dr Brinda Bose, Dr Paul Boyce, Dr Debanuj Dasgupta, Dr Sayantan Dasgupta, Dr Sangeeta Datta, Dr Aniruddha Dutta, Professor Rachel Dwyer, Professor Radhika Gajjala, Shibansu Ghosh, Dr K. Moti Gokulsing, Dr Shamira Meghani, Paul Mondal, Dr Ila Nagar, Mas Naina, Bishan Samaddar, Pujarini Sen, Charan Singh, Noni Stacey, Dr Jean Stevens and Professor Ruth Vanita. Hilary and Pete, thanks for providing such a peaceful space for me to work every Christmas (the last phase of this writing would not have been otherwise possible!). I would also like to thank Manjul and Kanwar Saini for giving me permission to use their images in this book. I would also like to thank my former colleagues at the Winchester School of Art, University of Southampton and my present colleagues at the Institute for Media and Creative Industries, Loughborough University. Also thanks to the three anonymous peer reviewers for their useful feedback and Aakash Chakrabarty, my editor at Routledge. This book has benefitted from their suggestions. My heartfelt thanks to my family – Maa, Baba and Rittika. Finally, thanks to Tim for being a constant support over the last five years while I was working on this. This book is dedicated to Amma.

# Introduction

This book investigates everyday experiences of queer Indian men on digital spaces. It explores the ways in which queer male identities are formed on virtual spaces and how the existence of such spaces challenge and critiques Indianness. The book also looks at the role of class, language, gender, intimacy and activism within the discourse of queer identities. Drawing from ethnographic research conducted among queer men in Kolkata, New Delhi and the suburban area of Barasat in India, as well as virtual ethnography (Hine, 2000) conducted over multiple digital spaces (such as *PlanetRomeo*, *Facebook* and *Grindr*), the book investigates the various practices through which queer men engage with a digital culture that has permeated and become an integral part of queer social life in India.

The focus of this book is queer Indian males. It is important to clarify at the very outset my use of this terminology. 'Queer' is an umbrella term that encompasses sexual as well as gender non-normative identity positions. It is also a political identity that can be broadly defined as a resistance to regimes of heterosexuality. Queer in this book refers to both. Within academic and activist literature on queer identities (Bhaskaran, 2004; Dave, 2012; Shahani, 2008), it is used as a term that replaces and challenges heteronormative power and the status quo. Some of my research participants variously chose to identify themselves as gay or queer, while some were quite ambiguous about these labels. In addition, a few chose to identify as *kothi*. I do not want to homogenise the different identity categories and the nuances of each, but for the sake of simplicity I have chosen to use 'queer' men to distinguish my participants from the other non-normative male sexual categories that exist in India. Scholars such as Boyce (2012: 76) are critical about ethnographic research done on male-to-male sexual subject categories, which puts 'excessive reliance on reductive categories' (such as gay, bisexual, *kothi* etc.), to describe male-to-male sexualities in India. 'Queer' as a term is widely used in the Indian context, even getting transliterated in the various regional languages. I thus found it most appropriate to use the terms 'queer male' and 'queer community' in this book rather than using the narrower 'gay male' and 'LGBTQ community' (or even LGBTQKHIA). The queer male community in India, as wide scholarship points out, is far from a homogenous group (Narrain and Bhan, 2005; Shahani, 2008). Issues such as class, gendered subjectivity and religion play an important role in the social groupings of this 'community'. Rather than using queer as a singular category of interrogation, this research problematises it by showing the ways in which the term is used within the Indian context and the various ways through which it contests social practices within the online/offline component of the lives of my research participants. In addition, I have unpacked this in detail within my chapters, when research participants have had a different opinion about the ways in which they 'self-identify'. I have chosen to concentrate on only the queer male community, as it was beyond the scope of this book to undertake a project where I could use a singular lens to examine all the queer identities that exist in India and their use of online digital space. There have been some recent ethnographic studies on queer women in India (Banerjea, 2014; Dave, 2012), but none of these look at the digital aspect and as such there is definitely scope for further work in this area.

In a conversation with leading queer activist Pawan Dhall in India, Dhall articulates the ways in which being queer in India has entered a new realm of imagination where queerness is played out both on digitally mediated screens and popular cruising grounds in Kolkata. The story of queer Indian life online began in 1993 when two South Asian queer men, Devesh Khatu and his friend Marty, met at a university in Texas and realised how difficult it was for Indian queer men to meet one another. They set up the first discussion group for queer Indian people called the *Khush* List in the same year. The word *khush*, which literally means happy, is a term used by many South Asians to refer to lesbian, gay, bisexual, trans* and queer-identified individuals (Bhaskaran, 2004).

It is worth noting that the Indian queer movement in the last two decades grew almost simultaneously with the growth of new media. Roy (2003) notes that the Internet has played a pivotal role in the growth of the queer movement in South Asia.[1] In his ethnographic essay on the history of South Asian queer virtual spaces, Roy further states that many long-time activists became involved with the Internet in its very early phase, while many others 'cut their activist teeth on the Internet, having been instrumental in forming online groups' (Roy, 2003: 181). An interesting point Roy makes is that while many of these early online groups, especially in the West, catered to the 'South Asian community', the most active groups were in fact those in India.

As the Internet grew in popularity in India in the latter half of the 1990s, more people started having access to websites and emails. This was before home computers were common, and this period also saw a huge growth in public cyber cafes. It also became much easier to create and maintain e-lists through websites such as Yahoo! and other web-based e-groups. One of the first e-groups established in India was the *GayBombay* group in 1998. This group, as Shahani (2008: 27) notes, is 'a symbol of the radical change that has swept across gay and lesbian Asia (especially India) due to the emergence of the Internet'. In its early phase, *GayBombay* also provided support to several other metropolitan cities in India, such as Kolkata, to start their own e-groups and online networks.

In this book, I argue that new media, social networking sites and related technologies do not exist in isolation; rather they are very much embedded within other social spaces. Few studies have focussed on both the offline and online component of queer cultures that exist in India. This is important because digital culture is a burgeoning social phenomenon in India, and the last decade has seen a tremendous growth of Internet and mobile technologies. Second, queer culture in India, as I argue in this book, is an intersection of online and offline practices, and therefore to study queer male identity and practices in contemporary India, it is important to navigate and acknowledge the connectedness between online and offline spaces. The context that prompted this investigation is my own personal experience as a political, middle class urban queer youth growing up in India, where my queer negotiations of daily life were located within the online worlds of *PlanetRomeo*, *Grindr* and *Facebook*.

Finally, sexuality in India is significant because it offers an expression of nationalist anxieties, and it is also a marker of modernity through which subjectivities are formed in middle class India. It would be worthwhile to note that queer people are excluded from the grand narrative of nationalism and national identities that constructs queerness as anti-national, as I will demonstrate in this book. Indian nationalism is constructed across different media spaces, including the digital. As such, by combining queerness and the digital, I am also providing a new lens and site to study key issues of nationalism and belonging.

The growth of queer visibility and queer consciousness is intrinsically linked to the notion of liberalisation. Liberalisation in India can be traced to 1991, where a shift in India's social and economic policies signalled a rapid era of globalisation and the growth of an ambitious middle class. As Roy (2003) and Shahani (2008) have argued, the queer community were amongst the first to enter the digital folds of social interaction. Shahani (2008: 33) explains that pre-existing social conditions in the form of an educated English-speaking middle class, the advent of the Internet and a 'recovered' queer history of South Asia (Vanita and Kidwai, 2000) offered queer men in India new ways of imagining themselves and experiencing imagined worlds within the digital sphere. It also prompted queer people to interrogate their 'belonging' and the ways in which they navigated their national and local identities within this new transnational space.

Alongside the issue of liberalisation, one of the core concepts, which bind all the four chapters together, is neoliberalism. The meaning of neoliberalism has changed over time. In this book, I use neoliberalism in the Foucaldian sense. Foucault (2004) argued that neoliberalism emerged as a social rationality that sought to remove any obstacles to free market enterprise, turning the citizen subject into an entrepreneurial citizen subject – one who acts as an active economic agent. Neoliberalism in the Indian context is an entanglement of economic liberalisation and changing social order. In this case, neoliberal bodies are deemed as productive and respectable – reformulating the citizen subject to a respectable entrepreneurial citizen subject. In the four empirical analyses chapters, this has been interrogated in different ways – through the failure to achieve romantic love (Chapter 3), the queer subject seen through the lens of consumerism (Chapter 4), effeminacy subverting respectability (Chapter 5) and finally the fight to be rights-bearing and legally recognised citizens (Chapter 6).

The digital/virtual space is a complicated arena. While hailed as a disembodied utopic space where signifiers of gender, race and class cease to exist (Rheingold, 1993), I argue that it has instead become the very space that reflects and symbolises the anxieties and possibilities of inflection of these categories. Sexuality performs an important role in examining the attitudinal transformation and changes that are currently happening in India: the growth of queer politics, intersectional politics and assertion of disparate identities.

The digital space, as I suggest, is a site upon which the anxieties, views and political positions are declared and forged and is constitutive of the everyday lives of queer men in India. These groups are a symbol of change that has swept across India since the late 1990s. This book draws upon and extends the work on Indian queer identities by ethnographers such as Boyce (2007, 2012, 2014), Dave (2012) and Dutta (2012, 2013a, 2013b). There has been little work done on the digital component of queer lives in India and no extended research exists, other than Shahani's (2008) work on the *GayBombay* community.

## Framework

This book uses an interdisciplinary approach to examine the experience of Indian queer men in digital spaces and looks at the ways in which the online/offline component of their lives intersects with each other. In doing so, I look at four main issues: class; masculinity and effeminophobia; intimacies; and finally dissent and activism.

As I mentioned earlier, this book is focussed on the study of queer males and not the entire spectrum of sexual and gender minorities in India. Most of my participants are English speaking and live in the urban locales of New Delhi, Kolkata and suburban Barasat in West Bengal.

This study relied on three years of ethnographic research on virtual sites and two extended field trips to New Delhi and West Bengal. Situating my research within these two states puts it in dialogue with some of the work on Eastern India that has been undertaken previously (Boyce, 2007; Dutta, 2013a, 2013b), and at the same time provides a macro-level understanding of digital queer cultures in India.

Data was collected through 'lurking' (Mowlabocus, 2010a: 121), a method by which I would join online groups, clubs and forums observing the communication but seldom participating. In addition, data was also collected through participant observation, informal interactions as well as semi-structured interviews, emails and instant chat. I would like to stress that all names of individuals used in this book are pseudonyms, unless they are well-known public figures (e.g. Pawan Dhall, Anindya Hajra, Aditya Bandyopadhyay), in which case they have been explicitly mentioned. This was done in order to protect the identities and privacy of my research participants. Where possible, I have chosen pseudonyms that reflect their class, linguistic and community backgrounds. In addition, I have also provided pseudonyms for all my virtual participants, including their usernames and handles. Usernames and handles are generally computer generated which the users can edit. These are used in lieu of the user's 'real name'. I have assigned names that are closely aligned and reflect the usernames they had chosen themselves. At the time of writing this book, the usernames I have assigned my research participants were not in use on *PlanetRomeo* or *Grindr*. I have provided more details regarding the research framework of this book in Appendix 2.

## Overview of chapters

There are six chapters in this book and a conclusion. Together, they represent the main themes of this book.

### *Postcolonial residues and contemporary sketches*

This is the first chapter of the book and uses broad brushstrokes to introduce existing literature on queerness and queer identities in India. Looking at the colonial dialogues and the postcolonial reactions to queer identity, the chapter sets the 'scene' for the rest of the book. It provides a narrative history of the formation of queer politics and queer organising in India.

*Media, diversity and emergence of the cyberqueer in India*

This chapter begins with an overview of media development in India. It then proceeds to a discussion of queer representations in mass media. This media history serves as a starting point for a discussion of digital queer spaces in India that are a consequence of the shifting political and socioscape of urban and suburban India. The chapter concludes by reviewing some of the key debates on digital culture and queer studies, thereby situating the Indian queer digital space within the existing scholarship.

*Virtual intimacies on digital queer platforms*

Virtual intimacies are mediated through technology (computer, mobile phones and other electronic devices). In this chapter, through an ethnographic study of queer participants in India, I explore the ways in which digital platforms open up new spaces for queer men to be 'virtually' together. With many young Indians still living with their parents, privacy and private 'places' to meet are often non-existent, especially for those living in smaller towns. As such, virtual technologies act as both objects and mediators of feeling. Through the personal narratives of my research participants, this chapter examines the ways in which intimate relationships are mediated across virtual queer spaces.

*'Imagined' queer communities*

This chapter interrogates the concept of a 'queer community' (both online and offline). My participants report experiencing community differently – for some it was the friendships made online, while for others it was just being part of online groups that gave them a feeling of community. Some, however, dismissed this idea of an 'imagined community'. I critique the community discourse, especially on grounds of class dynamics. Based on a series of case studies conducted in the *Pink Kolkata Party* group on *Facebook* and empirical data collected from the participants, I challenge the problematic 'community' discourse within a city like Kolkata where certain voices experience additional oppression because of their sexuality as well as class.

*Effeminophobia, 'straight acting' and global queering*

I begin this chapter by exploring the notion of the 'global gay' (Altman, 1997) and global queer assimilation which is based on the primacy of a Western queer model. Taking this as a starting point, this chapter argues that homonormativity (Duggan, 2003) has in recent years perpetuated racial, class and gender discrimination. By looking at two sites, *Facebook* and *PlanetRomeo*, I argue that online queer spaces systematically discriminate against effeminate subject positions (effeminophobia). This chapter furthers the debate started in the previous chapter on the ways in which digital spaces critique and reflect the identity fractures and anxieties within the queer male community in India.

## Dissident citizenship

On 11 December 2013, the Indian Supreme Court ruling on Section 377 came in, striking off the Delhi High court's earlier ruling, which decriminalised homosexuality in 2009, and thereby reinstating the draconian Victorian law back into the culture and social fabric of the country. In this chapter, I examine the acts of collective resistance and simultaneous efforts by dissident citizens (Sparks, 1997), to challenge and articulate strategies to critique civil society's role in the Supreme Court decision. To study activism is to study the relationship between the virtual and the actual. Using two case studies – the TV9 sting operation in Hyderabad and the Global Day of Rage (2013) – this chapter argues that dissident queer citizens are attempting to create counterpublics (Fraser, 2008) on the digital space, claiming a dissident and participative form of citizenship. This chapter extends Dave's (2012) study of activism by drawing upon a range of experiences of activists and civilians 'within the field', alongside the digital articulation and assimilation of these movements.

## Conclusion

This section summarises the main conclusions that I have drawn in the book. It also reflects on my research process and the various ways through which the book addresses queer identity politics in contemporary India.

# Key sites

Before I conclude, I would like to introduce the primary sites for this research project and how they came to be chosen. Three online spaces were identified for the purposes of this research, after my initial literature review and pilot interview with five participants in Kolkata. In this section, I will provide further details of these spaces and the reason why I consider these sites to be the most representative examples for the issues this book addresses, with regard to queer Indian men's engagement with digital culture.

The first site that all my research participants indicated they used was *PlanetRomeo*, 'a place for dating, sex, making and meeting friends, sharing ideas and offering mutual support' (*PlanetRomeo* website). *PlanetRomeo* is currently used by approximately 1.3 million Indian males (*PlanetRomeo*, 10 August 2015). Jens Schmidt set up *PlanetRomeo* in 2002 in Germany. By 2006, owing to the complicated nature and strict provisions of the German Act for the Protection of Young Persons and Minors, the company moved to the Netherlands. In 2009, one of their biggest mergers took place when *Guys4Men*, which had a considerable presence in Asia (and particularly India), joined *PlanetRomeo*, making it one of the largest transnational gay/queer male sites with over 2.6 million users as of June 2014 (though accurate quantifiable data is unavailable). *PlanetRomeo* provides a perfect entry point in gaining an understanding of Indian queer male engagement with digital culture. The site is located at the centre of queer culture in the country and, at the same time, on the ostensible margins of mainstream Indian society. As such, it reflects the hopes and anxieties of Indian queer men. By providing anonymity to meet other queer men for friendship, sex and social networking, it provides a 'safe haven' (Campbell, 2004) for queer men away from the interference of the state.

The second site for this study is the mainstream social networking site *Facebook*, which hosts three of the groups that I look at in this book. The history and the global reach of *Facebook* are unparalleled, with over 1.44 billion worldwide as of March 2015. Set up in 2004 in the United States, it reached India around 2007. India records the second-highest number of *Facebook* users (currently 112 million) after the United States. Owing to its global reach and popularity, it also hosts a number of special interest groups and societies, including queer groups from India. In this book, I have chosen to look at three of these groups that provide a representative sample for the issues this book seeks to answer.

The first group I explored is *Pink Kolkata Party* (PKP), a closed/private *Facebook* group, used by queer men and women in Kolkata. The site functions as a platform to organise social meetings between (primarily) queer men in the city. It grew out of a need to provide safe social spaces for middle and upper middle class queer men and women in Kolkata. Unlike other metros (New Delhi and Mumbai), Kolkata has never had a sustained queer nightlife. This forum was started to address this need, by organising weekly coffee meetings and monthly club nights. However, in addition to being a social platform, it also provides a stimulating space for debates and discussions. What is interesting about this collective is that the weekly physical meetings have more or less been discontinued; however, the online space is still very active. It also includes members from all social backgrounds, something the physical meetings did not owing to economic reasons, with most of the venues being chosen for parties being in expensive hotels that often discriminate against certain social demographics, as I extensively discuss in Chapter 4. PKP is used by approximately 1,300 members. It is currently a closed group, and administrators approve membership. The administrators were made aware of my project, and permission was sought to approach members and conduct analysis of the discussion threads.

The second *Facebook* group I also look at is *Kolkata Rainbow Pride Festival* (KRPF). This group is community run. Members belong to various NGOs. However, KRPF is organised outside an institutional framework. This group is quite a politically charged space and has been the site for some fierce debates, which are part of the case studies discussed in Chapter 4.

In addition to the *PlanetRomeo* and the *Facebook* groups, I also look at *Grindr*. *Grindr* is a smartphone application used by queer and gay men to facilitate sexual partnering. *Grindr* uses global positioning system (GPS) capabilities to identify other app users, sorting users by current (or last identified) proximity. *Grindr* was launched in March 2009, and in September 2013 it had over six million user profiles in 192 countries. *Grindr* reports estimated daily traffic of 250,000 users, and an article from the *Times of India* in September 2013 reported that almost 11,000 Indians are using *Grindr*, a small but not insignificant number.[2] This has been brought about primarily through the growth of mobile technologies in the country and an upcoming smartphone-using group of middle class urban young people. *Grindr* works seamlessly on popular platforms such as Android, Apple, Windows and Blackberry, and runs exclusively as a downloadable application on mobile devices (with no online/website version). Crooks (2013: n.p.) notes that 'where other information and communication technologies (ICT) claim to obviate space and time, *Grindr* works through propinquity'. Users can find other users based on their location and distance. *Grindr* is an example of geolocative media that combine elements of a number of other technologies, including the connectivity of social network sites, the location services of cell phones and the spatial architecture enabled by the advent of smartphones. As Crooks (2013: n.p.) further notes, 'These are technologies embodied in access, spatial in operations, and place – based in content.' During my field trip, I discovered that while *Grindr* was very popular in New Delhi, it was still to gain the same level of popularity in Kolkata. This can be attributed to the socio-economic populace of both cities, with Delhi boasting a higher number of upper middle class professionals. By 2014, however, *Grindr* had reached a massive user market in Kolkata. It was, therefore, imperative that this application also became a part of my analysis of digital queer cultures in India.

## A final word

Through the key sites and approaches discussed, this book makes a significant contribution to knowledge. Widely available scholarship has explored the historical, literary and social debates on queer sexualities in India. To reach a more holistic understanding of contemporary Indian queer sexualities, it is necessary to engage with the digital landscape as India's global power stems from its digital development. By looking at the multiple ways that the queer male community engages with the digital medium, I investigate the multifaceted, complex and sometimes contradictory ways in which this community understands, accesses and performs their sexual identities within the context of the nation and their local space. This book also combines online and offline ethnography, thereby providing a new methodological tool with which queer cultures in India can be studied. Finally, this book engages in a critical discussion of contemporary queer male communities in India, and adds to the scholarship on queer studies and studies in digital culture.

## Notes

1  I would like to note that the growth of queer consciousness and queer organisations in India was also led by international HIV/AIDS funding (Boyce, 2014).
2  See Sonal Nerurkar (2013). Available at: <http://timesofindia.indiatimes.com/tech/apps/Indians-hit-mobile-apps-to-find-love/articleshow/22597148.cms>. Accessed on 5 July 2014.

# 1 Postcolonial residues and contemporary sketches

## Introduction

> Father waits for the day
> I bring a crimson bride
> Yet if I sit on a white horse
> It'll be an empty ride
>
> – Rakesh Ratti (1999: 103)

This quote, taken from Rakesh Ratti's poem 'Beta' (Son), was featured in one of the first gay anthologies to 'come out' of India – Hoshang Merchant's *Yaarana: Gay Writing from India* (1999). The poem succinctly captures the anxieties of a queer man in contemporary India where marriage and the heteronormative family are central to one's social life; but in doing so, it also captures the son's loneliness and negotiation of being queer in contemporary India. The queer citizen subject in India, as elsewhere, is formed through a rights-based struggle. In India, this has been around the British 'bequest' of Section 377 to the Indian penal code that justified violence and societal disapproval of non-heternormative sexual practices criminalising 'carnal intercourse against the order of nature' (Narrain and Eldridge, 2009: 9).

On 2 July 2009, the Delhi High Court ruled that Section 377 of the Indian penal code violated the country's constitution guaranteeing dignity, equality and freedom to its citizens. The judges read down Section 377 decriminalising consensual sex between adults of the same sex in private. This was a landmark judgement, as it finally overturned a 150-year-old law that had denied queer citizens the right to be open about their sexuality. In finding Section 377 contrary to the Indian constitution, it also moved the queer person into the realms of a citizen subject. It is important to point out that national identity and belonging are at the core of the ways in which one understands the queer citizen in India. Rao (2014), for example, explains that those who challenged the High Court decision insisted that homosexuality was foreign and culturally inauthentic, whereas those who were opposing criminalisation pointed to the rich tradition of homosexual art and literature in order to argue that queerness has always been a part of Indian tradition. Rao (2014: 8) calls this the 'nativist politics of authenticity' where anything 'foreign' or imported has no place in the postcolonial nation. In both cases, the national identity is being framed to either castigate or provide support for the queer subject.

My research into digital queer practices in India situates itself in a narrow fracture. When I began writing this book, Section 377 had just been struck off and there was an excitement at the ways in which this would lead to greater rights for queer citizens in what a new anthology termed 'New Queer India' (Hajratwala, 2012). By the time I had finished my fieldwork, in a dramatic development, a two-member bench of the Supreme Court dismissed the High Court ruling, thus recriminalising homosexuality. While I will be addressing the role of dissidence and activism in relation to this recriminalisation in a later chapter of this book, in this chapter, I will sketch out the historical and contemporary contexts within which the discourse of queer sexuality in India is based. The narrative of queer sexuality in India is vast and it is beyond the scope of this book to address the entirety of this history, which has been written and commented upon by several scholars (Arondekar, 2009; Vanita and Kidwai, 2000). In this chapter, I bring together some of these voices to provide an overview of the colonial and postcolonial reaction to queerness in India.

## Colonial incursions

The expansion of the British Empire in the 18th century also dictated the policies of sexual regulation in the colonies driven by a Victorian 'fanatical purity campaign' (Bhaskaran, 2002: 16). The British Anti-Sodomy law was introduced in Britain in 1860, which reduced the punishment of sodomy from execution to imprisonment. However, when enacted in colonial states such as India (which had no anti-sodomy laws before this), as Section 377 of the Indian Penal Code, it was seen as a retrogressive move.

The law states:

> Whoever voluntarily has carnal intercourse against the order of nature with any man, woman or animal, shall be punished with imprisonment for life, or with imprisonment of either description for a term, which may extend to ten years, and shall be liable to fine.
>
> Explanation: Penetration is sufficient to constitute the carnal intercourse necessary to the offence described in this section.
>
> (Narrain and Eldridge, 2009: 9)

Prior to the enactment of this law, queer sexuality was accommodated, if not approved, in Indian culture (Merchant, 1999; Vanita and Kidwai, 2000). Vanita and Kidwai (2000: xviii) have pointed out that there have been no records found so far of active discrimination against homosexuals in India prior to colonial rule. However, with the passing of this law, homosexuality was officially condemned by the state and framed as a criminal activity. This is not to say that colonialism entirely drove queer sexuality underground, but rather colonialism acted as a device to obscure the queer identity, creating an unwillingness to 'come out' in public. In colonial India, the marginalisation of queer sexualities was a political agenda, which sought to position queer sexuality as a 'special oriental vice' (Ballhatchet, 1980). Ballhatchet (1980: 1) suggests that sexual energy was another reason for imperial expansion; he mentions British men with 'tastes which could not be satisfied in England . . . agreeably satiated overseas'. However, there was a great deal of anxiety by the British administrators about the sexual freedom India posed for its people, and homosexuality was blamed on Indian customs. Lord Curzon once remarked: 'I attribute it largely to early marriage. A boy gets tired of his wife, or of women at an early age and wants the stimulus of some more novel or exciting sensation' (cited in Ballhatchet, 1980: 120).

Bhaskaran provides an example from an advice column in the Bengali magazine *Sanjibani*, dated October 1893, where schoolboys engaging in 'unnatural and immoral habits' were advised by the magazine to be cured by visiting prostitutes (Bhaskaran, 2002: 17). Ballhatchet, on the other hand, flags up Surgeon-Major Hamilton's comment on the situation in England:

> I have had a good deal of experience of schools, seminaries and colleges for boys, and, as I daresay you know, few of these institutions escape being infected with some immorality or other; but, once it creeps in, it is most difficult to eradicate.

(1980: 120)

Ballhatchet further describes the various debates that took place in the British Parliament, with respect to the possibility of sexual relations taking place between the white elite and the native people. Parliament agreed that British subjects in India needed sexual regulations, with one major point of concern being the presence of prostitutes in the army cantonments. However, 'the prospect of homosexuality was revealed in guarded terms by the authorities whenever there was a talk of excluding prostitutes from the cantonments' (Ballhatchet, 1980: 162). This might seem contradictory to the Victorian morals of that time, but I would suggest that the fundamental concern was for the preservation of power by the authorities – to regulate the lives of those under their command. Attitudes to sexual conduct are likewise correlated to the safeguarding of vested interests and the constitution of power.

Aldrich (2003: 4) argues that 'colonialism . . . encouraged sexual irregularity, heterosexual and homosexual'. He further notes that the colonies 'provided many possibilities of homoeroticism, homosociality and homosexuality'. Thus, there was a multiplicity of possibilities and perspectives in which queer bonding and queer desire could take place in the colony.

The British ascendancy in India also incited a series of attacks on homoerotic texts that were deemed to be 'filthy' and, it was believed, needed to be expurgated. Ballhatchet (1980: 5) points out that books like *The Arabian Nights* aroused concern which was 'full of the adventures of gallantry and intrigue, as well as of the marvellous . . . but the Hindu and especially the Muhammadan youth . . . gloats quite much on the former, to his own moral harm'. The homoeroticism displayed by the Perso-Arabic texts was further checked through a series of education and legal reforms. The British not only policed the corridors of literary imagery, but also framed homoerotic love as a 'criminal activity'. In doing so, the colonisers were attempting to undo earlier forms of national identity. Identifying the indigenous literature and culture as obscene was also a way to instigate a need to remove them and to usher in a new and 'better' version that would mirror British Victorian culture. Thomas Babington Macaulay, who designed the colonial education system that would teach South Asians 'civilisation' on British Victorian models, also helped frame the legislation that labelled sodomy and other acts of love between men 'unnatural' and made them criminal offences (Kugle, 2002: 37). Cultural readjustments and revisionism were conducted to purge literature of erotic themes, especially homoeroticism. Through the poets Altaf Hussayn Hali (1837–1914) and Muhammad Husayn Azad (1834–1910), a radical 'ethical cleansing' took place of the Perso-Arabic texts (Kugle, 2002: 40).

However, it was also during the colonial period that texts such as the *Kamasutra* were 'recovered' as sites of scholarship by Orientalists such as Richard Burton. As Sweet (2002: 77) states, 'To the brilliant adventurer and erotomaniac Sir Richard Burton, the KS [*Kamasutra*] was a heaven-sent opportunity to spit in the eye of late-Victorian sexual hypocrisy.' However, these views on Indian sexual practice also propagated anxiety and an anti-sex bias among Victorian puritans. Another form of distortion that took place, influenced by Victorian sexual mores, was putting forward the idea that India was a heteronormative place with little or no queer history. For example, the historian Basham writes that 'The erotic life of ancient India was generally heterosexual. Homosexuality of both sexes was not wholly unknown, it is condemned briefly in the law books and the *Kamasutra* treats it but cursorily and with little unknown enthusiasm. In this respect, ancient India was far "healthier" than most ancient cultures' (1959: 172). This is obviously a wishful conjecture that can be rejected when looking at the wide gamut of queer narratives available in precolonial and colonial India.

Arondekar (2009) looks back at the colonial archive that suppressed homoerotic texts for recovering the same from its state of loss and obfuscation. In *On Sexuality and the Colonial Archive in India*, she mentions *Queen Empress v Khairati* (1884) as one of the earliest sodomy cases recorded. Arondekar treats homosexuality in the colonial archive as both 'obvious and elusive'. In this case, Khairati is framed as a 'habitual sodomite' whose unnatural sexual practices needed to be checked. He was initially arrested for dressing up in women's clothing and subjected to physical examination by the civil surgeon. On examination, as Arondekar notes, it was found that he had 'the characteristic mark of a habitual catamite' (68). Despite no records of the crimes' enactment, testimony or victims of the crime ever being located, Judge Denniston rendered a guilty verdict. When the case came up again in front of Judge Straight in the Allahabad High Court, the lack of evidence led him to overturn the previous judgement. However, he noted that the plaintiff was 'clearly a habitual sodomite' and he appreciated the desire of the authorities to 'check such disgusting practices' (69). Surprisingly, this case set a precedent for further cases where Section 377 was enforced, and has been cited numerously in legal commentaries on unnatural offences as a cautionary tale. This is what fascinates Arondekar; despite being a 'failed' case, it became a precedent which the British Empire used to regulate 'sexual irregularities', thus providing a fascinating display of the anxiety queerness had on the administrators. The elusiveness and ubiquity of queerness being played out rearticulate Macaulay's claim, when he passed the law:

> I believe that no country ever stood so much in need of a code of law as India and I believe also that there never was a country in which the want might be so easily supplied.
>
> (Cited in Bhaskaran, 2002: 20)

The anti-sex views and anxiety over non-normative sexualities espoused through colonial puritanism had a major influence on the development of the Indian national identity. As Bose and Bhattacharya (2007: x) critically note, 'Questions of identity are complex to begin with, and they become even more so when one has to relate questions of sexual identities or preferences with questions of national specificity.' The major factors that are commonly seen to contribute to the particularity of the Indian experience are the legacy of long-term colonialism, uneven economic development and the complex socio-ethnic diversity of the Indian society. Chatterjee (2004) emphasises that the heightened division between private and public life in Indian society, which despite being a normative proposition of modernity, was greatly exacerbated in India by the colonial presence. The private realm within which sexuality is firmly placed is most assiduously maintained as a realm of traditional and indigenous social practices. The persistence in postcolonial India of the tradition and modernity binary, with a significantly gendered dimension, remains a very distinctive feature of social life. It is, therefore, no surprise that the homophobia that was introduced through colonialism was also internalised by modern India.

Anxieties about homoeroticism circulated in a variety of spheres. An illustrative example of this is the short story collection *Chocolate* by Pandey Bechain Sharma 'Ugra' in 1924. The collection purported to denounce male homosexuality and cast a shadow on the stability of heterosexual manhood. In the words of Ugra (translated by Vanita), 'Chocolate is the name for those innocent tender and beautiful boys of the country whom society's demons push into the mouth of ruin to quench their own lusts' (Vanita, 2009: xxix.). However, the real purpose of this collection remains ambiguous as one of the other things the collection did was to locate the vice of homosexuality to hybrid Indian–Western elements. The characters in these stories legitimised their 'sexual offence' by not only invoking Shakespeare, Socrates and Oscar Wilde, but also by quoting *ghazals* from Urdu poets. Vanita (2009: xv) calls the publication of Ugra's stories as 'the first public debate on homosexuality in modern India'. Vanita further argues that while the collection claimed to denounce homosexuality, many readers received positive representations of same-sex male love. She points out: 'While wonderfully encapsulating how ineradicably Westerness is a part of modern Indian identity, it [Ugra's stories] also works to "normalise" male-male desire.'

## Postcolonial reactions and modern homophobia

Early postcolonial Indian nationalism can be divided into two major phases. The secular nationalism espoused by Jawaharlal Nehru can be traced up to the 1970s, owing mainly to India's key integrative policies under the Congress government. The years following 1970 are characterised by the growth of the Hindu nationalist party BJP (Bharatiya Janata Party), which can be attributed to the unpopularity of the then Prime Minister Indira Gandhi (Varshney, 1993).

Benedict Anderson's concept of 'imagined communities' is a useful framework for understanding the nationalist rhetoric of modern India.

The term 'imagined community' suggests a source of identity that is bigger than oneself. It rests on the assumption of 'imagining' and 'creating'. The national integration of India was possible by imagining this concept of a common history, and thus creating a common citizenship. However, sexuality fractures this idea of sameness. The heteropatriarchal ideology, through which nationalism was constructed and discussed in India, lead to the erasure of queer sexuality. Puri (1999), who studies the relationship between nationalism and sexuality, contends that nations and states uphold certain sexualities as respectable and others as abnormal or unacceptable. Puri argues that individuals are inclined to construct their sexuality, often with unsatisfactory results, according to the mandates of the state and the nation, and notes, 'Queer narratives have arisen in organised contexts where truth claims are structured in competition with hegemonic discourses of the nation state. In these queer narratives . . . not only the politics of nationalisms but also transnational cultural discourses are evident.'

It becomes problematic when homosexuality is placed within such a revisionist paradigm. Vanita (2006) argues that this desire to rewrite India's past as one of normative purity is, in part, the result of defensiveness against Western attempts to exoticise that past as one of unbridled sensuality. This was aimed specifically at the decadence of Indian princes who were described as 'ignorant and rather undisciplined' (Ballhatchet, 1980: 119). However, modern critics such as Nandy (1983: 45) use the queer effeminacy and anti-masculine image of Gandhi to critique colonialism. He writes, 'It was colonial India . . . still preserving something of its androgynous cosmology and style, which ultimately produced a transcultural protest against the hyper-masculine worldview of colonialism in the form of Gandhi.'

Twentieth-century India still frames same-sex desires as an import from the West. Vanita and Kidwai (2000) argue that structured by this myth, most 20th-century texts still strive to reinforce an imagined pure Indianness of manhood or womanhood. Expressions of queer sexuality, as various scholars have shown, have a much older history than colonialism. Earlier forms of sexuality and identities were reconstituted to fit the new norms of the colonial establishment, and this in turn became a part of the modernising nationalist rhetoric. Menon suggests that 'the normalisation of heterosexual identity [is] a part of the processes of colonial modernity' (2005: 38). Anxieties around homoeroticism have circulated in various spheres. Hansen's (2002) work on the Indian theatre shows the ways in which cross-dressing created various forms of unease at the desire being evoked between the male spectator and the cross-dressing male actors. Evidence of this anxiety can be found in demonstrations against films with queer storylines such as *Fire* (1998) and *Girlfriend* (2004) by the Hindu right wing (Ghosh, 2007). In the instance of *Fire*, it caught the ire of Shiv Sena. Party activists stormed theatres in Bombay and New Delhi halting screenings and severely damaging theatres. These modern forms of homophobia are inherently connected to questions of nationhood and the rejection of all claims of histories of homosexuality in the Indian tradition. Menon (2007: 38–39) points out that in the Indian context, 'the heterosexual patriarchal family [is] the cornerstone of the nation' and 'any radical transformative politics today must therefore be post-national'.

## Contemporary sketches

The contemporary moment has seen the emergence of a more public queer articulation and consciousness in India. While the queer subject in India has largely been formed around the law incorporating the queer male citizen within the discourse of rights-based politics, it would be wrong to think of the queer male in India through only a discourse on liberal rights. Gupta (2005) provides a brief history of Indian queer spaces through the mid-1990s. He notes that during the 1990s organisations such as Good As You (GAY) in Bangalore, Humsafar Trust in Mumbai, Humraahi in Delhi and Counsel Club in Kolkata were formed, which began holding weekly support and social meetings for gay and queer-identified men. These meetings, as Gupta further elaborates, focussed on diverse issues such as being gay, the social compulsion to marry, family and so on. Over time, this moved to issues around sexual health practice and HIV/AIDS. At the time when these groups started, they were mostly at a nascent stage, unsure of the direction they would take in the coming years. Most of these meetings were held clandestinely and were at that time the only social space available to queer men. Hajratwala (2012) recalls her visit to Mumbai, India, in 2010, where she was whisked away to a party in Juhu hotel for lesbian and bisexual women. She recalls that she had missed this vibrant queer scene when she first visited India almost 10 years previously, when her friend remarked, 'You couldn't have found us. Back then we would spread the word by phone . . . Then we'd show up with a red rose, so we could find each other' (Hajratwala, 2012: 11). This remarkable change has come about in a matter of years. First with the public debate around the film *Fire*, as I discussed in the previous section, a growing queer public dissident sphere (which I will discuss in Chapter 7) and finally the Delhi High Court judgement in the 2009 striking off the unconstitutional Section 377.

Shahani (2008) provides a narrative of this history in Bombay. He states that Bombay in the 1970s and 1980s was already popular for the growth of a queer subculture. This was brought about through a distinct professional class of gay men, who were living there at that time or had migrated from other parts of India. Bombay also opened one of the first gay bars called

Gokul in the 1980s that became an important part of the queer social life in the city. This was followed by Voodoo, a dance club situated in South Bombay. Alongside this was the growth of private parties. Private parties are an important feature of queer life in New Delhi and Kolkata. Sunil Gupta (2011), with reference to his photographic work 'Mr Malhotra's Party', explains that private queer parties in New Delhi had to be held clandestinely in commercial bars and clubs. These parties were booked and hosted by the pseudonymous Mr. Malhotra. Since then, queer parties in New Delhi have called themselves Mr. Malhotra's Party. As a final point, I should mention (as I have already done earlier in the Introduction), the growth of queer organising and communities in India is also directly related to international sexual health funding that helped queer male communities converge and form under NGOs and charities.

I should also state that these were predominantly gay spaces (queer was yet to enter the lexicon) that were catered towards the urban middle to upper middle class English-speaking men. A moment of rupture occurred with outreach work on HIV when it became necessary to distribute condoms and sexual health information to the MSM community. Gay men would seldom want to go to these spaces, and it was the *kothis* and *hijras* who became the outreach workers (Gupta, 2005: 127). While this might have brought the disparate queer male communities together, what actually happened was further splintering of the groups. This was, however, slightly different in the case of Kolkata, as Pawan Dhall explained to me:

> When we were in the Counsel Club, you had people of different classes and backgrounds sit together and talk about being gay, marriage and life . . . unfortunately things have changed since then.
>
> (23 August 2013)

Unfortunately, Dhall's experience during the Counsel Club Days in 1994 has been replaced by more rigid class and gender-based queer male spaces that are not only policed, but also protected (discussed in Chapters 5 and 6). The social/party scene, on the other hand, while already established in places like Mumbai and later Delhi, had a very late uptake in other places like Bangalore and Kolkata.

Another way to track the emergence of queer consciousness is also through queer cultural productions in India. In addition to the literature that I have discussed above, contemporary India has a rich tradition of literary texts about queer desires. Hoshang Merchant's anthology *Yaarana: Gay Writing from India* (1999) (that I mentioned earlier) is one such volume. In addition, playwrights such as Mahesh Dattani and novelists such as Vikram Seth and R. Raj Rao have been pioneers in literary expressions of queer desires in India. However, most of this literature is in English. As Bose (2015: 504–505) explains: 'The politics of queer literary expression is very much bound up with the issue of language . . . that most of this writing is in English points to the fact that this movement is still confined to a particular class.' There has, however, also been writing in regional languages such as Bengali, like the serially anthologised *Holdey Golaap* and the Sappho anthology *Chi Tumi Naki* and in other regional languages such as Hindi and Kannada, amongst others. However, most of these have been published by small independent publishers and magazines, thus making their reach relatively limited. There is also a large output of 'queer media' that have furthered discussions on queer representations and queer issues in India. These will be discussed in detail in the next chapter.

# 2 Media, diversity and emergence of the cyberqueer in India

## Introduction

In this chapter, I offer a critical discussion on the media landscape in India, focussing on the queer media landscape followed by an examination of the intersection between cyberculture and sexuality in India. In the first half of the chapter, I briefly sketched out the media history of India, followed by looking at the media liberalisation period starting in 1991, moving on to a theoretical framework on queer cybercultures. Finally, in the last section, I chart the emergence of queer cybercultures in India.

Media refers to the different communication channels (such as cinema, print magazine, newspapers, radio, Internet and other digital media) through which news and messages are broadcasted. It is a form of mass communication that has evolved over time, and as theorists such as Athique (2012) and Hall (1995) have explained, the media is not neutral but guided by their own specific ideologies in constructing the messages that they disseminate. Media plays a vital role in constituting the political and cultural identity of modern India. The growth of Indian mass media can be traced back to the colonial years when Indian media was used by the anti-colonialists to reach out and gather support for their cause. This was followed by hegemonic state-controlled media post-independence in 1947. The post-liberal period began in 1991, with India opening up its borders for foreign trade and entering its globalised phase. This had a direct effect on media because the state-owned media were rapidly replaced by private channels and syndicated foreign programmes.

The communication revolution, which includes rapid technological advances, has created new locations of power, with consequences for both social and political spheres.

## Media development in India

Colonialism and nationalism have very complicated and important relationship with mass media in India. During British colonialism, the establishments of media institutions such as the All India Radio were specifically created to carry out the propaganda of the British government against the Indian National Congress and the Axis powers.[1] With the end of colonial rule, the anti-colonial movement set about to create their version of the 'nation state' with the backing of state-owned media. As Athique (2012: 38) notes, both arms of the state-owned media post-independence – the All India Radio and the Films Division – provided 'an endless celebration of scientific progress and state policy' and what the Government of India regarded as 'authentic Indian lives'. The legitimacy of media was only included within the political discourse in 1959, when television made its appearance in India through a gift from Philips supplemented by a UNESCO grant (Gokulsing, 2004). This led to the establishment of 'tele-clubs' in middle and lower middle class localities of Delhi, followed by the rolling out of a rural programme. The first regular daily television service was started in 1965, and by 1967 the most popular daily service was *Krishi Darshan*, a programme on agricultural development (Gokulsing, 2004: 8). Gokulsing (2004: 14–15) argues that while media development in India was intended to provide a platform for dialogue between the government and the people, by the 1970s it became the political voice of the government and used less for dialogue and more for 'talking to' the people. The broadcasting industry in India was an amalgamation of state ownership and servicing the public. This changed with the advent of the liberalisation period in 1991, which as Athique (2012: 69) points out marked the transition 'from an era of statist monopoly . . . to an era of popular entertainment, cosmopolitan internationalism'. According to Athique, this became 'a time for individualism to flourish and for the expression of a list of desires that were long suppressed in the name of national integration, including desires for regional expressions . . . unruly politics' (Athique, 2012: 69). These issues were reflected in the  multichannel and multi-format nature of television broadcasting as well as the content of tele-serials and chat shows which played up to the consumerist aspirations of middle class India by production houses such as UTV, Zee Entertainment and Balaji Telefilms, to name a few.

The first phase of this liberalisation was the deregulation of Indian television, which followed the rapid growth of private entertainment-based television stations against the state-owned Doordarshan in 1991, and the ensuing growth of regional television and print media. As of November 2014, there are 800 television channels in India, with the big players being the News Corporation–owned Star TV and Sony-owned Sony Entertainment Television and Zee TV. The Ministry of Information and Broadcasting in India has announced that a complete switchover from analogue to digital will take place by November 2015.

The early 1990s marked the beginning of the information age characterised by economic liberalisation and computer technologies. Castells (2009), one of the leading theorists of globalisation, marks this as a new social order driven by the rise of informational technology and political processes. This new form of networked society is driven by the exchange of knowledge. Given the ambitious aim of Nehruvian politics of advancing India's technological and scientific objectives, it is not surprising that India's postcolonial elite made their way to Silicon Valley and other 'nodes' of information and technological revolution. The importance of the information technology sector has always been central to the Government of India. The Nehru-led Congress government in India invested significantly in tertiary education for technology and engineering studies through setting up the elite Indian Institutes of Technology (Athique, 2012).

The Internet began in India in 1995 (not long after Tim Berners Lee invented the World Wide Web in 1991) with the launch of services by Videsh Sanchar Nigam Limited (VSNL).[2] However, broadband technologies offering higher speed connectivity started only in 2004. According to the Internet and Mobile Association of India, there are 278 million Internet users in India as of October 2014.[3] India's success story, as Athique (2012: 102) points out, can be directly attributed to the growth of the information technology sector. Currently, India is the world leader of providing offshore services in business process operations that was made possible due to the scaling up of Internet and communication technologies since 1995. Gopinath (2009: 299), writing about Internet usage in India, has written that the growth has been in depth and not in spread. 'This is to be expected in a highly stratified society as exists in India . . . the penetration of Internet amongst urban Indians being around nine percent and amongst all Indians about two percent.' Athique (2012: 103) gives three reasons for the low penetration of the Internet in India: namely, the slow growth of computer ownership, capacity shortage in telecommunications and the fact that the content of the Internet is delivered in English. The Internet was relatively free from Government interference until 2000, whereby through Section 292 of the Indian penal code, online pornography was made a punishable offence. In addition, as of 2004, a new enforcement law came into practice that required Internet/cyber cafes to log details of their users, thus beginning a series of regulating frameworks to control the Internet in India (Rangaswamy, 2007).

There has also been a huge surge of mobile phones in developing countries around the world, especially in places such as India, Sri Lanka and Bangladesh. A report from the Telecom Regulatory Authority of India (TRAI), published in May 2012, projected a monthly growth of 0.91 per cent in mobile phone uptake and an overall mobile density of 76.8 per cent of the total Indian population. These figures are very encouraging; however, poor network connectivity and 3G uptake means that it will take a while before the Internet can reach the majority of mobile phone users. Currently, mobile phones are being put to several uses such as education, development and trade. Sirisena (2012), in her ethnographic study of mobile phone usage amongst students and young people in Sri Lanka, also found that mobile phones are being used to mediate intimacy within romantic relationships, an area I will be exploring in the next chapter.

One of the most popular media artefacts of India is, of course, the cinema. Cinema in India consists of films from all over India, even though the global hegemony of Bollywood (the Hindi language popular variety) remains unchallenged. There are almost 1,000 films produced each year by the various regional industries, and the Bengali and South Indian industries are set to compete internationally with Bollywood. While it is not within the scope of this chapter to go into a detailed analysis of the Indian cinematic landscape, the role of Indian cinema within the global sphere is unchallenged, making more films than Hollywood and moving Indian cinema from the peripheries to the very centre of the global cinema discourse (Gokulsing and Dissanyake, 2012). The Hindi cinema industry received 'industry status' only in 1998 by the Central Government. As Ganti (2013) has noted, despite India being the second-largest film industry in the world shortly after Independence and of much economic significance, it received little government support with respect to distribution and promotion, unlike Hollywood which received strong support from the US government. However, considering the mass appeal of the medium, the content of cinema has always been regulated since colonial times, when the British Government set up stringent regulatory bodies that have survived under the postcolonial government.

Gokulsing and Dissanyake (2012) remind us that the presence of regulatory bodies under the Ministry of Information and Broadcasting of the Government of India still have the power to rate and review audio-visual materials meant for public consumption. This is exercised stringently by the Central Board of Film Certification (CBFC), which was constituted by the Cinematograph Act of 1952 and the Cinematograph Certification Rules, 1983, for Indian films. The guidelines governing this body are so wide that the 'State can, if it desires, restrain any film from public viewing on grounds of security or morality or some other issue' (Gokulsing and Dissanyake, 2012: 160). The CBFC has a strong record of denying certification to films with queer storylines. As a case in point, Gokulsing and Dissanyake (2012) refer to Sridhar Rangayan's 2003 film *Gulabi Aina* (*The Pink Mirror*) about trans people. The film was denied certification on the grounds that it had vulgar and offensive content. The film-maker appealed twice but failed to obtain a censor certificate, without which films cannot be distributed or screened for commercial purposes. However, in the last five years, a few films with queer storylines and queer characters (*Dunno Y Na Jane Kyun*, *My Brother Nikhil*, *I Am*) have managed to obtain censor certification and screen their films for adult audiences.[4] Much more recently, the Censor Board has come under strict criticism again for giving Hansal Mehta's film *Aligarh* (2016) (based on the real-life incident of Professor Ramachandra Siras who was fired from his job because of his sexuality and subsequently committing suicide) an adult certificate, making it a restricted viewing. In the next section, I will briefly sketch a picture of 'queer media' that has existed in India from 1991 to 2012.

## Queer media in India: 1991–2012

Queer media in India can be found in various platforms and in various languages. In this section, I have chosen to look at both print and visual media. I recognise that trying to document the entire media coverage related to queer issues since 1991 would be too vast for the purposes of this book, and therefore have chosen to provide some representative examples from three areas – the English language print media, Indian cinema and television. These, in turn, will lead to an entry point to look at digital queer spaces. Newspapers and other forms of printed media are still very important in India, despite the growth in digital technologies with newspapers such as *The Times of India* having a daily circulation of more than four million, being one of the world's largest-selling English newspapers.[5] Therefore, to begin this discussion on queer media in India, it is necessary to start from the printed media.

Mainstream press coverage related to queer issues in India can be traced back to the early 1990s. Shahani (2008: 175) provides a few interesting examples of the tone these articles take. He writes that 'some of these articles were positive and almost evangelical in their tone'; on the other hand, there were also articles which were 'uninformed, replete with negative stereotypes about homosexuality and gay men; and downright silly'. Roy notes that some of the first stories about queer people that were written within English language print media were a 'Gay 101 story' which featured an interview with a psychiatrist, quotes from queer people with changed names and finally an activist intervention (SAJA Forum, 2008). However, publications such as *The Times of India*[6] and *The Telegraph*[7] have in recent years published several opinion pieces arguing for acceptance of queer people within Indian society. The *Telegraph* piece, for example, interviews parents of LGBT children and their concerns about their children's sexuality. Not all coverage has been positive; there is an element of sensationalism that drives the approach to queer-related issues. Examples of this include the 2006 media coverage of police-aided harassment of the queer community in Lucknow, in which one newspaper used the headline of 'Cops bust gay racket'.[8] The sensational report revealed names and addresses of all those who were involved in the 'racket' that, as the report explained, included 'chatting with gay members at an Internet site' and 'meet for physical intimacy'. However, running parallel to this form of homophobic media was the establishment of queer publications such as *Bombay Dost* by Ashok Row Kavi in 1990. *Bombay Dost* began a queer revolution in mainstream media as one of the first queer-led print media to counter the silence and hostile queer representations within mainstream press. This was followed in succession by other magazines and ezines such as *Gaylaxy, Pink Pages India* and *gaysifamily*, to name a few.[9] Indian media, in general, is perceived to be historically reticent to discuss private matters such as sexuality; however, as the examples above demonstrate, there has been a considerable shift within this discourse.

Indian television has also played a key role in the public perception of queer people in India. Chat shows such as *Kuch Dil Se* (*From the Heart*) telecast in 2004, *Zindagi Live* (*Life*) and *We the People* (2001–2013) have time and again invited queer-identified people onto their panels as guests and have been sympathetic towards queer-related issues. In fact, Barkha Dutt, host of *We the People*, proudly declares that it was one of first television shows to advocate for the decriminalisation of homosexuality in India and has worked tirelessly to support the rights of queer people.[10] Reality television shows such as *Big Boss* (Season 1, 2006), which featured the openly queer actor Bobby Darling, further pushed queer consciousness into the domestic space of India. However, their departure from the show in the first week could be argued to constitute a testimony to the passive homophobia of the contestants as well as the viewers who voted Darling out. In 2010, a new Hindi television drama, *Maryada: Lekin Kab Tak* (*Honour: But for how long?*), was credited for being the first national primetime television drama to feature a gay storyline. This was a watershed moment because previous television dramas such as *Jassi Jaisi Koi Nahin* (*No one like Jassi*, 2003, an Indian version of *Ugly Betty*), *Pyaar Ki Ek Kahaani* (*This Is a Story about Love*, 2010), reduced queer characters to stereotypes in order to provide humour or a subplot to the main story. Similar changes can also be noticed within regional television: Kaushik Ganguly's Bengali television film *Ushnatar Jonnyo* (*For Her Warmth*, 2002), a homo-erotic story about two female friends, signals this magnitude of transformation that Indian television has been witnessing in the last decade. However, incidents such as the sting attack carried out by the Hyderabad television channel TV9 in 2011 (which I discuss in Chapter 6) exposing gay men on social networking sites have drawn widespread criticism from queer activists as well as the mainstream media.

## Queer Indian films

The film medium in India has also played a significant role in influencing and establishing public consciousness about queer identities and issues. As mentioned in the last chapter, Deepa Mehta's film *Fire* (1998), which drew the ire of the Hindu Right wing for portraying a lesbian love story, opened up a lively debate around female sexuality and queer identities in India. Gokulsing and Dissanyake (2012: 17), writing about Indian popular cinema, argue that 'the discourse of Indian Popular Cinema has been evolving steadily over a century in response to newer social developments and historical conjunctures'. Cinema in India participates in the continual reconstruction of the social imaginary. Gokulsing and Dissanayake further argue that, in addition to being a dominant form of entertainment, Indian cinema has also played a role in instigating dialogues on social change. While popular Indian cinema has a long history of featuring cross-dressing male stars in comic or song sequences (Dasgupta, 2015), films in the 1990s and the 2000s, such as *Mast Kalandar* (*Intoxicated*, 1991), *Raja Hindustani* (*Indian King*, 1996), *Dulhan Hum Le Jayenge* (*We will Take the Bride*, 2000), *Mumbai Matinee* (2003), *Rules Pyar Ka Superhit Formula* (*Rules: The Super Hit Formula for love*, 2003), *Page Three* (2004), saw a shift from the stereotypical effeminate gay characters in earlier films to more complicated multilayered gay characters in the latter films. This was followed by Onir's path-breaking film *My Brother Nikhil* (2005), which for the first time featured an HIV-positive gay character in the title role. In addition, two other films, *Kal Ho Na Ho* (*If Tomorrow Never Comes*, 2003) and *Dostana* (*Friendship*, 2008), using the trope of 'mistaken identity' and 'misreading' (Ghosh, 2007), represent and stage homoerotic play and queer performance. Dudrah (2012) questions if these films simply offer cheap thrills and comedy or whether they actually engage meaningfully with queer representations and possibilities. Dudrah (2012: 45) recognises this as the 'secret politics of gender and [queer] sexuality in Bollywood'. He argues:

> These codes and their associated politics are attempted to be spoken, seen and heard cinematically that little bit more loudly; not yet as radical and instant queer political transformation, but as implicit and suggestive queer possibilities that are waiting to be developed further.
>
> (Dudrah, 2012: 61)

In addition to these and numerous other mainstream Bollywood films, there are also significant queer films being made in regional film industries such as Bengal. Rituparno Ghosh's queer trilogy *Memories in March* (2010), *Arekti Premer Golpo* (*Not Another Love Story*, 2010) and *Chitrangada* (2012) paved the way for a public discourse on queer identities in Bengal. I have argued elsewhere (Datta, Bakshi and Dasgupta, 2015: 223) that these films firmly brought queerness to the middle class dining tables of Kolkata and are quite progressive (and reactive) of its time (also see Dasgupta and Banerjee, 2016). There is also a very strong non-commercial film sector in India spearheaded by queer film-makers such as the late Riyad Wadia, Nishit Saran and Sridhar Rangayan.[11] The establishment of several queer film festivals across India is a testimony to the growing number of such films being made each year. Owing to the limitations and focus of this book, I do not have the space to explore queer Indian cinema beyond this brief sketch; however, Datta, Bakshi and Dasgupta (2015), Dudrah (2012), Ghosh (2007) and Gopinath (2005) provide further information and insight. Now that I have provided a background to Indian media and queer representations within Indian media, I turn to the digital landscape that is the primary concern of this book. It was important to provide this media background because it provides a context and history within which digital media usage in India can be placed. In the next few sections, I detail some of the existing theoretical literature that is available on queer digital culture, before turning specifically to online queer spaces in India.

## Online queer spaces

Space is a loosely bound area which one can understand both physically (our immediate surroundings) and cognitively (Hall's concept of home or multiple homes; Hall, 1995). Queer public spaces can be thought of as spaces that cross, engage and transgress social locations. According to Desert (1997: 21), queer space 'lends an inflected turn of meaning' to existing spaces. The general perception and belief is that most public spaces are heteronormative, and thus a queer space becomes a 'wishful thinking or desire . . . of the reading of space where queerness at a few brief points . . . dominates the (heterocentric) norm' (Desert, 1997: 21). Queer cyberspace allows public sites on the Internet to be co-opted, doubling up as a public space to form 'community' and a private space for intimate encounters. Queer space is thus not about claiming territory, but rather identifying new possibilities out of the existing space.

Media representations of queer people in India have changed at different periods of time. While some sections of the media have been sympathetic to queer people, other sections of the media, fuelled by jingoistic nationalism, have castigated and portrayed queer people in a very negative light. These have been major factors and a driving force behind the emergence of an alternative social space offered by the Internet.

The emergence of the Internet has brought about some significant changes within the cultural and social landscape around the world. By destabilising the boundaries between the private and public, it has opened up new spaces for social interaction and community formation. Swiss and Hermann (2000) examine the Internet as a unique cultural technology where several complex processes come together:

> The technology of the World Wide Web, perhaps *the* cultural technology of our time, is invested with plenty of utopian and dystopian mythic narratives, from those that project a future of a revitalised, Web based public sphere and civil society to those that imagine the catastrophic implosion of the social into the simulated virtuality of the Web.
>
> (Swiss and Hermann, 2000: 2)

The idea of a utopian world being created through the Internet envisages cyberspace as a safe and accommodating sphere where communities can interact and grow. Howard Rheingold first advocated the concept of an online community in 1993 when he coined the term 'virtual community'. Taking on Anderson's (1991) idea of an 'imagined community', Swiss and Hermann argue that 'virtual communities require an act of imagination to use . . . and what must be imagined is the idea of the community itself' (2000: 54). Others such as Gajjala, Rybas and Altman (2008) suggest that cyberspace is not a place, but rather a locus around which modes of social interaction, commercial interests and other discursive and imaginative practices coalesce. Shahani argues that queer lives are not divided between online and offline spheres; rather they merge together in interesting ways:

> I do not find this virtual versus real debate useful or productive. People do not build silos around their online and offline experiences – these seep into each other seamlessly.
>
> (2008: 64)

Concurring with Mowlabocus (2010a: 2) and Shahani (2008), who also see 'gay male subculture as being something that is both physical and virtual', I would suggest that queer male digital culture in India needs to be understood within the larger context of the social history of the country. The need for a safe space is probably the single most important factor that underlies the formation of digital queer spaces. The engagement of queer people using the Internet and other digital spaces reveals one of the many forms of 'expression of the personal self within the public sphere' (Pullen, 2010: 1).

Woodland (2000), in his study of the relationship between sexual identity and space, shows the ways in which spaces shape identity and identities shape space. Woodland writes that 'the kinds of queer spaces that have evolved to present queer discourse can be taken as measure of what queer identity is in the 1990s'. Woodland's study of four distinct queer cyberspaces, which are private bulletin boards, mainstream web spaces, bulletin board systems (BBS) and a text-based virtual reality system, shows that all these spaces deploy a specific cartography to structure their queer content. However, 'one factor that links these spaces with their historical and real life counterparts is the need to provide safe(r) spaces for queer folk to gather' (427). Mowlabocus (2010a) points out that the relationship between the online world created by new media technologies and the offline world of an existing gay male subculture complicates the questions concerning the character of online communities and identities. Mowlabocus (2010a) further argues that the digital is not separate from other spheres of gay life, but in fact grows out of while remaining rooted in local, national and international gay male subcultures.

Mowlabocus's statement about the digital being rooted in local gay male subcultures is important in understanding queer cyberspace. While anti-discrimination laws exist on a national level in the United Kingdom, in some countries in Europe and parts of the United States, sodomy laws still exist in many parts of the world, especially in South Asia, as a remnant of the colonisers.[12] It is within this hostile space that I situate queer men using the Internet in India. Research by Alexander (2002) documents that most queer Internet sites is similar in layout, design and intent. Mowlabocus' study of *Gaydar*, a popular British gay cruising site, also points to the similarity of multiple queer digital spaces. He goes on to say that 'many of these websites may in fact be peddling the same types of bodies and the same ideological messages as each other' (2010a: 84). However, queer space does not just exist in primarily queer-identified sites (such as *Gaydar*, *Guys4Men* and *PlanetRomeo*); rather the prevalence of queer individuals coming into contact with each other via mainstream websites such as *Facebook*, *MySpace*, *Twitter* and *Orkut* (which has recently been shut down as of September 2014) has added another dimension to discussions of queer identity and its representations on the Internet. Drushel (2010) points out that:

> Online social networking websites such as MySpace and Facebook, in the few short years since their introduction in 2003, have grown immensely popular among teens and young adults especially. They present the possibility of providing a virtual social support function in an environment which appears non geographically restricted.
>
> (62)

The Foucaldian idea of space and its subversive potential can be harnessed in the context of queer cyberspace, which can be read as a Foucaldian heterotopia – a place of difference. Foucault describes heterotopia as 'something like counter-sites, a kind of effectively enacted utopia, in which the real sites, all the other real sites that can be found within the culture, are simultaneously represented, contested and inverted' (1986: 24). The queer cyberspace can be considered heterotopic where the utopic place is not only reflected, but also reconfigured and revealed.

## Online queer identities

Identity is a complex construct through which belonging is declared to a particular group or community. A more appropriate and easier way to think about identity is to understand what it is not. It is, first, not merely a marker of nationality, ethnicity, religion or gender, though of course these are implicit in their appellation. The primacy that these markers have gained at the cost of other identities – namely sexuality, by focussing on commonalities and obliterating the differences – has fuelled extreme brands of identity formation. These markers demonstrate the essentialist notion of looking at the subject as static, and thus the identity as a fixed phenomenon.

Weeks (1995: 98) calls identities 'necessary fictions' that need to be created, 'especially in the gay world'. If we concur with Weeks, then identities can be seen as sites of multiplicity which are performed, contested and constantly reshaped.

> Behind the quest for identity are different and often conflicting values. By saying who we are, we are also trying to express what we are, what we believe and what we desire. The problem is that these desires are often patently in conflict, not only between communities but within individuals themselves.
>
> (Weeks, 1995: 115)

Identity is at the core of digital queer studies, as Nina Wakeford in her landmark essay, 'Cyberqueer' (1997), critically notes:

> The construction of identity is the key thematic which unites almost all cyberqueer studies. The importance of a new space is viewed not as an end in itself, but rather as a contextual feature for the creation of new versions of the self.
>
> (Wakeford, 1997: 31)

While I recognise that our social and cultural lives are determined by a fairly universal heteronormative code which validates heterosexual signifiers, the cyberqueer identity recognises multiple sites (in cyberspace) and discourses which give rise to alternative readings of identity and allows us to read the multiplicities and complexities within individual profiles. Alexander (2002) suggests that instead of offering a one-dimensional view of the gay body, the Internet allows a multidimensional image to develop. The profile is created through an assemblage of written text and visual cues. Mowlabocus (2010a: 81) asserts that 'If gay male digital culture remediates the body and does so through a pornographic lens, then it also provides the means for watching that body, in multiple ways and with multiple consequences.'

The profile picture unsurprisingly is a formal unit of this identificatory process. It identifies the user, evidences his desires and implicates his intentions. Farr (2010: 89) argues, 'the use of photos helped to assure one knew what they were getting into should they meet someone offline'. Therefore, the shifting crowd on the Internet is given shape by the profile pictures. The pictures are relied upon to tell the presence or absence of 'fats, femmes, fish [and] trolls' (Alexander, 2002: 90).

Queer male digital culture is an example of participatory culture.[13] Participation can take place in a variety of ways. There are websites such as *PlanetRomeo*, *Manhunt* and *Gaydar* that are cruising/dating sites as well as websites that have a more political and/or health-related output and several websites/blogs featuring coming out narratives. McLelland, in his ethnographic study of Japanese gay culture, notes:

> The extent to which Japanese gay culture has spread on to the Internet is remarkable – Japan's online gay culture obviously relates to offline life but also comprises its own independent world. Japanese gay culture now online is far more accessible than the traditional gay world of bars and beats ever was – particularly for international observers and participants.
> (2002: 391)

McLelland's statement is certainly true in the contemporary queer context, where public queer cultures are the subjects of 'both online and offline systems of security and surveillance' (Mowlabocus, 2010a: 119). The subject of online identity is a complex and shifting one. Like every other element of cyberculture, identity is centrally bound to the use of language, from the choice of a name to the representation of the physical self.

Cooper (2010: 76) argues that 'virtual communities offer the opportunity for identity testing, preparation for coming out, if one chooses to do so and a support system throughout the entire process'. The Internet thus provides queer youth with tools to create and redefine their queer identities, from dating and sexual bonding to politics and activism. Cooper further notes:

> For many of them, the online community was extremely important in identity testing and working out issues before doing so in their families and community, where the consequences may be very high. Community members even assisted in aspects of negotiating identity in potentially unsafe areas. In this way the community was a sounding board, but one which remained engaged by providing support throughout the process.
>
> (2010: 83)

The Internet is entering a phase remarkably linked to the concept of identification. With the proliferation of sites such as *PlanetRomeo*, *Facebook* and *Twitter*, the garb of anonymity that dominated the Internet in the first decade, when users were translated as stock information that was hidden by a username and information endorsed through their registration, is slowly lifting. Campbell and Carlson have called this 'exchanging privacy for participation' (2002: 591). Cooper and Dzara, writing about queer groups on *Facebook*, argue:

> The ability to join LGBT groups on Facebook creates access to information and resources. For many especially those in isolated rural areas, these groups may be the individual's first contact with others who share similar interests.
>
> (2010: 106)

Cooper and Dzara's point echoes the earlier view of Woodland (2000: 428), who has argued that 'identity is formed and strengthened by membership in a self aware community . . . In the fluid geographies of cyberspace, community boundaries shift as the discourse changes'. Woodland (2000: 430) goes on to argue that 'community is the key link between spatial metaphors and issues of identity'. According to Woodland, individual voices are informed by the 'community', in determining what is appropriate in tone and content, and therefore shaping individual and community identity.

Early work by scholars such as Rheingold (1993) and Swiss and Hermann (2000) see the utopic possibilities of the Internet in offering a new space for political and ideological formations through debates about power, identity and autonomy and heralding the beginning of a new democracy that is not impinged by race, colour and socio-economic status. However, scholars such as Tsang (2000) dismiss these utopic declarations, arguing that 'given the mainstream definition of beauty in this society, Asians, gay or straight are constantly reminded that we cannot hope to meet such standards' (436). As an example, he states the case of a college student from Taiwan who, after changing his ethnicity to white, 'received many more queries and invitations to chat' (435). Gajjala, Rybas and Altman (2008), writing about race and online identities, critically note:

> Race, gender, sexuality, and other indicators of difference are made up of ongoing processes of meaning-making, performance, and enactment. For instance, racialization in a technologically mediated global context is nuanced by how class, gender, geography, caste, colonization, and globalization intersect.
>
> (2008: 1111)

Campbell concurs with Tsang's views about queer cyberspace retaining its disenfranchisement of the 'other'. He contends:

> Far from being a means of escaping the body, online interaction constitutes a mode of rearticulating our relationship to the physical body and, at least for these interactants, resisting dominant models of beauty and the erotic.
>
> (2004: 191)

This book will go on to argue that online spaces make the differences around class, gender and body, central to the narrative of disenfranchisement. In this regard, I am in agreement with scholars (such as Tsang and Campbell) that the Internet and queer digital spaces should be critiqued and its role in promoting a certain kind of body/identity challenged.

## Queering cyberspace in India

The online presence of queer South Asians can be traced back to the establishment of the *Khush* list, which was founded in 1992 and which is one of the 'oldest and most established discussion spaces for LGBT identified South Asians' (Shahani, 2008: 85).[14] With the establishment of the *Khush* list, other similar lists such as *SAGrrls* and *desidykes* (a women-only group) emerged in quick succession. Sandip Roy, editor and later board member of the *Trikone Magazine*, writes that *Trikone* was the first ever queer South Asian website to be hosted online in 1995 (Roy, 2003).[15]

In this section, I turn to the creation of online queer spaces in India (and the diaspora), which engage with a new form of queer geography. These spaces act both as a point of resistance to the hegemony of patriarchal heterosexual Indian values and at the same time as a response to 'the desire for community' (Alexander, 2002: 102). There has not been a significant South Asian presence on the Internet in the years following the last decade. This might be due partly to the fact that the Internet remains a domain of privilege which most people in South Asia and likewise India had little access to. Leung (2008: 7), in her research on online geographies of Asia, remarks that 'one of the main limitations of the study of Asian online identity and activity is that it has been confined to a narrow socio economic demographic'. While it is true that the Internet 'is not as white as it was once thought to be', it is also true that it is restricted to those who have the advantage and the socio-economic means to access it. Leung argues:

> Access to cyberspace requires the use, if not the ownership, of a computer, a modem, a telephone service and an Internet provider. These resources are surely not equally distributed amongst the diverse groups of lesbians, gay men, transgendered and queer folk.
>
> (22)

It is, therefore, not surprising that the South Asian diaspora, and more specifically the Indian diaspora, were amongst the first to inhabit cyberspace by virtue of their economic standing, in comparison to their counterparts back home.

Queer individuals in India are constructed as 'Un-Indian' and a threat to national cohesion and identity, as I mentioned earlier in Chapter 1. Gopinath (2005) articulates the ways in which sexual minorities of Indian origin (citing the case of South Asian Lesbian and Gay Association) were denied representation at the Annual India Day parade in New York City in 1995, claiming that the group represented 'anti-nationalist' sentiments. Thus, it would be safe to assume that the particular brand of Indian nationalism, currently espoused by the state of India, systematically denies and has been denying queer citizens representation and voice. As Narrain and Bhan (2005) in their landmark anthology *Because I Have a Voice* point out:

> It is not just Section 377 that affects queer people – laws against obscenity, pornography, public nuisance and trafficking are also invoked in the policing of sexuality by the state and police. One also has to pay heed to the civil law regime where queer people are deprived of basic rights such as the right to marry or nominate one's partner.
>
> (8–9)

Queer online spaces in India can be mapped as a vast terrain of digital sites that range from gay blogs (Gajjala and Mitra, 2008) to listservs, created specifically for queer people (Roy, 2003) to social networking sites such as *PlanetRomeo* and more generic social networking spaces such as *Facebook*.[16] Since 2010, with the proliferation of smartphones and mobile technology, queer locative applications such as *Grindr* have also become popular, especially in the metropolitan cities such as Delhi and Mumbai, for those who can afford such hardware and data connection. Scholarly material focussed on digital culture and queer identity in India is scant, and at the time of writing this book, I found only a handful of sources who have written on them. Roy's (2003) work on South Asian queer lists and queer websites in the 1990s is one of the earliest examples. Gajjala and Mitra (2008) and Mitra (2010) have undertaken research into queer Indian blogging, and finally Shahani (2008) has published an ethnographic study on the *GayBombay* community.

Roy (2003) affirms that South Asians living in the West saw the first proliferation of personal computers at home, and this afforded South Asian queer individuals in the diaspora – the privacy to log in to chat rooms on gay websites. However, he also notes that in recent years it has had a very wide impact in the homeland:

> In recent years, the Internet has also impacted on countries in South Asia. The proliferation of cyber cafes in India means checking e-mail is not so difficult anymore. As a result, more and more South Asians are logging on. It is noteworthy that the more locally focused Gay Bombay list actually has more members than the more international Khush-list.
>
> (182)

Roy also makes a critical observation about the difference between the queer listservs in South Asia and those in the diaspora. He argues that while South Asian queers in the diaspora are creating visibility for themselves in a largely white gay mainstream, 'groups in South Asia are much less interested in the ramifications about being 'Indian *and* gay' as they are about being 'gay *in* India'. Gajjala and Mitra (2008) do not see the Internet as a 'liberator of all oppressed populations', but rather their study examines the ways in which queer presences of Indians are manifested online. Gajjala and Mitra's work concerns the poignant appeal for members of a stigmatised group (in this case, queer Indian men), to create spaces of relative safety and belonging. These are men who are not only marginalised because of the oppressive impact of homophobia, but also whose opportunities for self and community formation is constrained because of the lack of social acceptance.

In their work, Gajjala and Mitra state that queer Indian bloggers are not just celebrating their queerness, but also 'negotiat[ing] a balance between their identities as "Indian" and as "GLBT"' (408). This is in contrast to Alexander's (2002) early work on queer blogging, where he argues that 'discussions of the intersections between personal and professional life are all but non existent' (98). Thus, in the last 10 years, not only the content but also the kind of queer narratives that proliferate on the Internet have changed. Bachcheta (2007) points out that transnational queer representations are produced in a variety of sites that involve different actors. South Asian queer representation can be traced to three well-defined categories – academia (both in and outside South Asia), activism related to queer activism and finally the Internet. She writes, 'The actors tend to be privileged on a number of accounts: most are located in educated sectors of the West, and most are male. Their activities are differentially disciplined, whether by national laws, the academy or modalities of censorship' (104–105).

Additionally, Roy (2003) states that the Internet was invaluable for those growing up in small towns that did not have an active queer community. The anonymity offered by the Internet along with the possibility of meeting people from other parts of India, and perhaps even other parts of the world, was a great impetus for those queer men using the Internet in these small towns. Gajjala and Mitra, writing about Indian queer men living in the rural and small towns of India, critically point out that:

> Even gay men in the smallest, least industrialised, most rural towns of Indian heartland scout for tricks online . . . email and guys4men.com is a great way to make their presence felt in their tiny district (and even though they probably never imagined) in cyberspace.
>
> (2008: 416)

While it is true that processes of globalisation and liberalisation have made queer people a part of the public discourse in India, the change is still concentrated in select areas only. Chandra (2008) writes:

> This, however, should not give the impression that all is well for the queer in India. The change . . . is to be noticed in the urban metropolises and among the educated, middle or upper middle class. Besides, the extent of the change is small and often entails stiff resistance from the entrenched heteropatriarchal anti-gay lobbies, interestingly comprising the Hindu Right, the Church and the Muslim clergy. Away from the urban centres, in small towns and villages, among the lower and lower-lower classes, homosexuality continues to be feared, hated, and stigmatised, and lesbians and gays generally lead closeted (read oppressed) lives.
>
> (n.p.)

Shahani (2008) has noted that the reasons for people signing up to an online list such as *GayBombay* were varied: 'For some it was just curiosity, for others a way to know more about the emerging gay world in India.' Shahani (2008: 28) goes on to quote one of the users who said that he was 'fascinated at being able to interact with other gay people in Bombay, while being anonymous at the same time'. However, the slow penetration of the Internet in the suburban and rural parts of India and the digital divide have a huge impact on the voices that get heard and those that do not. Gajjala and Gajjala optimistically respond:

> Increasing access and widespread participation in ICT will bridge the 'digital divide,' allow a cacophony of voices to participate in cyber community building, encourage intercultural awareness, put an end to racisms and cultural domination throughout the world.
>
> (2008: x)

However, the truth remains that the digital divide in India is a significant one. Roy (2003) points out that the digital divide has a real impact in squeezing out voices that do not respond quickly enough. Issues around censorship of the Internet and what can and cannot be viewed are also central in discussions around access to Internet sites. As I pointed out earlier in this chapter, one of the reasons for the slow penetration of the Internet in India is because of the lack of computer ownership in relation to mobile telephones and television. A possible answer to this has been the burgeoning growth of cyber cafes in India, especially in the suburban and rural belts. Rangaswamy (2007), in her work on cyber cafes in Mumbai, is however quick to point out that rather than being spaces of possibilities, they also take on the role of censorship. Rangaswamy points out that all the cyber cafes have notices banning pornographic content from being accessed and, despite having women clientele, are predominantly male spaces. Thus, the cyber cafe, far from becoming a spatial outlet to the limitless possibilities of accessing queer content and media, has also become a space under constant surveillance that queer individuals might hesitate to use. The regulatory discourse surrounding illegality and what Rangaswamy (2007) calls the 'greyness of youth Internet activity', characterised by virtual chatting and social networking, thus becomes a site suffused with coded practices and non-formal boundaries which have to be time and again negotiated for safety and privacy.

With India's increasing urbanisation and economic liberalisation, there has been a significant change in the assertion of the queer identity. Financial independence and political consciousness have made queer men access the Internet for a variety of reasons, including participation in more political dialogues. This has also led to a growth of cyberactivism where individuals not only voice their opinions about their own sexuality, but also increasingly challenge political and media representations of queerness (Gajjala and Mitra, 2008; Mitra, 2010). Mitra (2010: 167) writes that 'queer Indian bloggers "talk back" to institutional normativity, and appropriate an institution-engendered divide between "practice" and "person/body" in terms of civil identity, online representation, partial anonymity and partial review'. Through a process of transnationalisation, the individuals actively explore and 'queer' popular discourses.[17] Drawing on Anderson's notion of imagined communities, Mitra argues 'with the growth of CMC (computer mediated communication), particularly from the use of the Internet, a new set of possibilities for community, and nation formation have emerged' (2000: 677). As Mitra (2000: 678) points out, electronic spaces such as social networking sites allow users to 'recreate a sense of virtual community through a rediscovery of their commonality'. While online new media might seem to offer a democratic scope for queer men to engage with issues around subjectivity and identity, it must also be remembered that this is fragmented and disconnected. The online space cannot simply be viewed as emancipatory or all-encompassing; rather issues such as class, gender and the socio-economic background of the users need to be engaged with, as the following chapters and case studies will evidence.

## Notes

1 Axis powers refer to Japan, Germany and Italy, who were part of the anti-British military alliance.
2 VSNL began in 1986 and was one of the first Public Sector Undertakings (PSU) to be listed in the New York Stock exchange. VSNL still exists, although the Government no longer owns it. It was acquired by the Tata Group, a big player in the telecommunication sector in India, in 2008.
3 See Internet and Mobile Association of India (2014). 'Internet in India, 2014 Research Report'. Available at: <http://www.iamai.in/rsh_pay.aspx?rid=4hjkHu7GsUU=>. Accessed on 6 July 2015.
4 The Indian Censor Board, CBFC, is a body attached to the Ministry of Information and Broadcasting which is well known for its lack of transparency and 'conspiracy of silence' (Bhowmick, 2013: 303). Their policies have changed from time to time relative to the state machinery and the government in control. It is mandatory for any film wanting a commercial release to obtain a censorship certificate. For more information, see Bhowmick (2013).
5 See Brendan Daley (2014). Available at: http://www.edelman.com/post/india-print-media-alive-well/. Accessed on 6 July 2015.
6 Poonam Gupta (2011). 'Do desi parents accept their gay children'. *Times of India*. 11 July 2011.

7  Arundhati Basu (2008). 'Breaking free: Indian gays are getting organised and boldly coming out'. *The Telegraph.* 31 August 2008.
8  'Cops bust gay racket, nab SAT official, 3 others'. *Hindustan Times.* 5 January 2006. Available at: <http://www.hindustantimes.com/News-Feed/ NM4/Cops-bust-gay-racket-nab-SAT-official-3-others/Article1–38816. aspx>. Accessed on 4 November 2012.
9  These are available at: http://www.gaylaxymag.com, http://www.pink-pages.co.in and http://www.gaysifamily.com respectively.
10  See Barkha Dutt. 'We the People'. Available at: <http://www.youtube. com/watch?v=x5_1aXfyw74&feature=share&list=SPE77B5BBB6220A 28F>. Accessed on 4 November 2012.
11  *Bomgay* (1993), *A Mermaid called Aida* (1996), *Summer in My Veins* (1999), *Pink Mirror* (2006), *Yours Emotionally* (2007), *68 Pages* (2007) and others.
12  Homosexuality is currently illegal in Afghanistan, Bangladesh, Bhutan, Pakistan and Sri Lanka in South Asia, with only Nepal legalising homosexuality in 2007. India legalised homosexuality in 2009 following a judgement by the Delhi High Court, only to recriminalise it in 2013 by the Supreme Court. In addition, seven countries (which include Iran, Saudi Arabia, United Arab Emirates, Nigeria, Mauritania, Sudan and Yemen) punish homosexuality with the death penalty.
13  Jenkins (2006) explains participatory culture is a contrast to the older notions of passive media spectatorship. Rather than seeing producers and consumers of media as separate, Jenkins argues we should see them as participants who interact with each other. Participants are actively participating in the creation and circulation of this content.
14  *Khush* list is a Bulletin Board. At the time of writing this chapter, the last activity/message posted on the Khush list was on 9 February 2012. The list can be accessed via http://dir.groups.yahoo.com/group/khush-list.
15  *Trikone* and *Trikone Magazine* (started in 1986) are based in San Francisco. *Trikone* is one of the earliest South Asian LGBT support groups.
16  A blog is a regularly updated website or webpage, which works like a journal. I would like to explain why queer blogs should be read as a space rather than simply a text. Gajjala and Mitra (2008) have noted that by blogging, Indian queer people were not simply being whisked away to some kind of virtual reality; rather they were creating inclusive spaces, where sexuality was one of the many identifications that the users engaged with. Queer texts have the ability to work as a 'social glue'. As Pullen (2014: 81), in his recent work on the 'It Gets Better Project' vlog campaign, remarks that through bonding these stories together, a more robust LGBT community is being created. It is because of this that I argue blogs function as a space.
17  Transnationalisation can be defined as a series of processes that heighten the interconnectivity amongst people through multiple ties and activities across different nation states and regions. Transnational communities are, therefore, not attached to specific cartographic regions. Vertovec (2010) has argued that this can be traced to the growth of communication technologies and digital media.

# 3 Virtual intimacies on digital queer platforms

## Introduction

> The real change had already taken place: the landscape of dating had changed completely. Everything was now just a click away.
>
> (Kauffman, 2012: 4)

Jean Claude Kauffman in his book *Love Online* (2012) states that with the turn of the millennium something remarkable happened. The landscape of human interaction shifted considerably, particularly with respect to the ways in which one establishes intimate connections. The use of online spaces had become a 'normal and legitimate way of finding a sexual partner – long term or otherwise' (2012: 5). Social networking sites and new media technologies have created opportunities for queer men in India to establish intimate connections. In this chapter, I interrogate the idea of virtual intimacies and the potentials for new kinds of politics nurtured within virtual intimate formations. McGlotten (2007: 123) defines virtual intimacies as 'intimacies mediated by technologies, by screens in particular'. My analysis in this chapter engages with two different virtual spaces – *PlanetRomeo* and *Grindr*. I introduce a series of case studies and narratives to explore the notion of virtual intimacies. These case studies began as semi-structured interviews and informal conversations with research participants, followed by participant observation and lurking on *PlanetRomeo* and *Grindr*. To interrogate the concept of virtual intimacy, I use four main themes to frame my discussions – intimacy, privacy, kinship and friendship. These themes speak to each other and intersect one another in multiple ways on virtual sites. I begin by discussing the literature around virtual space, intimacy and virtual intimacies with regard to the four main themes I have outlined, to foreground my research sites (*PlanetRomeo* and *Grindr*) as a space through which a sense of intimacy is forged. I follow this by introducing a range of case studies about the ways in which queer men on these virtual spaces articulate intimacy. In conclusion, I argue that virtual intimacies play a crucial role in understanding queer male subjectivity in India, beyond the legal and national discourses within which queer politics currently situates them. As a concluding point, I would like to point out that this chapter is not planned or grouped around specific platforms, but rather it is thematically led.

## Intimacy in the age of social media

Kuntsman (2012: 2) has argued that there is increasingly a need to 'think about feelings, technologies and politics together, through each other'. Arguably, digital technologies are changing the ways in which we connect with others – our sense of belonging and experience of love and sexuality. I draw on a number of scholars working on digital and queer studies, to investigate the ways in which these different categories intersect. Ahmed (2004) points out that texts have emotionality, arguing that texts use a variety of metaphors and allusions to generate affect. By this she means that the words and visuals that make up a text generate meaning because of their history and context. This is useful in contextualising and considering new media texts and the online interactions that take place on webpages, blogs and discussion forums.

Giddens (1991: 123), writing about the transformation of intimacy, comments that it is 'an intrinsic relation between the globalising tendencies of modernity and localised events in day-to-day life a complicated, dialectical connection between the "extensional" and the "intensional"'. He argues that romantic love is a product of modernity and has accompanied the process of modernisation. It is a form of storytelling where the self is narrated. According to Giddens (1991: 38), romantic love based on intimacy was impossible in the social environment where 'most marriages were contracted, not on the basis of mutual sexual attraction, but economic circumstance'. He further explains that romantic love is related to the question of intimacy and takes the form of an emotional communication.

Following Giddens, McGlotten (2013: 9) argues that intimacy has always been virtual. It is scripted, even if those scripts are 'diverse and contradictory . . . virtuality is one way to conceptualise intimacy'. Within the digital landscape, intimacy is generated and the 'emotional culture' it gives rise to is authenticated through public display and through the intersection of private and public lives. This view is supported by Giddens (1991), who argues that intimacy is part of a democratised process and structurally corresponds to the private sphere. Within the digital sphere, especially aided through social media, the perception of the private and the public is ruptured beyond recognition. According to Boyd (2008: 19), new media technology has made 'social information more easily accessible and can rupture people's sense of public and private by altering the previously understood social norms'. It is not that the traditional private and public distinction ceases to exist in cyberspace, but rather that they are reformulated.

Authors such as Reiman (1995) do not consider the act of sharing personal information as a way of conceptualising intimacy. Reiman argues that the revealing of personal information, then, is not what constitutes or powers the intimacy; rather 'it depends and fills out, invites and nurtures, the caring that powers the intimacy' (Reiman, 1995: 157). Reiman finds the value of intimacy within scarcity and exclusivity, a sort of restricted emotion. I disagree with Reiman's position. I believe that rather than being exclusive, the process of sharing enables my research participants to blur the private/public divide and articulate intimate scenarios in ways that do not restrict it. As my ethnography reveals, intimacy, while displayed and exhibited publicly (and often in public places), the language of its expression is still a 'privileged knowledge' that is only understood by those to whom it is directed.

Parallel to this also runs the issue of privacy. In what ways does intimacy manage to remain private? If intimacy, as Gidden has pointed out, is based on the narrative of self, what does it mean to share this narrative publicly through a social networking site? As research by digital and queer scholars (McGlotten, 2013; Mowlabocus, 2010a) demonstrate, intimacy can be shared and disclosed in private or public networks. Contemporary articulations of intimacy are being increasingly represented within public realms. This is emancipatory and additionally has the ability to constitute a powerful gesture, as my case studies in the following sections will reveal. Giddens (1991: 190) argues that 'intimacy should not be understood as an interactional description, but a cluster of prerogatives and responsibilities that define agendas of practical activity'. New media technologies have aided queer men in this quest, by offering them scope to explore various forms of intimacy. Privacy is also a contentious concept in a country like India, where my research is based. The family in India is seen as an idealised, traditional, secure structure, where privacy is anachronistic to the social dynamics that a family seeks to create. The domestic space, while seen as a private sphere, offers little privacy to its family members. Many of my research participants, for instance, still live with their families and their families police these spaces. Shahani (2008) articulates that having a private place to meet is uncommon in India, and often meetings and sexual encounters have to be planned around the absence of other family members in the house or using public spaces. The digital sphere, in a sense, provides a "lifeline" of private intimacy for these queer men.

The next two themes I introduce are kinship and friendship. In this book, I do not see friendship and kinship as exclusive sets of relationships. Weston's (1991) study found that chosen families of friends created by queer people are not merely compensating for the absence of biological families. The new relational ties that queer men seek to create, based on intimacy and trust, have characteristics that can be applied to both friendship and kinship. According to Rumens (2011: 38), 'these new relational forms help to destabilise heteronormative notions of family and friendship.' Butler (2002) astutely argues that queer kinship is not the same as gay marriage; rather it should be read as a reworking and revision of the social organisation of friendship and community to create non-state-centred forms of support and alliance. Same-sex friendship in India is also a staple component of the Indian popular culture, especially the popular cinema genre (Bollywood) where *dosti* and *yaarana* (friendship) are celebrated even at the expense of heterosexual love. I agree with Rumens's (2011) thesis that friendship and kinship work as a strategy for emotional and material support. These structures also help to overcome isolation and to find support, both of which were highlighted by my research participants as being extremely important while growing up. In addition to the themes of intimacy and privacy, friendship and kinship allow a useful way to read virtual intimacies. I am in agreement with Ahmed (2004) that emotions are produced through attachments (kinship and friendship). In this regard, Ahmed also talks about the ways in which certain signs and symbols become interpellated with certain associations. For example, *PlanetRomeo* and *Grindr* for my research participants were also objects through which they could not only make intimate attachments, but also reject certain forms of attachments.

In this chapter, I define intimacy as an assemblage of bodies, feelings and connections, mediated through new media technologies. In order to sketch the ways in which intimacies are experienced virtually by queer men in India, I am constructing a shifting virtual world where the screen-body interactions between my research participants and the sites they navigate twist the public dimensions of cyberspace by suspending normal rules of social intercourse. Through a close reading of their stories, they demonstrate the ways in which queer lives are intimately intertwined and informed by new media technologies bearing potentials for a new kind of queer politics in India.

## Haider's story: close encounters on *Grindr*

Haider (26) currently lives in Paris, France. I met him during my fieldwork in New Delhi in 2013, when he was preparing to move to Paris with his French partner. Haider has a degree in English and he has taught English at various private institutions in New Delhi. He is 'out' to all his friends but not to his family. He lived in a one bedroom apartment in the upmarket area of Hauz Khas Village (a popular trendy destination for young middle class professionals and expatriates) when I met him. He spoke at length about using *Grindr* and *PlanetRomeo* to meet other queer men in New Delhi, even meeting his current partner on one of these sites.

Haider told me that he preferred to use a social application like *Grindr* because of two factors. First, it let him 'hook up' with people almost instantaneously, as these were people who were already in the neighbourhood. Second, and in his words, 'It kept the riff-raff away.' I was very interested to hear more about this and pressed him to elaborate. He said:

> *Grindr* is much better than PR [*PlanetRomeo*]. I mean it is an app. Also unlike PR which anyone can login to and use, *Grindr* acts like a filter. It keeps the 'riff raffs away'. At the moment to have *Grindr* you need to own a smart phone *isliye sab koi nahin aa sakta* (so that is why not everyone can use this).
>
> (11 July 2013)

Haider demonstrates the privileged nature of using an application such as *Grindr*, which by locating itself as a smartphone application caters to a 'classed' community of users. Queer politics in India subsumes and makes the social actors almost indistinguishable. Talking of queer politics as it emerges across class/caste and religious background on Pride days does not translate in the same manner in the everyday lives of queer men. Clearly, class still matters to men like Haider. While social stratification and stigmatisation across caste and religion may have changed on a surface level over the years in India, inequalities still remain and make their presence felt, even when Haider is mapping his desires and looking for sex or love on *Grindr*. Smartphones, in this case, become what Ahmed (2004: 91) has described as the transference of emotion that she calls 'sticky'. In her words, stickiness is about 'what objects do to other objects – it involves a transference of affect'. Owning a smartphone or being a *Grindr* user conceals other silent concepts within it such as being from a certain (upper/middle) social class and (higher) economic and social background. As such, *Grindr* is creating a kind of social enclave that only the privileged few can access. On one hand, it is creating a form of acknowledgement and recognition of one's own social position as Haider does, and on the other hand, the technology itself is contributing towards perpetuating an unconscious (or even conscious) classed experience. Inadvertently, mobile applications such as *Grindr* work as a screening device by which certain people ('riff raffs' in Haider's words) are kept away because they do not have the economic means to own this mobile technology and enter the queer enclave created by these applications.

Haider also explained the ways in which *Grindr* helped him to create interactive intimate scenarios (McGlotten, 2007: 128). It was a part of his evolving relationship with digital culture. Intimacies and intimate sessions could now be initiated through his smartphone. It no longer needed him to actually go out or look for porn to 'satisfy urges' (Haider, 11 July 2013).

> I don't have to search for free porn. I can just switch on *Grindr* and enter into a hot texting session now.
>
> (11 July 2013)

The interface for *Grindr* includes a homepage that displays a number of profiles (usually 200 for free users) within the user's vicinity, with +/− 20 feet accuracy. The interactions are private. They are initiated by users clicking on the profiles of other users who are online at that time. Participants cannot engage in public conversations, so all interactions that take place are private. The example below is typical of what transpires when a private chat has been initiated. Haider gave me permission to quote this verbatim, disguising any identification information.

HAIDER:  Hello
HOTBOY:  Hii
HOTBOY:  See ur more pics?
HAIDER:  Yes (sends picture). What you looking for?
HAIDER:  Where in Delhi?
HOTBOY:  Fun. U hv any plc thn w cn full night [Do you have place? then we can have fun all night]
HAIDER:  I live in HKV.
HOTBOY:  Kkk. Thn cn w mt now. If u intrestd wth me. [Okay. Then can we meet now, if you're interested in me]

(6 July 2013)

The procedures for these interactions are fairly consistent. They begin with a greeting (Hello/Hi), and then move on to an exchange of personal information such as pictures, sexual roles (this was not discussed in this case because they had both stated their sexual roles on their profiles), the kind of activity that is sought (fun) and whether or not the person has a place to meet for 'fun'. As mentioned before, the ability to have a place to meet is often a key currency in some of these interactions. Haider himself told me:

> Not many people have their own place in Delhi. A few do and this is attractive to many people who want to hook up. Often conversations can be stopped if it is discovered that neither of the interactants have a place.
>
> (11 July 2013)

Sumit, interviewed in Kolkata, also stressed the same point:

> When I want to meet someone to have fun, one of the first things I ask for is if they have a place to have fun. If the answer is negative we often just stop talking. Of course this also depends on what I am looking for at that moment. If it is just a hook up, there is no point carrying on the conversation is it? I don't often have a place to myself. I have to plan it around my parent's timetable. After making sure the other person has a place we then start talking about our sexual fantasies and exchange of pictures.
>
> (22 June 2013)

It would be worthwhile noting here that despite the supposed disembodied nature of virtual 'chatting', the user's body is very much a constant presence in all these conversations, which are of an intimate nature (Mowlabocus, 2010a, 2010b).[1] The body is also incrementally constructed, first through the use of textual descriptions followed by an exchange of more intimate photographs

> HOTBOY:  Nce body. Whats ur stats? [Nice body. What are your stats?]
> HAIDER:  30 w 34 c, 80 weight
> HOTBOY:  Gud gud. You have any nude pics?
>
> (6 July 2013)

As the conversation progressed, I noticed that the body becomes more present within the discussion. The disembodied Haider transforms first into a textual body with his vital statistic information shared, and then slowly transforms into a visual body with an exchange of photographs.

Digital images abound on *Grindr*; in fact, there are very few profiles which choose not to have an image even if it is without their face. Mowlabocus (2010b) argues that these images operate as a culturally important resource that offer a specific force for identity formation and what it means to be a gay man in contemporary culture (body types, looks etc.).

The kind of intimacy that *Grindr* offers its users is the kind that one would not parade in public or advertise amongst friends (McGlotten, 2007: 130). However, it is something that Haider is sharing with a complete stranger. This form of negotiation and intimacy is also quite different from what Haider would have experienced if he were cruising in physical spaces, where glances and gestures (visual communication) would play a far more important role than the text. The interaction between Haider and HotBoy thus characterises a move from its disembodied nature to a more embodied one. As the chat progresses, the participants become visual forms, and finally physical forms from their initial textual description when they meet up.

HOTBOY:  I m cmng. Tkng 30 t 40 mins [I am coming. Taking 30 to 40 minutes]
HAIDER:  Ok
HOTBOY:  Gvur no [give your number]
HAIDER:  XXXXXXXX
HOTBOY:  XXXXXXX
HAIDER:  See you in sometime

(6 July 2013)

Talking to Haider, I realised that there are no clear lines between virtual and physical intimacy. While he used *Grindr* primarily to pick up men, he also frequently used it to initiate a 'hot chat session' that sometimes, as in the case of Sumit, led to a 'video session'.

SUMIT:  There was this one time I was chatting to a guy on PR [*Planet-Romeo*]. He was really cute and into me. However he lived in the other side of the city and it was such a drag having to go all over there, so instead we decided to have a video session. It's almost the real thing and worked as a good substitute to get off to rather than watching porn.

(22 June 2013)

What Sumit elaborates in this statement is the ways in which the screen mediates intimacy offering an intense relationship that is 'almost the real thing'. It not only intensified Sumit's relationship with technology, but also allowed him to successfully enact his desire with a sense of seriousness. The very act of initiating a video session functioned as a substitute for one's affective presence and transformed a technologically mediated space (of Skype, in this case) into a zone of virtual intimacy (Kuntsman, 2012). The immersive nature of an application like *Grindr* offers users such as Haider a sense of closeness to other users both geographically and on an intimate level.

## In the chat room

Moving away from the 'private space' of *Grindr*, this section will focus on the chat room that is understood as a 'public space'. This section will further problematise the private and public binary of digital space. The chat room is situated within an interactive media paradigm, which allows the participant to construct interactive 'intimate' scenarios. *PlanetRomeo* has several 'clubs' with active forums that facilitate 'chats' between participants.

For the purpose of this research, I joined the PR_Hindi[2] Club, which had one of the highest numbers of members from India. The forum has a variety of threads under which discussions take place. Unlike the Instant Messaging Chat Rooms available on *Gaydar*, group discussions/chats in *PlanetRomeo* can only take place through the various clubs and threads.

Initial research into chat rooms has focussed on the environment. Subhramanyam, Greenfield and Tynes (2004: 653), in their ethnographic study of an online teenage chat room, observe three typical characteristics of this space: several topics are discussed parallel in overlapping groups, people contribute to several conversations at the same time and finally the conversations are quite short. According to Subhramanyam, Greenfield and Tynes (2004), teenagers spend a considerable amount of time talking about sex and looking for spaces where they can explore and understand their sexuality. The chat room is one such space that aids in the construction of sexuality. Scholars such as McGlotten (2007, 2013) conceptualise the chat room as a subversive space that allows various kinds of conversations to take place. McGlotten (2007: 129) remarks:

> Chat rooms let you sidestep the rules about talking in the right way, about being honest, they let you in short sidestep 'good' communication . . . what mattered was your ability to draw someone out . . . to quickly construct hot chat scenarios.

The subversive potential of the *PlanetRomeo* forums also speaks to issues of class and assimilationist politics. While spaces such queer groups on *Facebook* rigidly protect the hierarchies of class (as I will discuss further in my next chapter), the chat room with its relative anonymity and potential for all forms of dialogue challenges and creates a space that destabilises some of these assumptions. Despite the public nature of the forum, I contend that it is less policed than other spaces and speaks to the issue of the 'lack' of private space for queer men in India.

Most people using these threads speak about issues such as religion and sexuality, marriage and sexual violence in the country. However, many users such as Johnnyred find it hypocritical that some users and administrators of these forums (which are called 'Clubs' on *PlanetRomeo*) also act as moral guardians who think that 'there are more important things to talk about than sex'. Johnnyred writes:

> The guys at the club are too pretentious, I suppose. Talking sex is taboo for majority of them. This is contrary to the need of the average online guy.

(28 December 2011)

This is indeed an important insight because, for many of these participants this is the only space where they can articulate their erotic and sexual desires/ fantasies that they feel compelled to hide in their social surroundings. The chat room, which is situated as a 'public' site, works very differently in the Indian context. The chat room, despite its 'public' setting, allows a sense of privacy outside the domestic space of the family. Unlike narratives found elsewhere in cyberspace, which are ambivalent and register a range of intimations, this space allows for direct communication, where intimacy plays a central role.

Muscle_ind, a 43-year-old bisexual man from Orissa, is a frequent participant on the forums. He described his time on *PlanetRomeo* as 'unfettered'. He not only enjoys chatting to men from his city on the forums, but also likes to use his time there to build connections with men in other cities that he visits for work.

> I enjoy the threads. People talk about many things here. There are threads where we rate the guy before us and say if we want to sleep with him or not, but there are also threads where we can talk about other things like what are the safe places for cruising. I do get quite sad if someone rejects me but then I just move on.
>
> (15 November 2012)

The issue of emotional investment raised by Muscle_Ind here is crucial. For Muscle_Ind, virtual intimacies are very real. Sites such as *PlanetRomeo* aid him in his search for potential friends and sexual partners, and the hurt of rejection is not just confined to the site. Mowlabocus (2010a) points out that there are no clear lines between the online and the offline and they seep into each other seamlessly. Similarly, it could be argued that Muscle_ Ind's sexual and emotional investment with the site also had consequences for his offline life – the hurt of rejection and the sadness associated with it are 'real' emotions that he feels. In the same way, when he talks about 'moving on' he displays optimism at the possibility of the site still helping him to meet a potential date/sexual partner.

Some of the other threads I closely followed on the forums engaged with self-doubt and homophobia. In one such thread, Muscle_ind asked why certain Indian men feel guilty after having sex. To give further context to this question, the thread was focussed on Indian men who have sex with men, who do not necessarily identify as queer or gay. The thread invited several responses with people ascribing this to internalised homophobia, an inability to come to terms with being gay and social guilt. One of the most interesting responses was by a-kshays. In a revelatory confession he declares:

> There can be many reasons behind the guilt. Religious, social, cultural, ethical. I have sexual feelings for a man,i have suppressed them for

long, coz of my religion. And in end up releasing my tension. I feel guilty.

I am a married and a committed man. I feel guilty about cheating on my spouse and partner.

I have seen how men are automatically considered effeminate and thus denigrated if they are known to like another man. I do that momentarily and i feel guilty.

I have fear or hatred about my own sexuality. But in the heat of moment I end up having sex with another man. I start doubting my own sexual orientation. I feel guilty.

(5 October 2013)

I would argue that this was not a conversation that a-kshays could have had in any other space. In fact, when I contacted him about his post, he was initially hesitant to talk with me. After several days of participating on the forum, he finally responded; writing that there are very few places where he can be so 'open about himself' and declare his true feelings. He was not 'out' to any of his family members or co-workers and he was married to a woman due to familial pressures. When he did end up meeting other men, the encounters were purely sexual and as he put it 'to release tension'. The forums/chat rooms provided him with a form of intimate space that he shared with other men living similar lives or strangers who would not be judgemental of his choices. He remarked that he would not have shared his story in any other setting outside the *PlanetRomeo* forum.

I don't have any close gay friends who I can know [*sic*] my story. I only tell on PR cos [*sic*] they will understand. I also know when I meet other men from here it is mostly just for sex and I don't think he would be interested to hear about my double life or my depression. He has only come to release his frustrations like me, so I tell on the thread and people give me support.

(23 October 2013)

I would like to use a-kshay's case as a way to think more closely about the ways in which *PlanetRomeo* offers friendship and intimacy for a-kshay, and the kind of kinship and relationality that gets created in this context. The current fight for decriminalisation in India is based on the provision of the state guaranteeing the queer male subject the right to love and privacy. The right to love is then being constructed as something that can be consumed in private by the modern queer subject. Privacy, as a number of scholars in a recent publication (Dave, 2012; Shrivastava, 2013) argue, remains a class issue. For men like a-kshays and muscle_ind, they do not conform and nor want to conform to being an affective marker for the

Indian state to confer rights on. I will argue that their social backgrounds close their access to a private space. Thus, their articulation of being queer and forming intimate attachments is only made possible through a space such as *PlanetRomeo*. Despite the very public nature of the forums that they unhesitatingly participate in, they still feel protected. There is a conscious understanding that the other users of these forums are also 'like them'. In doing so, they are conveying a notion of embedded experience. It would be worthwhile to refer to Bourdieu's (1985) concept of habitus as a way to understand this. Bourdieu explains that social life cannot be understood as an aggregate of individual experiences alone, but rather social meanings are made manifest in bodies and practices, a series of 'dispositions' – lifestyle values, thinking and feeling – that the individual acts upon acquired through the experiences of everyday life. A-kshays and muscle_ind are a product of this habitus. The kinship structures that they are creating on *PlanetRomeo* do not strictly conform to the ways in which Weston or Rumens have theorised them, as I explained in a previous section. These are not necessarily people they trust or know, but rather they remain intransient users (anonymous like themselves) who they encounter at various points, with whom they can identify and share their stories with without fear of censure or being pushed into the neoliberal discourse of 'coming out' in public and being visible.[3] I will be complicating this notion of 'coming out' in the Indian context further in my case study on Ruhin.

## Intimate queer bonds: Sumit's story

Sumit is a 35-year-old man living in Kolkata. He works for a cultural organisation in the city and is fairly open about his sexuality (to his co-workers, friends and cousins). I met Sumit on a *Facebook* group that catered towards queer people in Kolkata (KRPF). Sumit was interested in my research and was happy to be interviewed. He informed me that some of the best friends and lovers (he added under air quotes) he had made had been initiated through social networking sites. He was quite involved with the queer scene in Kolkata and regularly used the Internet to 'hook up' or meet other people. Like many other queer men, Sumit was searching for intimacy and companionship and hoped the Internet would provide him with potential intimate connections. When we first met, he wanted to talk about his love life:

> I met Rohan on PR [*PlanetRomeo*] two years go. We met on a forum thread where we were discussing what kind of queer films should be made. We hit off instantly. At that point there was no romantic connection but other people chatted about us on the thread. Even we had

begun to talk privately. Ultimately it led to us going out for a date followed by a yearlong relationship.

According to Povinelli (2006), liberal subjects are formed through the construct of romantic intimacy. In her definition of liberalism, Povinelli invokes the concept of freedom and the self-determining subject. She explains that the modern subject is constructed through romantic monogamous love fashioned through a set of pre-existing institutions and traditions. The modern Indian queer male subject is an individual who is inaugurated through the idea of romantic love. Sumit's desire for a romantic relationship with Rohan is formed through others on the thread suggesting a monogamous coupledom for both of them. The bestowing of conjugality is a form of regulatory mechanism for Sumit and Rohan's private chats. The private chats and the public threads are co-constitutive of each other, mirroring the co-constitution of virtual and real-time interactions between Sumit and Rohan. They eventually go on a date and engage in a year-long relationship. The year-long relationship signifies intimacy in the form of conjugal love, where Sumit and Rohan consummate their love in private. Giddens (1992: 58) argues that there is a 'transformation of intimacy' in modern society, where both parties 'entered into it for its own sake and continued only in so far as it is thought by both partners to deliver enough satisfactions for each individual to stay within it'. However, with virtual intimacies, it is not quite as straightforward as to simply leave, as Sumit later found out after his break up with Rohan.

> I was finding it simply difficult to go online on PR [*PlanetRomeo*]. I would invariably see if he was online and if he was I would get very jealous that he was courting other boys. PR also has a footprint stamp so if I visited his profile I knew he could see me and I would wait to see if he visited my profile as well. Unfortunately he never did and this made it even more unbearable for me.

Researchers such as Mowlabocus (2010a), Pullen (2010) and Shahani (2008) have demonstrated that the proliferation of new media is more than just contiguous to our physical identity. What Sumit's statement demonstrates is that the way in which he used new media to connect to a broken past and the ways in which the very textual and visual presence of his former partner creates a digital memory. Mackley and Karpovich (2012: 136) have described the communication media as an instrument of relationship, which facilitates and mediates it. One of the ways in which Sumit tried to cope with the ending of his relationship was by narrating his story (he blogged about it, as well as alluding to it on some of his thread conversations) on digital platforms. The relationship thus becomes an object, and Sumit used the community pages to share his memories and stories about it. Despite the fact that these were often disguised as general thoughts, it was not difficult for close friends to understand that Sumit was writing about his failed relationship. Mackley and Karpovich (2012: 129) remark that 'talking about things that mean something to us almost automatically involves some kind of personal disclosures: of taste traits . . . memories and experiences'. This act of self-narration is an emotional and intimate process of reflexivity. It is a complex interplay between the personal narrative and the social space where it is being narrated. The affective nature of this emotion is both a high risk (for the sensitive nature of the information) and has the potential for unexpected encounters.

The first time Sumit wrote about his relationship ending, he was chastised by a few people on the thread for 'baring his personal life on a public platform', but there were an equal number of sympathetic responses:

GO_2:  This is the story of our life. Cheating boyfriends and hostile city.
RAJIND:  My sympathies. You are strong and will recover.
KULFI:  I am not sure why you would share these details here but if it helps I am in a similar situation.

These three responses are examples of the discursive nature through which friendship and kinship is formed on virtual spaces. These companions and supporters could be anyone, from someone who is geographically distanced to someone who lives close by. Sumit did not know any of these three people personally, but he had spoken to one of them on *PlanetRomeo* before. This experience was an illuminating process for Sumit. He explained:

> I never knew that there could be strangers who would be there to give me emotional support, especially with no sexual intentions. My parents realised I was being slightly off for a few weeks but I could not explain to them I had just broken off with my boyfriend. Again it was the same space where I met Rohan that helped me heal some of my wounds.

It is worth noting that the affective charge of the conversations Sumit had with users on the forum provided him with an intimate space of comfort. His inability to articulate his emotions to his family, which is the microcosm around which social lives in India revolve (Menon, 2007), makes the digital queer space the only venue where he can seek acceptance and emotional support. Sumit's expression of intimacy on *PlanetRomeo* mirrors the ways in which dependency, exchange and attachment play a central part within queer kinship attachments. The idea of romantic love operates as haunting, and his failure to achieve romantic love resonates with comments made by other users (Go_2 and Kulfi both acknowledge that they are in similar positions). Further, Go_2 uses the phrase 'the story of our lives'. The 'our' signifies a kind of a hailing presupposing Sumit himself and other users on the thread all share a similar subject position. The hailing centralises the 'cheating boy friend and hostile city' as a kind of a loss around which the modern gay/queer male subject position is articulated. The shared intimacy on *PlanetRomeo* allows each of the users to mourn their (romantic and queer) injuries, and form affective bonds with each other. The modern gay/queer male subject is affectively formed through articulating intimate loss and mourning the failure of romantic love.

Another conception that this episode brings to the surface is the role of public mourning and intimacy. Butler (2004b: 19) argues that our vulnerability to loss and the mourning that follows creates a condition through which a basis for community can be found. Mourning and public display of loss serves a two-fold purpose – on one hand it is the acknowledgement that something has changed forever, and on the other it is an acceptance of the transformation that is about to follow. Sumit's grief by moving from a privatised zone to a public display transforms mourning, so that it does not remain a solitary situation. By making his grief public, he is sharing it with others and creating a sense of relationality. His experience makes clear that the exposure to grief on new media sites where memory remains intact far longer thwarts any effort to foreclose that vulnerability, but at the same time the public mourning that is elicited from these digital memories offers the possibility of new forms of kinship networks developing.

Berlant (2004: 10), in her introduction to *Compassion: The Culture and Politics of an Emotion*, argues that compassion implies a social relation between spectators and sufferers. The emphasis of this is on the spectator. The participants and users on *PlanetRomeo* share a strong similarity with offline support groups offered by non-governmental organisations.[4] The discussions on the thread also offer emotional support to participants. Sumit has spoken at length about the compassion that he received from other forum users when they found out about his relationship ending. Suffering can be understood as being circular and moving through a reciprocal function, a characteristic of intimacy. Raun's (2012) work with Transvloggers on *YouTube* proposes that the vloggers act as an online support group for each other, offering emotional comfort and practical help. I would argue that the experience of pain or loss (of romantic love, as in this case) acts as a locus around which different queer subjects are able to identify and associate with – a point of recognition.

Alex_amazing (19 March 2012) writes:

> I can see what everyone is going through on this forum. At times I cry because I feel no one understands me whilst at other times when I look at the people on this forum and I am reminded of my many brithers [*sic*] here, I smile contended. What I want you to know, Sumit is that we feel the ame [*sic*] as you. My words might seem empty to you right now but when I will be in your place some years later I would like someone to say the same supportive words to me, then.

As Berlant (2004) has suggested, cultural scripts for emotion are relatively mixed. In the above posting, Alex_amazing deploys a sensitive and compassionate approach to Sumit's relationship. With regard to compassion and its relation to virtual intimacy, I would like to draw three conclusions. As with other mediated intimate communications that take place on *PlanetRomeo*, compassion is also focussed on an emotion, suffering or anxiety (due to relationship, dating and coming out), which in this case is deemed to be a shared emotion. Returning to Berlant, I would suggest that readers of this narrative responded to it in an effective way that is collective and adds to the space's archive of feeling. Intimacy is initiated within the forum in order to feel connected, explore the virtuality of the community (or the fragility of it). Finally, I would argue that virtual intimacies in the form of exchanging sympathy and empathy is one of the ways in which many gay/ queer male subjects are formed against the imposed non-recognition and lack of compassion of this pain and loss in the physical world.

Sumit responded further:

> I have dwelled with my past lovers but now through my self-narrative I am forging new connections. These are people who empathise with what I have gone through and offer me some form of consolation, which I do not think I would have received elsewhere. They barely need to say much. The fact that they would post a simple hug, meant so much to me.

Intimacy, after all, 'is a sign of past and future connection' (McGlotten, 2007: 126), one that is constituted not only by memories, but also holds the intimation of a future. Sumit's way of coping with his past and forging intimate connections with his compassionate readers is a sign of the importance of virtual intimacy with respect to suffering and emotion.

Intimacy saturates queer interaction on cyberspace. Mediated by digital technology, the discourse of intimacy has not just been transformed, but has undergone a redefinition. Issues such as compassion, companionship, relationships and hook-ups on cyberspace remain central in understanding virtual intimacies. Mobile and digital media have defined new pathways and reconfigurations of public space. There has been a significant shift in the ways in which intimacy is played out on the public space through public postings, chatting on threads and blogs. Interactions have led to reciprocity, which is an important example of a way in which intimacy is performed on the digital screen.

Virtual presence is as important as is physical presence. Through continual reciprocal exchanges, this presence is maintained addressing issues of commitment and trust. Intimate spaces are also created through the very act of sharing personal stories and anecdotes. Intimacy is actualised when there is reciprocity. For meaning to exist, there has to be an interaction. As one of my other research participants Rahul explains, intimacies need to be actualised in the 'real' world. Scholars such as McGlotten (2013) note that finding love and maintaining it within an accepting community, even on the Internet, is no easy task.

Sumit, in the same way as Haider, a-kshays and Ruhin (who I will introduce next), is part of the regulatory neoliberal project of the respectable citizen subject. Sumit occupies a striatiated spatial arrangement within Indian neoliberalism. While a-kshays is articulating a sense of failure to articulate his queer desires in public and utilising *PlanetRomeo* to voice his frustrations, Sumit articulates his inability to form romantic attachments on *PlanetRomeo*. This articulation of failure connects the queer male subject to others in the same position. Through posts, threads and comments, a loop of intimate connections is formed. Sumit's story attends to this affective nature of entanglement that cyberspaces afford.

Messaging and chatting on these spaces is about managing the relationship and appreciating the role of each other in sustaining it. It is one of the many ways through which individuals occupy a social space and exhibit intimacy, carving a private niche within a public domain. This intimacy, whether exhibited on forums or managed through private messaging, exchange of images and footprints, is constantly being mediated and transformed. I would argue that my participants were asserting their identity and the validity of their relationships through creating intimate corners in an otherwise public space. Queer men, as everyone else, share the need for meaningful intimate contact that has allowed them to define new pathways in order to be able to express their love and sexuality.

## Speaking the language of footprints

When I examined the data on the role of Internet and digital technology in queer culture and queer relationships, I was witness to another level of meaning beyond the content of the messages that were exchanged between the users. This came about through the use of footprints (see Figure 3.1). Footprints, somewhat similar to 'winks' on *Gaydar* and 'pokes' on *Facebook*, are a prominent way through which meaning is also conveyed in conversations taking place on *PlanetRomeo*. Footprints are basically graphic animated images that convey certain meanings to users; these range from compliments such as 'gorgeous face', 'great body', to more direct references such as 'get in touch if you're interested' and 'wanna have sex'.

One of the ways in which one can make sense of footprints is by employing Miller's (2008) concept of phatic culture, a form of communication that Miller identifies as non-dialogic and non-informational. While I do not agree with Miller's argument that this form of communication is non-informational, I do, however, think it provides a useful framework to think about this form of non-dialogic communication.

Footprints are an ephemeral way of sending messages on *PlanetRomeo*. The recipient sometimes misses them and they only last for a few days. The user cannot save them and they only remain as a fleeting gesture and reminder of an intimate encounter with another person. Giddens (1991) argues that relationships engender trust through constant communication. Footprints are, by that logic, a quick and fast way to keep in contact and provide constant gestures of intimacy. Miller (2008: 389) contends that emotion is increasingly becoming detached from genuine moral commitment, and thus overt displays of emotion are also seen as a part of this strategy of having to constantly maintain social contact.

Miller (2008: 390) further argues that social networking sites allow more visual prominence at the expense of textual material. This contravenes the

*Figure 3.1* Footprints on *PlanetRomeo*. Screenshot from www.planetromeo.com.

actuality of some of these queer platforms where texts play an important role in the profile configuration, even if it is prefigured items such as body statistics, sexual information and so on. Additionally, the dialogue has the textual verbosity of an offline encounter alongside the sparing linguistic play of intimate gestures. In my interview with Rahul (26), I was surprised when he told me that he used footprints considerably more than he actually sent messages. I was intrigued by this and interpreted it as shyness. However, it was not the main reason why he used footprints; rather, according to Rahul, footprints were a way of being ambiguous about his intentions. He explained:

> Imagine if I actually found someone cute I would message him but then I know there are others messaging him as well and I don't want to come out too needy. So I could just leave a footprint saying 'Great profile' or 'You're interesting'. In this way if he is interested to get back to me he can and somehow I don't feel like I am being too pushy about this.
>
> (20 July 2013)

Berlant (2004) argues that intimacy is about being able to communicate with the sparest of signs and gestures. Rahul's use of footprints seems to fall within the same territory. He is cautious about not wanting to come on too strongly, and so he uses subtle methods such as leaving a footprint to make his presence felt and his intention known. Sumit had a somewhat similar experience with respect to using footprints and used them very frequently when he was still seeing his former partner.

> When I was dating Rohan we used to frequently leave footprints for each other. We were both really busy with work and did not always have the time to talk to each other. Of course we would text but leaving footprints felt quite cute. I could just remind him I was there by leaving him a 'Man of my dreams' footprint. He in turn often left me a 'great smile' or a cheeky 'I want to have your baby' footprint.
>
> (22 June 2013)

Drawing from Sumit's experience of using footprints, I would argue that footprints are embedded in layers of meaning beyond the simple content of the footprint itself. It is a contextual and deeply personal form of engagement. It means more than merely an exchange of messages. It is a way of reminding the other person of the relationship within the de-spatialised context of *PlanetRomeo*. In that sense, I disagree with Miller's thesis of phatic communication being merely a bare communicative gesture that does not inform or exchange meaningful information. The role of foot-prints is a social one, where the user expresses sociability and maintains his bonds with his friends and larger network. The footprints actively carry information for the receiver, and these are not just concerned with the process of communication as Miller has argued. The footprint implies recognition of the bonds and intimacy shared by the user and the recipient, as well as the possibility of carrying embedded meaning, despite the fact that the footprint itself might be contentless.

I would draw a parallel between the ways in which my participants used footprints to Sirisena's (2012) research on the role of mobile phones in romantic relationships in Sri Lanka. Sirisena discovered that 'ring cuts' or 'missed calls' speckled everyday exchanges in her participants' relationships. They were a way by which her participants could remind their lovers the space that they occupied in their lives. Similarly, Sumit used footprints to remind his partner that he was thinking about him, whereas Rahul used footprints to register his interest in someone. Footprints are an intimate gesture, imbued with a sense of reciprocity. Rahul's footprints would either generate another footprint from the person or that person would message back. There were times when the other person was not interested, but Rahul attributed it to 'the way this game is played'.

McGlotten (2007: 126–127) concurs that 'intimacy is a sign . . . of things barely communicated. Communicating with the barest of signs is similar to having a secret language, a language whose secrecy runs so deep that neither oneself nor the other with whom one communicates briefly, sparingly can claim literacy on it'. Footprints are a part of what McGlotten has called secret language. While footprints such as 'Man of my Dreams' or 'I wanna have your babies' have a surface-level meaning, for people such as Sumit and Rohan, they are imbued with a deeper level of intimacy both for their brevity and their underlying meaning which is only understood by the sender and the receiver, and herein lies its appeal.

By focussing on footprints, I have wanted to shift the lens from content to other forms through which meaning is created and experienced on the Internet. Sumit and Rahul's examples point out the ways in which ephemeral intimations such as this reveal much deeper aspects of queer culture and queer intimacies on the Internet. This ambivalence aids in the process of finding a companion or 'intimate other', as Rahul's case has demonstrated. These forms of ambivalent gestures occupy a central place within online culture, saturated with private meanings indexing a whole range of suggestions, yet to the outsider would only reveal the surface text. The confusion and the anxieties that result, for example, 'what if he hasn't left me a footprint?' (Rahul), are part of this assemblage.

## 'Coming out': Ruhin's story

For many queer people, particularly those living in suburban and rural areas, the Internet has been one of the most useful tools for connecting with others and for establishing a sense of identity and community (Gajjala and Mitra, 2008; Roy, 2003). I would like to argue that the existence of coming-out narratives offers a rather unique space within which to consider the boundaries between personal desires and public identities. In this section I will explore the ways in which queer men in India use coming-out narratives as a form of representational practice, and also the ways in which this intimate disclosure on forums and threads extends discussions of virtual intimacy.

Ruhin (19), a psychology student in Kolkata, recounted his own coming-out story to me:

> I was pretty young when I joined, PR [*PlanetRomeo*]. I was only 14. At that time I had gone to a cyber cafe to watch some porn when by chance I ended up on a gay website. And I realised there was something like this too (People being gay). It was my first time and I did not like it very much and closed it. In the back of my mind I was curious about this and wanted to know more. So I went back to the cyber cafe, this time on my own and googled some more and I ended up knowing more. Everything happened pretty fast. When I was 14 I used to think that I liked boys and thought that something was wrong. As popular culture shows us, only a man and woman can like each other so I used to think am I a woman trapped in a man's body? Then I realised no, I am a man who likes man [*sic*].
>
> (15 December 2012)

Ruhin's self-identification as a queer man took place relatively early on in his life. He believes that he would have eventually made this discovery, but that the Internet made the process considerably faster. He found images with which he could identify, and this in turn led to his own identification with that particular sexual category. Ruhin was, however, still not ready to 'come out' about his sexual identity to others. Drushel (2010: 61) argues that 'Self identification as a sexual minority and subsequent disclosure to another person typically is not a single event, but rather a protracted process.' This is characterised by 'unpredictability, starts, stops, backtracking and denial' (Drushel, 2010: 62). This pattern was evident in my conversation with Ruhin. I asked him if he had come out to any of his close friends or to his family.

> In the beginning I could not come out to anyone. I was too scared and ashamed of it. My coming out happened on G4M (*Guys4Men*

which later became *PlanetRomeo*). By joining G4M, I first came out to myself. In school people teased me at times but I always denied being gay to them. I have now come out to some of the close people in my life, these are the same people I met on the site and later became friends with. I do not think it is necessary to tell each and every person one meets. I have told my sister who is very important to me and some of my close friends and people I met at the Pride March. I do plan to tell my parents once I get a job. If they decide to throw me out of the house, who is going to pay for my education, who is going to back me? Not the government! They are pretty homophobic themselves.

(15 December 2012)

Ruhin's experience shows that he went through a period of identity confusion; however, through a queer social networking site such as *Planet-Romeo*, he managed to receive positive feedback and affirmation of his sexual identity. Drushel (2010: 63) notes that queer teenagers are coming out at younger ages, at least in part because of the support and interactivity offered by the Internet. The very nature of coming out, as Ruhin expounds, has evolved. His act of joining *PlanetRomeo* itself was the first step he took towards coming out to himself, followed by sharing intimate information about himself such as his sexuality to complete strangers.

Declarations such as the one made by Ruhin are intimately personal and highlight the importance of the Internet in everyday queer life. The interpersonal awareness that develops among the members of a group helps sustain this intimate exchange of dialogue. It evolves through reciprocity.

After I came out, two others followed suit. Obviously we all knew we were gay, why else were we on PR [*PlanetRomeo*], but the fact that I was sharing this intimate part of my life with them helped these other two to also come out. It helped lift the garb of being a stranger.

(Ruhin, 15 December 2012)

Ruhin's assertion demonstrates that intimacy cannot be catalogued as an emotional or physical response alone. The experiential nature of it, as described by Ruhin on a public platform, suggests that queer intimacy in cyberspace takes various forms. By showing reciprocity, the two other group members mutually engage in an intimate exchange of ideas, thoughts and memories. Alexander and Losh (2010: 42) argue that online spaces have opened up possibilities to explore different sexual subjectivities online before trying them out in real life. Ruhin used *PlanetRomeo* as a testing ground to experience his sexual identity before deciding to come out to people offline. He probably did not realise at the time that intimate connections were being forged by his action intimating others to follow suit.

> I did not really expect these two would also come out. They were very careful. They never displayed their pictures and always had text on their profile, saying they were just experimenting. I think it was definitely a huge step for them and we suddenly felt connected by our shared truth (coming out).
>
> (Ruhin, 15 December 2012)

Ruhin, similar to Sumit, is not out to his parents, but for the last few years he has managed to establish himself as a well-known gay man on both *PlanetRomeo* and within the city. Using *PlanetRomeo* and the discussion forums, he has not only established himself as a visible and 'out' queer man, but spurred by other members and supported by them, he also managed to come out to his sister. The issue of the family is a complicated and central one in Indian queer life, and more so within the context of 'coming out'. In one posting, Horizon33 writes:

> It is easy to come out to frndz. . . . way too easy than coming out to Parents!!!
> But one day, everyone of us will have to face the situation (Well, most of us) . . . What should be done then . . .
> What do you suggest??? I am thinking of coming out!!!!
>
> (28 September 2011)

This thread received several replies. Most of the respondents told Horizon33 that he was brave because he was thinking of telling his parents. At the same time, others cautioned him against it, arguing that there was an age gap and that they would not really understand. The following post by UnAmor, however, was interesting because he offers three possible outcomes. The post demonstrates how important the family is in India and how difficult any transformative politics would be to implement.

> Well According to me. . . . There are three possible things that can be done:
>
>> Be Selfish, Tell our parents & continue our own way of living – after all its our life & we should be owner of it.

> Accept what parents say & marry a girl – parents are god (according to religiuos teachings at least), they brought us to life, made us learn. . . . blah blahblah.
>
> Living in Self Denial (Well sorta, if not telling parents. . . . U r half out . . . not completely, even if whole world knows) & remain unmarried according to parents – Afterall it is matter of life of an innocent girl, Imagine what will u do, if someone will do it to ur sister/frnd.
>
> (16 April 2013)

Menon (2007: 38) argues that the 'heterosexual patriarchal family is the cornerstone of the nation', and thus any discourse on queerness would have to not only grapple with social constructs, but also national specificities and expectations. The online forum becomes a site where people like Sumit, Ruhin and Horizon33 can share their experiences with respect to their families and the fear that their families might not support their sexuality. However, it is important to also consider that in all these cases, the participants are invested in maintaining a relationship with their family, with the expectation that the family will come around and accept their sexuality when they do finally come out to them.

Coming out is a complicated concept within India. I would argue that 'coming out' is a part of the project of Indian modernity and neoliberal queer politics where the capability to be visible and articulate a (global) gay/queer identity is part of the civilising and affective marker of modernity. Several respondents such as Rahul have felt this pressure that in order to be able to take part in queer politics in India they need to 'come out'. He explains:

> Coming out is seen as the ultimate victory. If you come out you are liberated and 'modern'. People do not think you are progressive if you are still in the closet.
>
> (20 July 2013)

I find this view extremely regressive, and would argue this is a pressure to conform to a global queer politics (Altman, 1997) that places a certain degree of pressure on the role of visibility and coming out. It also creates a shame culture, where those who are not out are seen as regressive and backward. The queer citizen subject is being created on the template of Western modernity. In order to be respectable, subversive practices such as cruising and anonymity are seen as failures. The fight for the decriminalisation of Section 377 was, after all, the right to be 'open' and to be able to love in 'private'. In an interesting conversation on *Facebook*, a queer activist (who I would like to remain anonymous), narrated a very interesting incident to me. I am quoting it verbatim with translations:

aami takhan ek jon er shathe prem kortam . . . delhi te thhakto chhele ta-maane ekhano thhake – amar or break up hoye jawa shotteo he is someone my parents are very fond.
[At that time I was in a relationship with someone from Delhi. He still lives there. He is someone my friends are still very fond of]
i had never come out officially to my parents
but emnii o ashle amader baari te thhakto
[but if he was ever down, he would stay with us in our house]
etc
ma/baba ki jaanten aami jani na
[What my mother and father understood or knew, I don't know]
ekbar hoyechhe ki-aami ar ma – biye niye nanan conversations korchhi-in the kitchen
[There was this one time, I was having a discussion about marriage with my mother in the kitchen]
anek katha – aami kyano biye korbo na-aami to ektu err biye birodhi-mane str8 gay jai hok na kyano. . . .
[Many conversations. Why I was against marriage – Gay or straight]
anekkshan dhor ealochhona howar por ma jakhan bujhlen je aami serious – she paused for a while and asked me direct – achha taar mane ki XXX (my boyfriend) o biye korbe na?
[After a long discussions when my mother finally realised that I was serious – she paused a while and asked me direct. So does this mean that XXX (my boyfriend) will also not marry?]
aami to ei correlation e hotobaaak
[I was amazed at this correlation]
i remember my father telling me. . . . tomader madhye ja hoyechhe tomra mitiye naao
[I remember my father telling me – whatever has happened between you both, try to resolve it.]

(1 June 2012)

This conversation is very important because it demonstrates the language through which intergenerational understanding of queerness and queer relationships is articulated. It also explains the various ways in which Indian men are coming out, in a language that does not simply say 'I am Gay'. Similarly, the author Sandip Roy in a recent article 'What's It Like to Be Gay in Modern India' in *The Telegraph*[5] (27 January 2015) explains that coming out in India is really about marriage where the standard coming out line is 'Mom, Dad I don't think I am going to get married'. As I explained earlier, the family and marriage are important constructs through which India bestows respectability and subjectivity on its citizens. By choosing not to marry is thus an important statement and choice, and as both the activist I have cited and Roy explains, it is also a way in which to 'come out'. One way to articulate this, as this person further explained, was to say:

> O bondhu noy [He is not a friend]
> Bondhur cheye onek beshi [He is more than a friend]
> Aaro (Much more]
>
> (1 June 2012)

Interestingly, the phrase 'more than a friend' was made into a queer film (of the same name) by queer film-maker Debolina and Sappho for Equality, a lesbian charity in Kolkata, India.[6] My intention in using this case study is not to suggest that the promise of virtual intimacies replace familial ties, but rather as Sumit and Ruhin have demonstrated, virtual intimacies hold the promise of forming personal connections with other site users, and this has created intimate kinship networks outside the family circle. Second, I also choose to use this case study to further complicate the (Western) global notion of 'coming out'. In this sense, this ethnographic vignette, similar to the previous narratives, also problematises the respectable queer citizen subject as a product of neoliberal modernity.

## Conclusion

It is evident from this chapter that intimacies saturate queer interactions on cyberspace. Mediated by digital technology, the discourse of intimacy has not only been transformed but it has also undergone a redefinition. Issues such as compassion, companionship, relationships and sexual encounters on cyberspace remain central to understanding virtual intimacies on queer spaces.

New media technologies have defined new pathways and reconfigurations of public space. There has been a significant shift in the ways in which intimacy is played out in public space through public postings, 'chatting' on threads and blogs. Interactions have led to reciprocity, which is important to the ways in which intimacy is performed through the digital screen. Virtual presence is arguably as important as physical presence. Through continual reciprocal exchanges, this presence is maintained, addressing issues of commitment and trust. Intimate spaces are also created through the very act of sharing personal stories and anecdotes.

I have also alluded to Ahmed's work on affect and emotion. I situate the queer subject in online spaces as bodies that are forging spaces of comfort and intimacy. Virtual intimacies help us to resist normative codes of what intimacy means. These are 'actual' and 'real' emotions mediated through technology. Virtual intimacies demonstrate the importance of ambivalent gestures which might index a whole range of saturated meaning, a 'secret language' only accessible to some.

This chapter has reflected on some of the ways in which queer men in India are using the Internet to 'be together' and transcend conventional relationship structures. In narrating these stories, I was also moved by some of the romantic depictions of sensibility that populated online narratives. This challenged my own understanding of queer culture in India and illustrates the ways in which queer men are using digital technologies to redefine relationships and companionship. As Kuntsman (2012: 6) eloquently argues, 'Digital culture in itself can be a site of investment of feelings.' Queer social networking sites like *PlanetRomeo* undeniably inspire and create strong emotional attachments for its users. These sites exemplify the promise of digital culture in creating and reinstating a textual/visual language of intimacy and emotion. I would argue that this should be considered not as marginal but as explicitly embedded in human emotions and the expression of queer India's impossible desires. The relationship between modernity, queer desires and the Indian state is marked by the removal of the colonial anti-sodomy provision (Section 377), positing the queer subject as a project of Indian modernity and (his) capability to forge love and companionship as affective markers of modernity. In contrast to the virtual articulations of romantic love, my case studies suggest that a feeling of failure haunts the formation of the queer male subject. Virtual exchanges about failure to form romantic love, anxieties related to coming out and classed desires are narrated, creating the formation of a different kind of queer (male) self. The bonds forged on *PlanetRomeo* and *Grindr* do not cohere around conjugal coupling; rather they articulate failure of the romantic narrative. Intimate queer attachments are forged through narration of pain and a sense of shared compassion. As Katyal (2011: 136) explains, 'To be online is . . . a moving away from all that is entirely familiar It is the point of meeting other people, of individually entering hitherto unfamiliar circuits, of being a part of something. . . .' Throughout this chapter, I have shown through the case studies the ways in which a sense of self is being articulated within a specific cultural and social context. My ethnography in this chapter responds to the experiential realities of the diverse constitution of intimacies and the potentials of reading these virtual encounters as another way of thinking about queer politics and queer identities in India.

# Notes

1  In particular, see Mowlabocus (2010b) on the role of images in gay men's digital culture.
2  The club name has been changed to protect its identity, because clubs can be easily searched using the search facility available on the *PlanetRomeo* Website. The club's current membership is 4,431 members. The total number of members currently registered on *PlanetRomeo* from India is 111,908. Accessed on 6 October 2013.
3  Neo-liberalism refers to an ideology based on promoting rational self-interest through deregulation and privatization. According to Povinelli (2006), the economics of neo-liberalism should be seen as a strategic containment of potentially more radical futures. Duggan (2003: xii) makes a similar claim that neo-liberalism dismantles the welfare state, which strips down equality to a compatible form and maintains the upward distribution of wealth.
4  My earlier research in Kolkata showed that some form of counseling was offered by almost all the queer NGOs. SAATHII (Solidarity Against the HIV and AIDS Infection), however, also offers a unique online counseling service, a first of many in Eastern India. See Dasgupta (2012) for an analysis of SAATHII's digital response to sexual health monitoring and advocacy within the gay, MSM, queer populace in the city.
5  See Sandip Roy (2015). Available at: http://www.telegraph.co.uk/men/relationships/11365516/What-its-like-to-be-gay-in-modern-India.html. Accessed on 2 March 2015.
6  The film was called *Taar Cheye She Onek Aaro* directed by Debolina Majumder, which was screened at several film festivals around the world, including the BFI Flare Film Festival. A trailer is available at: http://youtu.be/7CDoLRQ8vmk. Accessed on 2 March 2015.

# 4 'Imagined' queer communities

## Introduction

In the previous chapter, I was concerned with issues of intimacy and the mediation of intimate relationships on virtual spaces and the ways in which these relationships create a sense of friendship and kinship. The participants in the last chapter conceptualised 'community' in terms of intimacy on gay/queer spaces such as *PlanetRomeo* and *Grindr*. In this chapter, I move away from the notion of intimacy and instead focus on the class dimension; I want to critique the concept of a queer 'community' as they exist both online and offline. Through looking at the ways in which community has been conceptualised by an online queer social group on *Facebook* in the city of Kolkata, India, I argue that queer community formations such as the one I discuss in this chapter often invisibilises class. By looking at intersections and tensions between class, gender and sexuality, this chapter will argue that these inflect our understanding of community and, more largely, identity.

Jean Ulrick Desert (1997: 18), in her definition of queer space, remarks that 'queer space is virtual space'. By virtual, Desert refers to the temporal simulated nature of queer spaces. While it can be argued that explicitly identified queer spaces do exist such as bars, cafes, cruising grounds and community centres, such spaces are ostensibly situated at the margins of public space. Desert argues that 'queer culture exists because of the dominant normative culture' (19). Borrowing Gopinath's (2005: 20) definition of South Asian public culture as a 'practice through which queer subjects articulate new modes of collectivity and kinship', my understanding of queer space builds on both Gopinath and Desert, who contend that such space is an 'activated zone' which is 'at once private and public' (Desert, 1997: 21). Desert argues that public space is considered a site of heterosexuality where 'queerness, at a few brief points and for some fleeting moments dominates the heterocentric norm'. Queer people occupying public space thus become a site of transgression, and in Appadurai and Breckenridge's phrase 'a zone of cultural debate' (1988: 6).

Mowlabocus (2010a) and Shahani (2008) have both commented on the role of social networking sites and technology in gay male subculture. Their recognition that queer male subculture lies between the physical and the virtual space is a position that my own book takes in relation to the queer male community in India. Rheingold (1993: 6), in his study of virtual communities, remarks that the migration of traditional forms of community to cyberspace can be traced to the loss of public space and 'a hunger for community'. It should also be noted that this is a very Western view of public space, one that is tied with issues of ownership and the growing privatisation/commercialisation of public spaces. The debate as to what constitutes a community is an ongoing one. The word *community* has no consensually accepted universal definition; rather it is a contested term and there are multiple ways of defining it. Anderson (1991) sees community as an embodiment premised on ideas of commonality – these could be shared allegiances, kinship or blood relations. He further argues that a community exists because people believe in this commonality. This is reinforced through the media and the use of ceremonial symbols such as flags, national anthems and figure of the martyr. Billig (1995) calls this banal nationalism, where everyday representations through these symbols build an imagined sense of national solidarity and belonging. He argues that these symbols are used repetitively and are effective because of their subliminal nature. This is quite important because the focus on overt forms of nationalism, while scrutinised and critiqued, often glosses over the subliminal nature of everyday 'banal' messages. Without oversimplification, it can be argued that a similar pattern can also be observed within queer community celebrations – observing Stonewall Day, Pride marches, the rainbow flag and, of course, the annual pride anthem, all of which subliminally seek to ascertain a commonality that can be called 'queer nationalism'. These symbols, along with the global discourse on the martyred queer figure, tend to construct an essentialised queer 'community' – one that subsumes any other form of identity and ideology as 'fringe'.

Ingram, Bouthilette and Retter (1997: 449) have defined a queer community as a 'full collection or select subset of queer networks for a particular territory, with relatively stable relationships that enhance interdependence, mutual support and protection'. This interdependence and support is predicated upon the interaction, solidarity and affirmation of queer men and women who position themselves and their ongoing presence within an allied commonality. I argue in this chapter that this community is far more stratified, concealing certain tensions that provide an illusory perception of an 'imagined' community (Anderson, 1991). Scholars (Boyce, 2007;

Dutta, 2013a) working on subaltern sexual categories in India have often commented that the queer community (mostly gay and male) excludes trans*, female and bisexual people.

A final issue this chapter addresses is the issue of intersectionality. While there is abundant literature on gender and sexuality in India, there are only a handful of texts that consider the interconnections between social class and sexuality (Khanna, 2011; Shrivastava, 2004, 2013). The notion of intersectionality is a feminist sociological theory that was first proposed by Crenshaw (1989) to address issues of race and gender within a composite framework. It acknowledges the power overlaps and the complexity of sexuality in interplay with other social categorisations and power differentials such as ethnicity, class and nationality. By taking an intersectional focus, this chapter aims to study queer digital space through the lens of class.

In this chapter, I primarily analyse a *Facebook* group PKP that diverges significantly from the opportunities offered by spaces such as *PlanetRomeo* or *Grindr*. There are two main reasons for the methodological decision to focus on and analyse this single group. PKP is an example of the ways in which a queer community has appropriated a mainstream site such as *Facebook*, thus blurring the divide between queer space as a segmented space and a queer space occupied by queer people defying heteronormativity and power (Oswin, 2008). Furthermore, because of its online/offline existence, the group provides an opportunity to study PKP without having to demarcate the physical and the virtual existence of the members, while at the same time it embodies and enforces certain strategic voices in constructing its identity. This web group is also location based (primarily for queer individuals in Kolkata), thus providing an archive of local politics and queer activity in a metropolitan city in India. There is also an ethical dimension that needs to be addressed in my methodology for this chapter. While the group is restricted to members, the members are mostly not anonymous, using their 'real' *Facebook* accounts to participate in discussions. I have, therefore, had to seek permission from the group administrators for conducting research on PKP as well as informing the members about my lurking in the group.

I have lightly disguised the name of the group under study here. All names of the participants and members have also been disguised, whereas posts have been quoted verbatim. These cannot be searched through search engines. Such anonymity was imperative for the group members, especially when they knew that their postings were being analysed. As I had been to one of the physical events hosted by the group, and because I originally lived in Kolkata, my presence on the group was not unusual. I intruded as little as possible in the forum discussions, and when I did that data was discarded and not used for purposes of this analysis. This was because I was concerned that it might compromise the way in which the discussions shifted due to my input.

## Whose community is it anyway?

> I don't talk like the rest or have coffee in fancy restaurants like them. How can I be them? I am gay but I don't feel like I am a part of any community shommunity.
>
> (Amit, 22 December 2012)

This is a statement from Amit when I interviewed him in December 2012, recorded at a crowded coffee shop in Kolkata, India.[1] He spoke hesitatingly, conscious of the people around him, thus giving the impression that he was not comfortable talking about himself (or specifically, about his sexual choices) in a public space, a space that is demarcated by default as heterosexual (Elder, 1998; Gopinath, 2005). Elder (1998), for instance, argues that the normality of heterosexuality is maintained through regulatory mechanisms which control people's use and manipulation of space. The public and heterosexual nature of this space meant that for Amit to 'claim territory' (Ingram, Bouthilette and Retter, 1997: 10), he would have to appropriate his queerness and make it apparent, something which remains a vulnerable position for many queer people in India. This quote was a response to my question about the newly formed PKP Community, which began as an online *Facebook* group in 2011 in response to the need 'to find a regular space to socialise during the weekends for the LGBT community in Kolkata' (from the group page accessed in May 2013). As Amit suggests, he does not feel himself to be a part of the larger queer community in Kolkata. He specifically references his class background and inability to access the same venues as the larger (publicly visible) queer community in the city. Amit's quote is a starting point to explore the ways in which the queer virtual community in Kolkata enables new possibilities for self-representation, community building and friendship, while also marginalising and rejecting a section of the queer populace of the city because of their class (and language) position. As Amit explained to me in the interview, there is little support for those people who cannot speak English and who do not live up to the class identifiers and gender performance (I discuss this in detail in Chapter 5) of the majority in the group.

In an interview with me, Pawan Dhall, a prominent queer activist, recounted his early days of trying to build a queer community in Kolkata:

> In the early days it was very difficult to meet other people in Kolkata. There was of course Counsel Club but we needed to reach out to a

wider range of people. The Gaybombay group in Bombay were very helpful in setting up e-forums for the other cities and very soon we had a Gay Calcutta e-forum. This meant we could connect with others all over India. In the beginning there were only around five members and there were mostly arguments and fights, nothing concrete ever came out. I was often frustrated at the lack of dialogue in these spaces and left the forums many times. However within a very short space of time, we were suddenly inundated with members and it also helped that service users could remain anonymous or keep their details confidential.

(11 July 2013)

The primary aim of using such sites, as Dhall's comment articulates, is to establish connections with others and as a way of breaking into a world that is under constant threat from the societal hegemony of heteronormativity. Physical queer spaces in Kolkata are often transitory spaces that are vulnerable to change and are at the constant risk of ceasing to exist. As Raj, a 32-year-old IT consultant, explains:

There are very few spaces for gay men to socialise in Kolkata. We used to earlier congregate around the Dhakuria Lakes or Minto Park. Both of these spaces have undergone huge changes in recent years and are no longer in existence.[2] I used to frequent these places after work on my way home but with strong lights, clearing away of trees and more visitors, gay men find it more difficult to meet or hook up with others now. Everything seems to be changing in the city. I started using PR [PlanetRomeo] in 2007 after I thought I was losing my community.

(14 December 2012)

Raj articulates one of the many anxieties faced by queer people in general, the anxiety of wanting to be part of a community, especially because of the transitory nature of queer social spaces in the city. This anxiety was also articulated by many of my other research participants, although there was an equal number who vociferously criticised this idea of a 'community'. Queer communities are shaped by multiple interactions within the various contexts of nationality, class, religion and race. Kuntsman and Miyake (2008) in a recent volume, *Out of Place: Interrogating Silences in Queerness and Raciality*, examine some of these interstices. They argue that some of the attempts made by scholars in considering the idea of race alongside queer identities often result in the submergence of raciality within queerness. They further argue that '[t]hese situations often leave the very racialised groups in question silent/silenced – "out of place" – within supposedly queer spaces' (7). In the Indian context, this silence and the issue of feeling out of place can be observed most acutely within the different class dynamics present within the queer community. Henderson (2013), in her cultural critique and exploration of race and class in the United States, argues that social class makes a significant difference to queer subjectivity and representation. Henderson (2013: 1) contends that we 'cannot see queer cultures clearly enough when we ignore class, nor can we see con-temporary class outside the production of sexual difference'. In his inter-view with me, Pawan Dhall recounted his horror in 2000 when he first realised that most gay men on the Calcutta e-forums were relatively trans-phobic, and the users of these forums advised him to 'stay away from these low class people'.[3] What this reveals is interesting because class location and identification are significant in India (Donner and De Neve, 2011). Donner and De Neve (2011: 9) explain that consumerism is one way to think about the growing middle class and contemporary society in India. Fernandes (2006: xviii), writing about the middle class in India, remarks:

> The new Indian middle class represents the political construction of a social group that operates as a proponent of economic liberalisation . . . a process of production of a distinctive social and political identity.

While there are multiple articulations of class in India, and consumerism as Donner and De Neve (2011) explain is one of these, and what Fer-nandes (2006) illustrates is that class determines power and creation of a social/political identity that then determines the agency of the individ-ual. Within the Indian queer community, it is vital to look at class within the discourse of inclusion and exclusion. Sexual identity politics has not replaced class politics; rather it is embedded within structures of constraints and opportunities.

There has been debate on the democratising potential of the Internet and the manner in which it has been perceived to have broken down some of the barriers encountered within physical space. Wakeford (1997), for instance, in her essay 'Cyberqueer' argues that the LGBT community was amongst the earliest to embrace cyber resources. This is hardly surprising because the Internet offers a myriad of opportunities for queer-identified men and women, including but not limited to queer activism through mobilisation of community support, as Pawan Dhall has pointed out. It also provides opportunities for coming out and meeting other queer men, as Raj articulated in his interview. However, one of the issues which is not considered in Wakeford's text is who is actually a part of this community – in terms of the class of its users, and even more so the digital divides that exist and continue to exist in many parts of the world. This meant that the LGBT community that embraced these cyber resources was not only of a certain privileged class, but also from a section of the globe that had access to these digital resources. The increase in queer visibility and queer awareness can be attributed to the growth of Internet groups such as PKP, *Planet-Romeo* and so on. Berry, Martin and Yue (2003: 1) argue that 'the recent emergence of gay and lesbian communities in Asia and its diaspora is intimately linked to the development of information technology in the region'.

For queer individuals, the advent of transnational media connections across diverse nations offers new scope for sexual identification. Vertovec (2010: 15) observes that 'cheap telephone calls, faxes, email and frequent modes of travel have allowed for continuous and real time communication'. Pullen (2012: 6) argues that this has allowed 'the discursive potential of an imagined gay or LGBT community [to] seem vividly real, enabling coalescence, interactivity and identity formation'. Consequently, I would argue that this 'imagined' community is enabled not so much by a shared commonality, but rather by individuals, personal agency and disparate community groups that have sustained a common dialogue so far against the mainstream state-led queer minority oppression.

From a subaltern studies perspective (Spivak, 1988), tracing queer virtual communities in Kolkata is not only about studying the text available on websites, but it is equally important to recover those voices that are subdued and have no place within the forums. More often than not, particular individuals, groups or subsections of the LGBT population have been rendered voiceless on the basis of their class and linguistic affiliation, thus making it imperative to read into what has not been said, and interrogate the textual site to reclaim the narratives and dynamics that are buried or not given a space for expression. Of relevance here is the work of the subaltern school, and in particular Spivak. Spivak, in her essay 'Can the Subaltern Speak' (1988), argues that the benevolent coloniser by prohibiting *sati* silences the widow who wants to die on her husband's funeral pyre. Spivak reminds us that in order to uplift the 'plight' of the subaltern, colonisers were effectively silencing their voice, and thus any subaltern voice was merely a representation created and framed by a Western perspective. Borrowing Spivak's argument, in my own attempt to recover the queer subaltern who is absent and often silenced on the online site, I have used empirical evidence from interviews with a range of participants and contextualised and placed these within the 'silences' and 'gaps'.

I should note that the subaltern school in South Asia has largely left out sexual minorities from their discourse, and by bringing them in to this chapter, I am also extending the scope of subaltern theory in queer studies (even though Spivak herself is quite critical of subaltern being used in other contexts). The subaltern school was engaged in 'excavating' history from the voices of the disenfranchised classes in colonial India. In a similar tradition, this chapter is constructed from the voices of subaltern queers which are missing from these online spaces, and at the same time examining the silences and gaps that exist within the 'queer community' discourse.

Before moving on to a description and analysis of the PKP group, it is essential to sketch a brief picture of the queer (male) history/movement in Kolkata and place the group within this context. One of the earliest queer initiatives in Kolkata was the establishment of the Fun Club between 1990 and 1991. This was envisioned as a 'fun spot' for queer men in Kolkata. Later, the key members envisioned that they needed to grow in a similar manner to their counterparts in other cities and decided to start holding discussion sessions on HIV/AIDS. This did not last long, and became inactive within a year. This was followed by the publication of *Pravartak*, a newsletter in 1991, and finally the establishment of the Counsel Club in 1993, which initiated social activities, community programmes and activism around queer issues. By 2000, this group had diversified and opened satellite centres in other towns and cities in West Bengal. The Counsel Club was also involved in the queer social life of the city organising film screenings, dance performances and regular meetings. The Counsel Club closed its doors in 2002, but by then the people involved in the club and others had established numerous other queer organisations and NGOs in the city (Dhall, 2005). Unlike other metropolitan cities (New Delhi and Mumbai particularly), there have been no gay/queer male socialising venues outside the NGO structure or private parties in Kolkata. The need for a socialising venue outside these was long felt, and PKP, established in 2011, filled this space.

## Pink Kolkata Party

PKP was formed to cater to the socialising needs of the queer populace in the city of Kolkata. It started off as a *Facebook* group to reach out to the queer community and float the idea of a regular physical meeting. Very soon, the group organised a regular Wednesday meeting at a popular coffee shop in central Kolkata. Subsequently, the administrators and group members followed this up with regular Pink Party events at popular mainstream clubs. The group initially began with 50 members, growing to 800 members by the time they celebrated their first anniversary in April 2012. Currently, their *Facebook* group has more than 2,500 members. From the outset, the idea behind these events was to queer the mainstream urban space instead of creating separate queer spaces. Oswin (2008) identifies queer space as space that is either occupied by self-identified queer people or those who are defying and contesting power and heteronormativity. These spaces are highly segmented and are under constant threat of accessibility (Ingram, Bouthilette and Retter, 1997). Virtual spaces, in theory, help circumvent some of these threats, although as Usher and Morrison (2010: 279) point out, with the decline in 'gay neighbourhoods', gay people have gone online and these spaces are 'located both globally and locally', unbounded by geography. In recent years, online spaces have played a very important role in the growth of queer consciousness and mobilising towards queer rights. In line with what Oswin argues, PKP occupies and queers a mainstream heteronormative space like *Facebook*, defying and contesting the heteronormative social spaces that are available in the city. Second, as Raj has pointed out, physical queer spaces in the city are constantly transforming with some ceasing to exist as a queer space, signalling the decline in 'gay neighbourhoods'. PKP thus acts as a connecting node, a space for queer people in Kolkata to meet and socialise. Finally, PKP connects to the larger diaspora. During the time of writing this book, many queer men I spoke with, who have migrated from Kolkata, used the group to find out about the next social meeting/party and often planned their visits around them.

People have to request membership to join the group and this has to be approved by the two administrators. The homepage does not have a cover image like many other *Facebook* groups, but instead after approval, members can see who the other members are, read the notes on the 'wall' (where users can post content) and post anything of interest there. On clicking the 'About' tab, one can read the description of the group and the general rules for members. The description of the group reads:

> A need to find a regular place to socialize during weekends for the LGBT community in Kolkata has led to the formation of this group.
> Regular updates about Events will be put up here.
> Please spread the word and invite people in to make this network grow continuously.
> Lets reach out to the rest of our diverse communities and friends and allies.

The first 'party' that emerged from the discussions on the online group was held at an upmarket five star club in the city called Rocky at The Garden Hotel. The move was seen as a masterstroke because for the first time a mainstream club with restrictive policies was allowing a queer party to take place on its premises. The party soon turned awry when many revellers who had arrived were turned away by the club management for 'dressing inappropriately' (Amit, 30 July 2013). As Amit explained to me they were not wearing any 'gender transgressive clothing' but were wearing 'normal' shirt and trousers with some embellishments such as glitter and female scarves. To contextualise this, the club is a popular space for celebrities, and by virtue of it being part of a five star hotel chain, it caters to a wealthy and elite clientele who, as I have observed on my several visits there, dress smartly or in smart casual clothing (a lot of designer wear was also sported). When news of this 'screening' reached the group, there was uproar about this prejudiced behaviour of the club, and the members and administrators took to the *Facebook* group to vent and discuss their grievance.

Anindya Hajra,[4] prominent queer activist and one of the administrators of the group, stated:

> It was a humiliating and emotionally debilitating experience for many who arrived early to be denied entry at the gates, despite being 'appropriately' dressed without citing any reason whatsoever – and in a case of clearly homophobic/transphobic screening allowing others over members of this group the right to entry.
>
> (21 July 2011)

I recount this occasion in order to consider the politics of recognition within everyday life that marks this event. First is the club's hostile recognition of the group member's dissident sexual and gender (trans*) identity, and then, second, my own recognition of understanding this within class terms. As I mentioned earlier in this chapter, class in India is linked intrinsically to sexual identity, with identities such as *hijra* and *kothi* seen as non-metropolitan subaltern sexual identities as opposed to the neoliberal, modern, urban and socially mobile 'gay' identity. I argue that knowledge and recognition of one's identity (sexuality) does not automatically help recognise the other (class). This class issue is linked to the idea of community, one that is conceptualised and imagined as a homogenous group. It is important to also acknowledge the class tensions through which this community is being constructed, silencing the voice of the subaltern.

Henderson (2013: 71) states that 'recognition takes many forms, though some categories of social difference like sexuality have been more amenable to a positive politics of recognition, while others like class have been less so'. This is certainly true in relation to this incident because while a simplistic reading of the incident might indicate sexual identification was the reason for exclusion, a closer reading reveals a class-based bias. The management was aware of the fact that a queer party was scheduled for the evening and they allowed entry to some of the patrons while denying others. It is interesting to observe the ways in which this debate played out across the members within the community belonging to different classes. Rudranil Mukherjee, a fashion designer who could be classified as belonging to an upper middle class, wrote:

> Well i hv been publically out for many years now, and i have never faced any prejudiced behavior from any1 at The Garden, i hv made out

wth guys on the floor in Rocky, Sutra, Regis & TRC infront of The Garden management even before the decriminalization of the 377 act, yet The Garden has been very gay friendly & nice to me. . . . It is just unfortunate to find out that few PINK members were mistreated at The Garden!!

(21 July 2011)[5]

Rudranil's point is important because he stresses that the issue had nothing to do with sexuality. On previous occasions, when he had visited various clubs of the hotel (Rocky, Sutra, Regis and TRC), he had not been discriminated against. In fact, to vouch for the queer friendliness of the administration of the hotel, he recounts 'making out with guys on the floor' without being asked to leave. His inability to understand the administration's decision is, of course, much more insidious and has to do with the non-recognition of the power of class dynamics and the social class of those who were turned away. The clothes worn by group members are another visual indicator of one's class status, and in this case also of gender subjectivity. By turning away people because of 'dressing inappropriately', the club was actually making a statement that only certain types of people (dressed smart, in expensive clothes, normative and not in drag) would be allowed entry while excluding those who did not 'fit' this model. This echoes McDermott (2011: 64), who has argued that 'social class [is] a major axis of power which positions LGBT people unequally and unjustly'. Thus, while some queer members were allowed entry, others were excluded.

## Class identification and the fractured community

McDermott (2011: 66) argues that queer theories are based upon a politics of visibility by which dominated groups unite through their signs of oppression and demand recognition as an oppressed community. However, she notes that 'these classless sexual identity politics are compounded by cultural representations of lesbian and gay men which are predominantly, middle class, affluent and white' (McDermott, 2011: 66). This is perhaps exemplified (in an unreflexive fashion) in the response given by group member Jash Khanna, who found the entire incident to have been blown out of proportion and was angry that group members were even debating such 'triviality'. He wrote:

i dont understand what people are trying to say here
    if rocky freakin wants to be elitist its thier choice. if you have a problem with that take your ass to some other club which is not 'elitist' according to you

i mean cmon. why are people screaming homophobia and transphobia ? wtf, there so so many of my straight friends who were very well dressed but were still denied entry just because the manager dint want them to enter.

its a club and thats how clubs function. deal with it

leave to a bunch of gay guys to stir up trivial drama even when it is not required.

(21 July, 2011)

There are various ways in which Jash's statement can be read. Jash does not recognise or see himself as one of the members who were being deprived entry. As such his swift gesture, to resist any kind of discussion on the issue, registers the difficulties that subaltern queer voices face from within and outside the community. Jash's own queer elite position (which was evidenced by his *Facebook* profile) – the acceptable face of queer India and the club's own position in terms of class – signal the different forms of marginality working within this space. It was surprising that only two people who were denied entry actively discussed this on the thread. Most of the others were silent or did not participate in this dialogue. Drawing on the work of Spivak (1988), as discussed, I would argue that the issue is not only the lack of an opportunity to speak and be heard, but also the discursive mechanisms such as Jash's comment, which through equating the club's policy as acceptable renders any oppositional statements (such as class-based bias) useless. The subaltern's voice, as Spivak has argued previously, is only mediated and represented but never fully replicated. Amit was one of the revellers who was turned away at the gate. He narrated his version of the story to me and said:

I went to the club with two other friends. We had never ever been to this hotel before, but because this was a community party we pooled together money (It was 850 rupees per person) to attend. But when we went to the gate, the manager; a woman looked at us up and down and told us rudely that we cannot go in. When we asked why, she said it was 'couple's only'; which was obviously a lie because I could see other single men entering. I did not want to argue as I was embarrassed and ashamed. We went away feeling very humiliated.

(30 July 2013)

On being asked why he did not share his story on the group thread, he said that this incident reflected his own (class) background, and as a result he was not able to live up to the class identity of the other group members who were able to access the venue. He had not read Jash's comment, but on being told about it, he looked unsurprised and told me that this was the reason he did not tell other members that he was one of the people who had been turned away at the entrance. He felt safe hiding his class from others. Judging by the speech, style and appearance of Amit, I would suggest that he belonged to the lower/working class youth populace of the city. His statement highlights his recognition of the apparent discomfort in the revelation of his class background and the vulnerability of his class position.

Writing about virtual queer communities in India, Mitra (2010: 167) argues that '[t]he construction and representation of online queer identities is problematic however, in that it involves both "critical silences" and strategic negotiation, which are likely to engender a particular stream of queer identity but leave others out'. While communities such as PKP talk back to institutional social hegemony by their very existence on global websites such as *Facebook* and queer it, it also leaves certain voices out of the process. It then becomes imperative to challenge the queer history that is now being written which ignores the class disenfranchised. People like Amit are marked 'out of place' not just by door attendants and the elite patrons of the club, but this event also marks a conformity to the neoliberal project of creating the respectable, socially mobile (and economically sound) queer citizen subject.

Cooper and Dzara (2010) have argued that queer users of *Facebook* seek to form friendships and find a sense of companionship through shared interests by joining groups that cater to these interests. These communities are thus based on a shared purpose or common interests – in this case, socialising with other queer people in the city. PKP is a place for communication and discussion, and also a space for socialising and forging connections. While voices such as Amit are silenced, other voices such as Jash and Rudranil take a hierarchical position and ultimately become the dominant voices of the community. Neither Jash nor Rudranil actively tried to become the 'voice' of the group; rather I would argue that their class entitlement gave them the confidence and capital to take on the dominant voice in this instance. McIntosh (1988), in her seminal essay 'White Privilege and Male Privilege', argues that white people are not taught to recognise the privileges that come with being white. It is important to recognise that white privilege can and does exist without the conscious knowledge of its presence. Jash and Rudranil's stance here can be read through a similar lens. Their argument that they were not denied entry even though they were queer affirms what they perceive as the queer solidarity of the management at The Garden. What they, however, fail to realise is that it is their class privilege that was also recognisable and afforded them this mobility. In this instance, middle class/upper middle class-ness is positioned as that which is invisible to the bearer of this identity (i.e. Jash and Rudranil).

Henderson (2013: 88) contends that cultural systems of class attribution are always partial. They signify a cultural capital as well as other attributes such as middle class modesty or a self-conscious entrance into another class. Jash's misrecognition and hostility towards those who were denied entry expresses less about the absolute class position or Jash's habits and more about class compliance (with Rudranil's sentiments, in this case) and resistance.

## Language matters: 'only speak in English, please'

Owing to globalisation, consumerism, market liberalisation and a growing consciousness of queer identities, the last two decades have seen a considerable increase in queer visibility in India. Pawan Dhall recalled the Pride celebrations in Kolkata in 2006 and 2007, when the only form of queer visibility was trans*/*kothi*/*hijra* visibility. There were very few gay men who were comfortable with walking publicly in a Pride parade, and many did not want to associate themselves with the subaltern vernacular queer people of the city. Dhall recalls the overt transphobia, when he first started working with the community.

> When we started organising the Sidharth Gautam Film Festival and the Pride marches in Kolkata, I would face a barrage of people on the e-forums who would tell me: Pawan, you are not doing any 'real' activism. Why are you working with these transgender and hijra people. They are the scum of the society who only beg and cheat. These were middle class, upper middle class, gay identified men who had access to these e-forums. There were also some apologists who appreciated what I was doing but thought I wasn't doing enough to address their 'gay' concerns.
>
> (23 August 2013)

This has changed in recent years with more queer/gay men taking part in the Pride marches and taking on the dominant voice within the queer discourse both online and offline. Such has been the change that for the first time in the history of Pride marches in Kolkata, there were two separate marches in 2013 because the trans* community felt that they were being sidelined in the march by the gay men. One of the other manifestations of this visibility has also been the power afforded to the English language. It is not surprising that most of these gay identified men are educated to university levels, belong to middle class and upper middle class families and speak in English. Bernstein (1960: 271), in his essay 'Language and Social Class', attests that different modes of speech can be found within people belonging to different socio-economic classes, and that the resulting form of language orient the speakers towards different and distinct relationships with objects and people.

As I mentioned earlier in Chapter 3, the ability to speak English is related to class in India. In India, the English language has a very distinguished history. Lord Macaulay (who also drafted the infamous Section 377) drafted the 'Minute on Education' in 1835, by which funding for Indian languages was reduced and instead money was allocated to fund education in Western subjects with English as the language of instruction. In his own words, 'Whoever knows that language [English] has ready access to all the vast intellectual wealth, which all the wisest nations of the earth have created and hoarded in the course of ninety generations' (Macaulay, [1835] 2004: 313). The underlying motive was to create 'a class of persons, Indian in blood and colour, but English in tastes and opinions, in morals and in intellect' (Macaulay, [1835] 2004: 313). This elevation of the English language has remained a distinct part of the social fabric of postcolonial India. As Ganguly-Scrase and Scrase (2012: 198) point out, 'English proficiency [in India] emerges as a cultural capital that serves to secure middle class status.'

PKP does not have any rules regarding which language can be used within the group. However, there have been frequent posts by group members asking non-English speakers to refrain from using the vernacular. Ratul, for example, in reply to a post writes:

> Please do comment in english [*sic*]. Its an english [*sic*] forum do write up in english (If you are capable, otherwise humble apology).

From this statement, Ratul indicates that he is aware that the group member he is referring to might not be proficient in the language and very clearly makes an allusion to his 'capability'. The language divides on the forum follows the language divide in India, and is a reflection of the broader social class and cultural division. Ganguly-Scrase and Scrase (2012) maintain that the Indian classes see a distinct social advantage in maintaining English proficiency. Ratul's comment is indicative of his own class subjectivity and the way in which he views the class status of the person he is critiquing. Interestingly, several of the member profiles on *PlanetRomeo* also state that proficiency in English is essential before contacting them, as Confounded2007's profile text reads:

> Writing up something intellectual seems necessary to attract the cerebral faculties of profile visitors. Please have something more to start with than the infamous 'hi'. Please know how to speak the Queen's language before trying to get my attention.

Shahani (2008: 274) notes that the predominance of English in India has proved to be beneficial in the formation of queer digital spaces. Shahani argues that when the Internet emerged, predominantly in English, there was already a constituency of English-speaking, upper middle class gay men, who were ready to exploit its opportunities and utilise it for their own benefit. Roy (2003: 190), however, notes that despite the hegemony of the English language on the Internet, there is evidence of 'more people from small towns logging on' as well as 'people with different proficiencies in English'.

Most of the people I interviewed were of the consensus that PKP catered to a narrow English-speaking, upper middle class segment of the queer populace in Kolkata. By contrast, Amit directed me to a new *Facebook* group that had emerged called KRPF. While the group emerged primarily to organise the annual Pride marches in Kolkata as an independent non-funded body away from the organisational and NGO structures, it also aimed to provide an alternative online/offline space for queer party revellers in Kolkata, and instead of hosting parties in expensive clubs and hotels with exorbitant entry /cover charges, KRPF hosts parties at smaller venues with a diverse clientele. The stratification within PKP, however, was also a source of comfort for many. As Rajeev pointed out to me:

> I prefer to hang out with people of my own socio-economic background. I do not think PKP is posh. I think it is quite mixed. People of all backgrounds can access the venue and we can use our own discretion about who we want to talk to or not. I do get a bit frustrated when some of these LS (low society) people start using vulgar vernacular slangs. It spoils the ambience within the group.
>
> (12 August 2013)

Rajeev's quote suggests that marginalisation is evident within a space like PKP. PKP, despite its democratic outlook of wanting to provide a space for 'all queers' in Kolkata, works within this stratified paradigm. As Henderson (2013) points out, class disrupts the dominant queer arena (i.e. gay, male, white). Rajeev, in his contradictory statement, accepts that PKP is mixed, but also shows his discomfort at the inclusion of the 'LS people'. Rajeev's views have, however, also come under criticism by others such as Anindya Hajra, the moderator on PKP who believes that some amount of vernacular should not only be allowed, but also encouraged on the forum. In response to Rajeev's complaint on the forum about the 'disturbing trend of having entire conversations in vernacular' (13 January 2012), Hajra remarked:

> I agree posts, essentially need to be in a language that can be accessed by an imagined 'all', but (and this is no defense of Bangla alone but

ALL language that gets classified as 'vernacular') if I may also put this in here that an equal number of people may sometimes feel comfortable speaking in that vernacular – and if this space can also sometimes factor that in.

(13 January 2012)

Hajra's comment is illuminating because he critiques the notion of the 'imagined all'. While users such as Rajeev believe that using a vernacular language on the forum distances many users who cannot follow the language or the idioms, Hajra is quick to point out that there are an equal number who may not feel comfortable expressing themselves in English and are more comfortable using the vernacular language. It should be stated that some of the users who use the 'vernacular' language do so using the Roman script and writing in Bengali or Hindi; and in a city such as Kolkata, there would be very few who do not understand one of those two languages, thus challenging Rajeev's theory of vernaculars distancing certain users. In fact, all my 25 research participants understood all three languages with varying degrees of expertise. Khanna (2011: 195) contends that 'the queer body, the urban, working class/lower middle class, has existed in a space of tension, or marginality . . . This especially as it begins to distinguish itself from the body of the *Hijra*, from the class or community that has been accorded particular places in hierarchies and social matrices'. Hajra's comments can be read alongside Foucault's (2001) work on the history of sexuality, where Foucault argues that subjectivities are discursively produced through internalising certain regulations. As this section highlights, the queer subjects on PKP construct themselves based on the model of a universal sexual identity (Altman, 1997), while relegating subaltern indigenised identities as 'disturbing', 'low society' and 'scum'.

## When race meets class

At this point, I would like to relate a second incident that played out on the Pink Party forum more than a year after the incident at The Garden. In recalling this incident, I would like to focus on the intersection between class, race and queer subjectivity in the city and the ways in which the different voices merged on the online forum. Not only does the incident expose the fractures within the group a year later, it also enables me to further critique the community discourse. This time, a party was held at a private farmhouse owned by a white expatriate of Canadian origin living in Kolkata and group members were asked to pay a cover charge for entry. What should have been a safe party with no issues around accessibility took a turn for the worse when the following day accusations of classism and racism were levelled against the organisers and the host on the *Facebook* group.

Some of the group members claimed that they were thrown out of the party late at night while they were drunk and in a somewhat vulnerable state. These group members claimed that while certain members were allowed to stay the night, many others were unceremoniously asked to leave the property immediately after the advertised time. For a long time, none of the organisers or the hosts made any comment until Carl, the expatriate host, decided to intervene and defend PKP and the party.

> Seriously Rocky and others that find it necessary to critique the PKP events. You really have to understand that PKP is not a professional event company, hotel or caterer. It is organised by private individuals who donate there [*sic*] time and energy towards it. I know exactly what your options are in this city – cheap smoke filled dark and dingy bars.
>
> (24 October 2012)

Carl's comment, while potentially objectionable, is also illuminating about what he considers to be the options for queer men in the city. His comment highlights the ways in which income, wealth and class privilege roots queer identity and queer entertainment in the city. Queer men do not have the privilege of accessing other venues, and so their criticism regarding the event was unacceptable to Carl. By choosing to exclude some people, Carl is making a personal choice, but the subtle decisions behind it would benefit from being interrogated within the framework of class privilege. Carl was not alone in his defence of the party. Another group member Richard Vernen, who also attended the party, chimed in, 'id say be grateful ! and stop whining ! why does everyone whine here !! ???' (24 October 2012).

Richard and Carl echo the earlier comments made by Rudranil and Jash and their inability to perceive class privilege in this context. In my attempt to explore the ways in which class types structure queer difference and queer specificity, I return to Henderson (2013: 57), who claims that any mode of queer class analysis throws up patterns of 'comportment, familialism and legitimate acquisition of the good life in the commercial ratification of queerness'. Carl and Richard's comments defending PKP resonate with the earlier defence made by Rudranil and Jash. I would argue that this evidences the promotion of a certain class-inflected queer male identity over queer solidarity. The implicit discomfort with other class types was made evident with Carl's decision to ask some people to leave over others. Research shows (McDermott, 2011) that social class is implicated in the ways in which LGBT people choose to identify themselves and the social choices they make. In this instance, it reveals not just the motivations of Carl (who decided to throw some group members out), but also of those who decided to protest against this perceived injustice. Sushovan, one of the group members, protested against the elitism being shown by some of the members in the forum. In reply to one of Richard's comments about the members 'demanding too much for the little paid':

> dont come looking for caviar with an entry fee of Rs .1100 . . Next time u organise a party and make sure caviar is on the menu and id like some wine with it . . while ur at it . . .

Sushovan wrote:

> This comment by Richard is absolutely in the league of 'if they dont have bread . . .' not that I ever had a very high opinion of PKP being a socially responsible forum (its after all populated by the likes of XXX) but this is outrageously classist, elitist and condescending comment. I demand an apology!!!
>
> (24 October 2012)

Sushovan's comments succinctly capture the two sides of the PKP community. Not only does he compare and attribute the elitism of some of the group members to the elitism shown by the French monarchy before the revolution (by which he also displays some of his own cultural capital), but he also bluntly critiques the PKP administration for this debacle. Interestingly enough, Richard replies to this comment asking Shushovan, 'who are you?' (24 October 2012), to which another group member replied, 'why will social profiling him help you better on how to address your comments towards him?'

My attempt here is not to discredit the PKP group, but rather to critique the elitism of its members. PKP have very publicly declared that the group caters to all queer people, that is, 'open to all' people within the community. Although they have never positioned themselves as a civil rights/political pressure group (as institutional organisations and NGOs do), they do hold a strong grip on the queer imagination of the city. Most recently, one of the moderators of the group again echoed their commitment to embracing everyone and opening a forum that is accessible to all.

> Pink parties was created with the belief and aim to bring together people from the community and beyond . . . Pink Parties have had always been a non profit making body and primarily helping the community people and beyond to get together at public spaces . . . Rest assured Pink party is just taking a break from the social overdose and it will

be back soon with a new format of parties in the usual prominent and comfortable venues along with open arms to people from every kind of background.

(15 July 2013)

Agreeing with Henderson's (2013: 59) critique that 'queer class life has nowhere to go and nothing to do except to live with the limits dominance imposes, learning class rules from the cultural ether . . .' I want to use this event as an example where the silenced voices of the group spoke up, a marked difference from the earlier event at The Garden. While the administrators ultimately tried to openly engage with group members in explaining (albeit defending Carl) the events of the previous night, this also opened up deep divisions within the group, something that had happened only intermittently before this event. Sushovan also used the event to critique the racism (again, along class lines) of the host. In reply to the moderator, he asked:

> shaheb je eto gulo brown skinmiddleclass bachha chhele ke nijer bungalow theke ghaar dhaaka diye ber kore dilo, sheta niye to ekta kothao shona gelo na?
> (The fact that this [rich] white man chucked so many brown skinned working/middle class boys out by their neck, how come that is not being addressed?)

(24 October 2012)

Although this question remained unanswered, it foregrounds some of the issues and disjunctures around class within the queer community which in some senses were heightened by a failure to engage.

## Inclusion/exclusion

PKP offers an alternative space for queer entertainment and queer intermingling in the city. While one of the primary implicit aims of the group when it was formed was to help in creating and sustaining a community, this has not been entirely successful. When I interviewed some of the group members, they all described it as a community space and many referred to themselves as 'pinkies' (members of PKP). In an interview conducted with Raj, he described PKP as 'a highway stop where all the gays of Kolkata meet at some time or the other'.[6] These are 'people you may know or will get to know from the forums'. The group's 'open to all' ethos further encourages people from around the globe, especially those with a connection to Kolkata, to come together. While the name PKP indicates a geographical specificity, I would argue that the space addresses a potential global queer

community, challenging border divides and opening up a global intercon-
nectedness. Pullen (2012) argues that such transnational identity challenges the notion of a Western-centric LGBTQ model. Pullen (2012: 6)
writes, 'In this sense of a new shared imagination, enabled by transnational
potential challenges the notion of a Western queer subjectivity.' I would
argue that most group members on PKP actually structure their identities
along this Western subjectivity, although the presence of subaltern queer
identities on the group also unsettles this.

What is also important to highlight is that PKP is probably more successful as an online forum than its physical counterpart. It has allowed people
like Amit, who are in the closet and not comfortable coming out about his
sexual preference, to extend the territory upon which he can express his
queer self into realms that will not be policed. However, this also comes at
a cost levied on the subaltern body. As PKP demonstrates, the marginality
imposed on the classed body is both implicit and explicit.

Mowlabocus (2010a: 87), in his exploration of the sociality of online
queer spaces, notes that 'websites such as Gaydar have provided important
resources to combat the isolation and marginalisation that growing up gay
in a straight world often engenders'. The space offered by groups such as
PKP affirms queer existence and queer expression by emphasising and cen-
tralising the participant's sexuality through discussions around queer issues
and organising queer entertainment options. However, such affirmation
comes at a cost, as demonstrated above. Alexander (2002: 90) comments
that queer online spaces impose various forms of boundaries and unfortunate bigotries, 'a biting reminder that in-group membership status within
the gay male community often comes at a certain price, extracted on the
body of those seeking inclusion'.

Amit's first comment of not being able to identify with a community
addresses the mechanism of inclusion and exclusion within the PKP community and the relation of power and dominance of certain voices. The
people I have quoted and those who spoke unhesitatingly to me, 'stands
as an invitation or beacon, a brightness on the social horizon through
which painful, sometimes shameful, experiences and feelings are pressed
into recognition' (Henderson, 2013: 97). Their collective narratives act as
a redemptive device. Voices such as Amit's, who are in possession of their
own circumstance and position, critique dominant groupings. As a significant minority, they hold the right to dissent (Appadurai, 1996). Appadurai
contends that in the liberal imagination, large majorities lose their rationality as they are shaped by outside forces such as the state or other dominant
voices. The same can be seen with dominant queer voices. Thus, voices
such as Sushovan, Amit and Anindya transcend those that are dominant,
offering diverse opinions and approaches.

The assumption that all queer men on the Internet are affluent rearticulates the classism within participatory media culture. I would like to argue that social exclusion is not just limited to access to the Internet, but it is also about being able to fruitfully engage in a conversation with others without being subject to class-identified backlash. As the examples given here articulate, the notion of access and representation is subject to hate speech, which reinforces the power dynamics within the group.

Issues around class are rarely addressed in queer media (Henderson, 2013), and even less so on social media platforms. As Amit told me, 'Class is not considered important, everyone who is going to these parties can pay quite a bit of money, it is people like me who need to talk about it.' Shahani (2008: 253), in his ethnographic work on the *GayBombay* community, points out the hypocritical nature through which class is mediated in queer social groups: 'While there was some resentment among *GayBombay* people to interact socially with people from the non English speaking classes, many of them had no qualms in exoticising them in their sexual fantasies.' This remark was echoed by Jasjit in his interview, when he remarked: 'These men act coy and submissive on anonymous sites like *PlanetRomeo* but when they see us on PKP they feign ignorance, actually they are scared to tell people about their low class escapades' (13 August 2013).

## What makes PKP tick?

PKP occupies a unique position within the queer imagination of the city. By situating itself within a mainstream site such as *Facebook*, it appropriates a heteronormative space and queers it. It does not work in the same way as sites such as *PlanetRomeo* or *Gaydar* function; rather it strategises itself like a cybercottage (Mowlabocus, 2010a). The group is not 'secret' but 'closed', which means people can easily find it but cannot view its posts until they have joined the group. It works on a referral system, whereby someone wishing to join the group needs to be accepted by the users and moderators while users can also add other users to the group.

PKP, despite its English language bias, has tried to engage with the larger community. As both moderators of the *Facebook* group have espoused time and again, they do support vernacular dialogue amongst members as well as trying to find spaces that will be welcoming to all. Perhaps, most importantly, PKP offers a social space that is not bounded through an organisational structure. This has been the most attractive feature of the group to its members. While the group strongly advocates not using the pages to look for sexual partners, 'This is not a hook up joint so kindly be aware and chat accordingly . . .', there have been many instances of members posting their body stats and availability to other members in the hope of a sexual encounter. This has usually been censured by proactive members and sometimes by the moderators, but this 'transgression' continues unabated.

Some group members have also suggested that they find themselves within a different standpoint not reflected in the mainstream within this space. Members are known to come from far-flung locations just to be able to 'shake a leg and dance with the community' (Jasjit, 13 August 2013). Boyce and Hajra (2011: 17), in their ethnographic study conducted with trans* people in West Bengal, note that for many marginalised sexual identities the marginalisation 'is one of restriction, where a sense of self is not commensurate with the world at large'. This sense of restriction is reflected most notably on the subaltern queer identities within the group. While power structures dictate the dominance of certain voices, PKP also offers a platform for dissenting minority voices like Amit and Jasjit to engage in a debate. Garcia-Arroyo (2006: 91) contends that 'in India there are no legitimate places for queer people, everything goes underground'. This has certainly been challenged in recent years with the politics and activism surrounding Section 377 that has spawned a wide range of debates on the queer body in India (Khanna, 2011). Queer activist Ashok Row Kavi, in his short autobiographical piece 'The Contract of Silence' (1999), writes that a typical day for gay men in Bombay (and by extension in India) is made up of two cycles. The morning represents family and work, but it was after sunset when the rest of the city slept that gay life began. The rise of social spaces on the Internet has altered this concept vastly. Shaw (1997), for instance, points out that while heterosexual people have access to participate in conversations outside Internet chat rooms (e.g. the bar, the store), not as many opportunities exist for queer people. The Internet and by extension groups such as PKP provide the means for queer people to meet and socialise. Shaw notes, 'In the gay world, a gay itch is satisfied by going out to a club or party which requires a certain time commitment while IRC is literally at my fingertips (at work and home)' (1997: 138).

Roy (2003: 191), however, claims that 'the Internet can also foster disconnections even as it potentially creates new connections'. PKP was set up with the hope of building a social space for queer people in the city that would include all sections of the community. However, people like Amit have been critical at what they perceive to be a misappropriation of their voice. Amit asserted that:

> This community talk is crap, as I have mentioned before I do not talk like them nor do I go to fancy places. I do not think we need to be a part of some happy family because we are not but it is as important to recognise this difference which is currently being appropriated by one overarching voice.

> (30 July 2013)

Amit's argument has resonance with the divides that plague the queer community in India and the West (Roy, 2003). Rather than arguing for one queer community, as Amit points out, it is more fruitful to recognise the differences and disjunctions and work with these.

Class is a contentious issue to talk about both within India and in discourses about the queer community, especially where mainstream media representation of queer people is within the narrow stratum of white, male and wealthy (Demory and Pullen, 2013). As Demory and Pullen (2013: 6) argue, representation politics of non-normative sexualities has always been positioned between a certain degree of tolerance and a superficial tokenism of the alternative. Queer continues to be a restricted identity category, especially for those who are economically underprivileged. This is exacerbated when media representations of queer people are skewed towards a white, high earning class, making it even more difficult for others to actively engage in a process of self-definition with limited forms of representation with which to identify.[7] Spaces such as PKP and KRPF have, in recent years, opened up a valuable space for dialogue. They have actively engaged individuals to ask questions and to socialise, and they have stated that they wish to foster acceptance; but in this process, they have also created discriminatory structures for some.

## Concluding remarks: building the 'invisible' community

I began this chapter by critiquing the very notion of a community (state created, locally created or organisationally created), which relies on a sense of commonality. This commonality is a conflation of certain points of convergence – sexuality, gender, class, race – but are not intersectional, as my case studies have shown. My attempt in this chapter has not been to idealise the subversive potential of a space like PKP, but rather to critique it and to use it as a case study to demonstrate some of the ways in which classism works within queer communities, and in particular within online queer communities in India.

As the previous sections have demonstrated, the subversive potential of a space like PKP in the discursive exploration of sexual identities and sexual kinship within a city such as Kolkata is immense. While for some joining the group was a necessity (not having recourse to a support structure), for others it offered the potential to connect with a larger queer populace of the city beyond gay dating sites such as *PlanetRomeo* or organisational support spaces (most queer charities also have online groups).

The issue of language, which is seldom connected to issues of class difference in queer communities, is another area that this ethnography has brought to the surface. Analysis of queerness and social class has seen recent scholarship (Henderson, 2013) arguing and offering innovative observations between the two. Within a class-entrenched society such as India, this approach towards thinking about class and queerness together, especially within an online space, yields a rich tranche of personal biases, politics and a critique of queer solidarity. PKP has allowed a space for activists such as Pawan Dhall and Anindya Hajra (who interestingly have some extremely divergent viewpoints) to feature alongside subaltern voices such as Jasjit and Amit as well as voices like Jash, Rudranil and others. The very fact that the space offers a platform for these voices is unique within the cityscape. What still needs to be interrogated are those silent voices which are yet to make their presence felt in the group. There are 1,400 members registered in the group, but only a small percentage can be counted as active. The interactions between the group members negotiated through a series of online and offline experiences have created a community culture (e.g. people calling themselves Pinkies), yet it is also characterised by the lack of a class-based diversity.

PKP offers a cosmopolitan vision (Beck, 2008: 3) which reveals 'a reflexive awareness of ambivalences . . . blurring of differentiations'. A universal community is not the solution and that needs to be critiqued. Rather the subversive potential of the PKP space in opening up a dialogue between unheard voices and dominant ones is crucial and encouraging both for human rights discourses and national queer politics. As Shahani (2008) explicates, mobility within the queer community is a privilege only a few can afford, and for those bodies which cannot travel, a space like PKP opens up a space for social gathering (both online and offline). As Rajeev revealed to me in a conversation:

> I left India primarily for studies and work and did not really get to know the queer community back home very well. A site (sic) like PKP is almost godsent. It has allowed me to connect with a few people who I had known in passing but more importantly it has helped keep me abreast of news and event within the queer community in Kolkata. I do not really post much, I am more of a silent observer. Being part of the group somehow makes me feel like one foot is still in Kolkata whilst the other is here.
>
> (12 August 2013)

To sum up, in this chapter, I have argued that PKP exists within a diverse constitution of queer identities in Kolkata. It has been an instrumental part of the queer social scene of the city. The very fact that its online group is much more active than its offline one (by June 2015, the Wednesday evening coffee meetings had more or less stopped) is indicative of both its failure in addressing certain class issues within its membership; but at the same its online presence has been an important ground for disparate voices to debate and challenge the myth of a queer community. Like many other online groups, the PKP community is characterised by certain progressive ideals towards open dialogue and creating queer spaces in the city, but at the same time fails to engage and offer diversity amongst the different class and economic backgrounds it purports to represent.

In the next chapter, I continue exploring the inequalities and tensions within these digital queer male spaces by critiquing the gender normative privilege and discrimination of effeminate and femme subject positions of users on these digital platforms.

## Notes

1  The interview space (i.e. the coffee shop) was chosen by Amit himself. I had offered to use other spaces such as my house or my friend's house, or the local university that provides space for public use.

2  Dhakuria Lake remains a popular cruising ground, unlike what Raj says, though Minto Park has indeed undergone a transformation. None of my research participants spoke about Minto Park, and I would believe if it is used as a cruising space this would be quite limited. Most participants I spoke to mentioned the Lake and Nandan (a publicly funded theatre/cinema and cultural space in central Kolkata).

3  By low-class people, he meant *kothis* and *hijras*, as Pawan explained to me when I asked him to clarify. For a discussion on *kothis* and *hijras*, see Boyce (2007) and Boyce and Hajra (2011).

4  Please note that all names have been changed to protect the identity of the participants and group members of the group, except when they are public figures (e.g. Pawan Dhall and Anindya Hajra).

5  All statements from the group wall have been quoted verbatim. I have only changed the names of the venues to protect the venue's identity.

6  I found it interesting that Amit made this reference to a physical space. Highway stops are transitory spaces and have a history of being used as potential cruising grounds. In fact, one of the higher-risk groups within the sexual health discourse are truck drivers in India who use the highways.

7  At the time of writing this book, Russell T Davies' new television shows *Banana* and *Cucumber* had just started on Channel 4, and, unlike many other shows, the characters here come from a range of social and racial backgrounds. However, I would argue that this is still limited. Even a very recent music video made by the United Nations Human Rights office to celebrate queer identities in India showed a rich, fair-skinned, privileged gay male gender normative couple. The video was widely debated on various forums and digital media, including a debate between the activist Ashok Row Kavi and myself. This can be viewed at Udayan Dhar (2014). 'Queer Reactions to Celina Jaitley Musical'. Available at: http://pink-pages.co.in/the-gay-agenda/queer-reactions-celina-jaitley-musical/. Accessed on 1 January 2015.

# 5   Effeminophobia, 'straight-acting' and global queering

## Introduction

Since the early 2000s, there has been an emerging alignment of non-Western queer cultures in countries such as India, with a global queer assimilation (Altman, 1997; Dutta, 2013a). One of the particular characteristics of this has been a tendency to be a part of the homonormative paradigm (Duggan, 2003), which configures some queer men as 'normative' masculine subjects while subordinating feminised/non-normative gender positionalities. Duggan (2003: 50) defines the new homonormativity as:

> . . . a politics that does not contest dominant heteronormative assumptions and institutions, but upholds and sustains them, while promising the possibility of a demobilized gay constituency and a privatized, depoliticized gay culture anchored in domesticity and consumption.

Effeminacy is not only denigrated by straight men, but has also been the subject of ridicule within gay spaces, where a certain section of gay men categorically shun and reject men who identify with effeminate subject positions. This 'effeminophobia', as Sinfield (1994: 15) so eloquently points out, is borne out of a sense of misogyny. He argues that 'the root idea [of effeminacy] is a male falling away from the purposeful reasonableness that is supposed to constitute manliness into the laxity and weakness conventionally attributed to women'. Richardson (2009: 528) argues that homosexuality is still identified as gender transitivity and effeminacy. This stereotype, according to Richardson, 'stems from the tradition of assuming that the gender binary (masculine/feminine) is the scaffold of sexual desire and that anyone who is attracted to another man must by definition, be feminine; while anyone who is attracted to a woman must, by the same reasoning, be masculine', thus conflating the effeminate man as being gay/queer in popular media representations. These contributing factors sit alongside a fear of disdain by a society which privileges gender normative behaviour (perpetuated through homonormativity). This has led to gay men 'playing up' to their masculinity and dispelling any notion of femininity in their behaviour. In this chapter, I explore the ways in which effeminate subject positions are derided within online queer spaces in India. In doing so, I would like to demonstrate two important points. First is that contemporary gay/queer politics in India (as elsewhere) has taken a homonormative position, which in its desire to conform to mainstream Indian culture (privileging gender normativity), subjectively discriminates against positions that are deemed 'too transgressive'. The concept of 'too transgressive' is an issue I discuss during the course of this chapter. The second point I seek to make in this chapter builds upon the work I have undertaken in previous chapters – that of critiquing the 'community' and the utopic discourse of online queer spaces – which, as I will demonstrate here, thrives on difference and discrimination rather than commonality. The digital space, as this chapter shall argue, provides for more visible and scathing attacks on effeminate subject positions. I would like to point out that while class is another useful avenue to pursue, in this chapter I am bracketing that off, as it was already the main focus of my last chapter. In this chapter, I shift the lens to gender.

## Gender and masculinity in India

One of the most important areas of research in gender and postcolonial studies has been the analysis of indigenous masculinities within colonial contexts (Nandy, 1983; Sinha, 1995). This exploration foregrounds the gender, race and class dynamics within colonialism and nationalism, and provides opportunities for interrogating alternative gender practices that challenge hegemonic structures imposed by a Western, middle class patriarchy. In theorising the production of masculinities in postcolonial systems, it is useful to remember that these hegemonies were created through a colonial system, where indigenous populations were effeminised, especially in the context of the Bengali *bhadralok* (Sinha, 1995). Historically, the *bhadralok* class was a group of tax collectors and clerics who occupied some of the highest positions in the colonial hierarchy. It is closely aligned with the Bengal renaissance, when the introduction of Western education led to the growth of a new class of intelligentsia. Chowdhury (1998) argues that the stereotypes associated with the Bengali *bhadralok* were a way of justifying colonial rule. From the early colonial paintings to the public discourse in colonial India, the *bhadralok babu* (gentleman) was depicted as effeminate, leading a scandalous life and being subservient to a domineering wife. In creating this idealised hegemonic *bhadralok* masculinity, the *bhadramahila* (the gentlewoman) was cast as the repository of the family honour, whose transgression had the power to dismantle this carefully constructed ideal of the Bengali joint family. Chakraborty (1997) notes that the figure of the chaste Hindu wife (the *grihalakshmi*) symbolised the *bhadralok*'s attempt to differentiate themselves from the colonisers. The self-sacrificing Hindu wife was seen as an anti-book to the Eurocentric model of individualism. However, Chakrabarty does not deny the violence concealed in this process of rewriting Indian womanhood through patriarchy. Sarkar (2003) reads this as an attempt made by the *bhadralok* male to exert dominance within the private domestic sphere, now that colonisers had subordinated his position in the public sphere.

Another argument is that masculinities in the colonies were created and perpetuated as a contrast to the coloniser's own masculinity. For instance, native African and Indian men were seen as hypersexual; their sexuality was considered to be a threat to the virtuous white woman in imminent danger from such unchecked sexuality, thus creating a justification for colonisers to check and discipline other cultures (Sinha, 1995). The constructed predatory nature of the colonised man was reviled by the White coloniser, who, having produced such a vision of predation, sought to violently subdue it through newly legitimated colonial practices. Practices such as polygamy, *sati*, and *burkhas* were seen as a part of the widespread uncivilised patriarchy that existed in the colonies, and provided the pretext for the 'white man saving the brown women from brown men' (Spivak, 1988: 297). The argument was that if Indian men were patriarchal and violent within the confines of their family, forcing their women to wear the *burkha* or practice *sati*, how could they be fair in their dealings with the British government (Sinha, 1995)? This essentialising of colonial masculinities through the White imaginary served to both obscure and appropriate an unsettling difference.

Much of the current scholarship concerning gender and nationhood has fixated itself on the role of women, who are constructed as symbols of the nation and 'motherland'. Thus, as Ray (2000) points out, more often women's bodies become sites of contested culture, tradition and the nation. However, in recent years, questioning this gendered version of nationalism has thrown up new questions on the role of masculinity and the male body. John and Nair, in their seminal work on Indian sexuality *A Question of Silence*, point out that 'questions of male sexuality have rarely been a focus of scholarly analysis except for celebrated instances of celibacy' (1998: 15).

Gender in India operates on myriad levels. On the one hand, there is the hypersexual predatory nature of masculinity, and on the other there is the effeminisation of the Indian male through colonialism and control, as I noted earlier. This effeminisation led postcolonial popular culture to recreate the Indian male as the virile masculine figure of the precolonial era.

This is most evident within the *Amar Chitra Katha* comic book series. The *Amar Chitra Katha*, which remains one of India's leading comic book series, promotes 'the route to your roots' and the 'glorious heritage of India', highlighting and appealing to the nationalist sentiments of consumers, thus equating masculinity as a form of national pride (McLain, 2009: 159).

Within the discourse of queerness and masculinity in India, the *kothi* continues to be a persistent figure. The *kothi* is often described as the only authentic/pan-Indian queer identity in the context of the Western-produced gay identity. This is a view scholars such as Khanna (2011) disagree with. Khanna claims that the *kothi* is a figure of globalisation, NGO politics and the HIV/AIDS discourse. Narrain (2004: 2–3) defines *kothi* as the following:

> Kothi is a feminised male identity which is adopted by some people in the Indian subcontinent and is marked by gender non-conformity. A kothi though biologically male, adopts feminine modes of dressing, speech and behaviour and would look for a male partner who has masculine modes of behaviour.

Khanna (2011) further argues that categories such as *kothis* in India and Bangladesh, *kathoey* in Thailand, *metis* in Nepal and *zenanas* in Pakistan are ways in which indigenous equivalences are created in response to disavowal of categories such as that of the homosexual, and their defining feature 'is that they are all, quite simply put penetrated'. While the *kothi* is penetrated, the masculine equivalent (who *kothis* usually identify as their partners/lovers) are known as *parikhs*, or *giriyas* in different parts of India (Boyce, 2007). Within this paradigm, the *parikh* figure is seen as the 'original man'. His sexual choices are not seen as an aberration due to his masculine gendered role. It should also be noted that *panthis* is rarely a category of self-identity; rather it is an identity ascribed by *kothis* to their partners as part of the *kothi/panthi* dyad (Boyce, 2007, 2012). *Panthis* and *parikhs* seldom identify as homosexual/queer. *Kothis*, on the other hand, because of their gender atypical performance are seen as demasculinised subjects. The figure of the *kothi* is much maligned, both because of their non-normative gender roles and their class/social background, with many *kothis* coming from an economically disadvantaged background. I would argue that homonormativity and global queering and a privileging of masculinity within Indian society, in general, add to this growing anti-effeminate behaviour within gay men, who in trying to assimilate to the societal expectations, discard and defeminise themselves, and in the process also display effeminophobic attitudes.

## 'Straight-acting': politics and performance[1]

The history of global queer politics is steeped with figures such as the radical faeries (in London, 1978–1979) and drag queens (in Stonewall, 1969), whose transgressive bodies have been at the forefront of the queer political movement. As already discussed in Chapter 1, India's queer history abounds with the figure of the 'third sex'. One of the most visible forms of queer India is the figure of the *hijra*. It is thus somewhat ironic that the trans*/effeminate/queer body is now being sidelined and dominated by normative, middle class, 'straight-acting' gay men.

Kimmel (1994) has argued that masculinity is not static or timeless; rather it is a historical concept which is socially constructed and defined in opposition to others. Masculinity, as Connell (2001: 78) explains, is based on a system of oppression. This positions homosexual masculinities at the very bottom of the gendered order, where gay men are 'symbolically expelled from hegemonic masculinity'. Connell demonstrates that there is not one model of masculinity but rather multiple masculinities. One also needs to be aware that when one speaks of masculinities, these are influenced by other variables such as race, caste, class and, of course, sexuality. From the point of view of hegemonic masculinity, effeminate subject positions are assimilated within femininity. Halberstam (2008) notes that the effeminate man is seen as traitorous to the politics of virility as one who has betrayed the patriarchal fraternity existing within heteronormative men. The conspicuous presence of the effeminate man within and outside queer communities also make them one of the most subordinated and stigmatised groups. The effeminate man is not only going against the hegemonic dominant position of masculinity, but is also exposing himself to powerlessness through his sexual choices. Edelman (1994: 98) explains the relationship between sexual passivity and gender: '. . . getting fucked . . . connotes a willing sacrifice of the subjectivity, the disciplined self mastery, traditionally attributed only to those who perform the active or penetrative and hence, masculine role in the active passive binarism that organises our cultural perspective on sexual behaviour'. Here, Edelman explains that through the act of being penetrated, the receptive partner is effeminised, evoking pleasures associated through the violation of phallic masculinity.

I agree with Connell (2001: 79), when she argues that normative definitions of masculinity are problematic because not all men meet this 'normative standard'. While the queer male position is subject to a gender-variant discourse within the mainstream, what can also be noticed today is the way in which gay men are increasingly constructing themselves as 'hypermasculine', whereby they are assimilating themselves within the normative masculine paradigm, and consequently a new hierarchical model is being created with 'straight-acting' macho men at the top of the pecking order. Kimmel (1994: 133) explains that young men are constantly negotiating gender boundaries, where 'the stakes of sissydom are enormous – sometimes [a] matter of life and death'. Richardson (2003: 233) concurs that within queer male culture, 'sexual passivity equals femininity which, regulated by effeminophobia, equals inferiority'. Richardson (2009: 529) further argues that 'effeminophobia is a wide reaching problem in contemporary British culture and often that which is labelled as homophobia should more correctly be termed effeminophobia. The effeminate man is either, depending upon his context, a figure of fun or a monster to be feared'. While I disagree with the conflation of homophobia and effeminophobia, especially within the Indian context where homosexuality has a strong nationalist, legal and religious specificity to it (see Chapters 1 and 4 and also Chapter 6), I agree that a masculine subject position within gay male culture is valourised over other more gender-variant positions. As recent studies point out, there is a growing distancing of MSM and gay-identified groups from public effeminacy and gender variance (Dutta, 2012). This anxiety grows out of the assimilationist politics of the contemporary queer movement in India. It would also be worthwhile to point out that while NGOs in India are constantly trying to standardise the usage of terms such as MSM and TG (trans*) within the development narrative, 'gay' as a category circulates freely within Internet chat rooms and mainstream media. Dutta (2013a), for example, in their ethnographic work in eastern India, found that while MSM as a non-gay-identified term exists within the development sector, 'gay' is used as a common signifier within English language media in India to indicate a range of gender/sexual variant persons. There is also a sense of sensationality (with pejorative connotations), where gay is not always distinguished from transgender within this lexicon. As Dutta (2013a: 281–282) further points out, 'articles on civic activism such as pride marches commonly use phrases like "gay rally", "gay pride" or "gay community" accompanied by pictures of gender-variant persons in feminine attire, including *kothi* – identified people in case of the annual Kolkata Pride Walk' (Figure 5.1).[2] However, Dutta also explains that emergent gay communities in India have disavowed this stereotype and affirmed an overt masculinity as the norm. My research supports this position.

Within online queer spaces, it is not uncommon to see queer men valourising masculinity by either self-identifying as 'straight-acting' or directing their desires towards other 'straight-acting' men only. While there is a misogynist tendency towards the ways in which effeminate subject positions are denigrated, this should not simply be understood as a copy of heterosexuality and masculine privilege; rather it is more productive to complicate the category of 'straight-acting' and see it beyond just a simple copy of patriarchy.

*Figure 5.1* Kolkata Pride Parade, 2015. Photographer unknown. Author's collection.

A series of vlogs (video blogs) on *YouTube* by Western gay vloggers, such as Davey Wavey,[3] have been instrumental in performing this kind of masculinity. I have chosen to discuss Davey Wavey here because he is a popular figure within the urban queer male circles in India; many of my research participants mentioned his vlogs when I interviewed them. In most of his videos, he is seen bare chested as he attempts to discuss 'gay issues' with his followers. Wavey is one of many gay vloggers who have become well-known figures after their vlogs gained a popular following within the queer male community. Wavey has three *YouTube* channels, and they have been collectively viewed over 150 million times by his followers worldwide. I want to briefly outline some of his vlogs, in order to discuss the ways in which he performs gay masculinity.

In his video 'Gay things straight boys do',[4] Wavey appears in front of the audience in a pink vest with the word Kween printed on it, which reminds the audience that it is a gay marker, referring to Queen, a gay slang which refers to a flamboyant gay man. Wavey goes on to talk about wrestling, and in the next scene we see him bare-chested wrestling with another similarly muscular man, before Wavey exclaims he is 'getting hard', again correlating this physical contact with another man with his gay desires. Similarly, in another video 'Can you make a straight guy gay?', we see Wavey standing shirtless with a male model. Wavey asserts that the male model is heterosexual, and then he attempts to 'turn' him gay by first making him take his vest off, followed by throwing glitter at him and finally ending with a kiss. Having sex with a straight man (and, by extension, a masculine man) is one of the most popular genres within gay pornography, and Wavey extends this fantasy through his vlog. Wavey is performing a stud role when we are introduced to him (the muscular bare body, addressing the audience directly and talking about his love of 'ass' in many of his videos). In most of his videos, he talks about straight men either as desirable objects or using them as a point of reference when talking about his own gayness or about other forms of gay performance. His online performance appears to intensify the erotic experience for both himself (his occasional guests) and the viewers, who are his regular followers. While Wavey would not necessarily come across to others as conventionally hypermasculine (his voice is quite shrill) and he constantly uses a range of gay signifiers (often sporting vests with Kween or #YesHomo), he uses his videos and his body to privilege a certain type of gay masculinity. Moreover, he very rarely discusses non-normative gay identities or bodies. Wavey is not trying to simply come across as a straight man. His masculinity is modelled as something different – a gay masculinity. I will argue that while Wavey's gay masculinity might still be seen as subordinate and 'different' from heteronormative masculinity, this can still be read as a privileged position on the gender privilege ladder where effeminate subject positions are relegated to the bottom.

In contrast, other gay Western vloggers such as J.W. Harvey and J. Merridew are seen more frequently in sleeveless shirts. Harvey, in fact, in one video explains that he had been told he would gain more followers if he took off his shirt, something he followed through in the video that had over 4,000 views.[5] While he does not mention Wavey, it is clear that his action is in response to Wavey. Merridew, on the other hand, is the youngest of the three vloggers and has used his vlogs to critique the gay community for its effeminophobia.[6] While *YouTube* gay vlogs are an important source, within which one can trace the valorisation of gay masculinity and the derision of effeminacy, digital social networking sites such as *PlanetRomeo* and mobile phone applications such as *Grindr* are two of the most visible sites, within which networks of effeminophobia can be found. In the following sections, I consider a range of profiles on *PlanetRomeo* and *Grindr*, alongside discussions around effeminophobia (and tangentially transphobia) that have emanated from discussion groups and interviews with the researcher.

## Acting straight

'Straight-acting' as a term refers to a set of attributes that are commonly associated with heterosexual men, which include 'manly', 'masculine' and 'butch' in opposition to other gay attributes such as 'queen', 'femme' and 'camp' (Payne, 2007: 526). According to Payne, 'straight-acting' is different from being masculine; it implies a level of performance (This is me acting straight!), and more pragmatically it might refer to a need to be discreet – to be able to easily pass as a heterosexual male. In addition, according to Payne, it also has an erotic connotation: 'naming the self or the other a 'straight-acting' subject or object of desire' (Payne, 2007: 526). 'Straight-acting' as a term also embodies the tension between gay men and other sexually dissident men (who do not identify as gay, e.g. *kothi* men in India). Despite the accusations levelled against 'straight-acting' in terms of being a manifestation of internalised homophobia, I would like to read 'straight-acting' as a reaction against and product of global queering and homonormativity.

On his *PlanetRomeo* profile, str8_ladind[7] describes himself as 'a laid back boy, into cricket, football and the *occasional* cheesy tearjerker'. Similarly, HotTop describes himself as 'masculine and a real man, not into uncles, sissies and pansies', while luvr4you makes it clear that he is 'into other str8 acting only, no gayboys or sisters'. These profiles make clear that 'straight-acting' appears to be a highly valued attribute, which is in many ways linked to heterosexual codes of masculinity such as, for instance, watching sports. 'Aberrant' activities such as watching an emotional film (tear-jerker) are categorically explained away as something that is occasional, in case anyone should question str8_ladind's manliness. Thus, even if str8_ladind does enjoy the occasional cheesy tear-jerker, an interest not necessarily associated with gay masculinity, he is also able to enjoy cricket and football. This double interest thus opens up the possibility for some 'slippages', beyond the expectations of normative gay masculinity. However, the fact that he mentions that he likes to watch cricket and football stresses his masculine interests and behaviours. The other two profiles, on the other hand, very clearly point out that they are only looking for masculine men and not 'gayboys' or 'sissies'. 'Gayboys' here is being used to differentiate gayness (one that is characterised by heterosexual gender conformity and homosexual desire) from one that is 'feminine' and camp. 'Gayboys' as a term is seldom used outside *PlanetRomeo* or *Grindr*. In fact, as I was made to understand from my analyses of the profiles, 'gayboy' works almost as a synonym for a 'sissy'. It is used to denote effeminacy and gender non-conformity in gay/queer men. Terms such as 'gayboy' here describe a feminine same-sex sexual subjectivity. Similar terms are also found in other languages such as *meyeli chele* or *meyechele* in Kolkata and Barasat. These terms, which literally mean 'girlish boys', are common terms in everyday discourse (Boyce, 2012). In addition, as I have discussed elsewhere (Datta, Bakshi and Dasgupta, 2015), terms such as *rituparno* (named after a well-known effeminate queer film-maker from Bengal) have become common in the last three years as a stand-in for queer/gay men who are effeminate/gender non-normative. The profiles, I discuss here, reinforce Connell's concept of hegemonic masculinity. As Payne (2007: 526) argues, 'The difference here between simple adjective ("masculine") and the grammatically complicated "straight-acting" signifies a shift in ontological certainty: a difference between self as being and as becoming.' Straight-acting thus becomes a way of being masculine, a substitute for what one wants to become.

Mowlabocus (2010a: 78, emphasis mine) explains that 'the identification of homosexuality continues to be a preoccupation for both the mainstream and the margin, and secondly *that being seen to be gay* continues to be problematic for many gay people'. In other words, for many queer men, the dissociation from effeminate subjectivities and conforming to an existing heteronormative masculine identity is one of the ways in which 'straight-acting' starts to become a reconceived identity. Homosexuality, as Richardson (2009) points out, is still identified in terms of gender transitivity. This presumption stems from the gender binary assumption (masculine/feminine). Scholars such as Butler (2004a: 216) have argued against this gender binary, explaining that the 'binary system of gender is disputed and challenged, where the coherence of the categories are put into question, and where the very social life of gender turns out to be malleable and transformable'. This is expressed in the various changing patterns of queer identities and roles. In same-sex sexual desire, it is (wrongly) widely understood that one must enact the masculine role and the other the feminine. Therefore, for a man to be attracted to another man, he must be feminine. This cultural stereotyping has become ingrained in popular media, thus making an effeminate man almost always read as queer/homosexual. Queer politics in India has a strong trans* presence, thus stereotyping the connection between homosexuality and gender variance.[8] On the other hand, trans* and gender-variant presences on online platforms are ignored and masculinity is given the pride of place. It is not uncommon to have someone like rahulversatile on *PlanetRomeo*, who writes:

> My expectations : Need sincere and decent guys . . not necessarily to be a high fi socialite . . . but one who can respect the secrecy and privacy of others would be encouraged as he can expect the same on from me . .!!
>    A good manly guys to tame my girliness (wat eva wud i call tat. But am damn sure. Am 100 % 'straight-acting' . . .!!).

Rahulversatile's profile text is interesting. While he identifies himself as 'straight-acting', he is also alluding to his gayness – he wants someone (presumably a masculine man) to tame his 'girliness'. In his profile, he demonstrates duality. He appears to not only need to assert his masculinity, but also demonstrates a desire for masculinity in potential partners. Gay and queer identification and recognition are a complicated terrain. Digital spaces such as *Gaydar, PlanetRomeo* and *Grindr* mechanise this (Payne, 2007). By mechanising, I mean choosing a set of pre-existing templates within which the profile is expected to sit comfortably. For instance, on *Grindr*, you can join different tribes (groups such as Daddy, Twink or discreet) and on *PlanetRomeo* you can choose to describe your gender attributes. Interestingly, while these labels do not occur 'naturally' within the gay community, and even less so within the Indian queer community, they become appropriated amongst gay and queer men in Kolkata and New Delhi, as gleaned through my interviews and informal conversations. I met Rishabh twice during the period of carrying out my research in Kolkata. He introduced himself as an English language teacher. One evening, I spent some time with him at a party in Kolkata where I described my research to him. He was very interested to know how I described myself (Are you genderqueer, trans\* or twink?). I explained to him that I did not really understand these labels and thought of my gender and sexuality as being fluid. Rishabh explained that he identified himself as 'a daddy', further adding, 'I think I am quite hairy, so I think people would call me a bear'. It was interesting to see how he had appropriated these labels within an Indian context. Rishabh was not the only person I encountered in my field trip who had appropriated such labels. There are various complicated ways in which users of these spaces identify, perform and become visible. The strategic queering of Rahulversatile's gender conformity is interesting because while in one sentence he identifies his desire for a masculine partner to tame his feminine side, in the next sentence he also alludes to being masculine and 'straight-acting. According to Payne (2007: 528), the 'straight-acting' label is both a construction of stereotyping and normativity. Many users such as rahulversatile or HotTop (mentioned earlier in this chapter) use the textual component of choosing their username to also make their sexual and gender attributes known to other users. In the context within which I am discussing these profiles, I would agree with Mowlabocus (2010a: 90) that 'the profile is created by the user in order to attract activity', that is, to commodify the user's attributes and make it desirable to other users. Rishabh's own PR profile was called Indian_daddy_bear 68.

The utopic argument (Rheingold, 1993; Swiss and Hermann, 2000) of the Internet dismantling the raced, sexed and gendered body falls apart when one considers online profiles such as those that I have mentioned above. The bodily performance of masculinity is carried forward with great posterity by users and ever present within the production of online queer spaces. Sites such as *Douchebags of Grindr* have been instrumental in making visible the production of these stereotyping categories within the juggernaut of online profiles on *Grindr*.[9] A simple tag search with femmephobia on the website displays a very large number of profiles users have submitted which include an effeminophobic element.

Sanchez and Vilain (2012), in their study of over 750 men in the United States which was carried out to assess the importance of masculinity amongst gay men, made three main findings: first, they found that masculine looks and behaviour were very important to gay men; second, most of the gay men who participated in this study expressed a desire to be more masculine and less feminine than their perceptions of themselves;[10] finally, Sachez and Vilain found that gay men relied on the behaviour of others rather than appearances to assess masculinity. I will now progress to assess to what extent these findings translate to the digital space, and the ways in which behaviour can be measured through online profiles. One of my interviewees, Raj explained:

> I am not sure what you mean by femmephobia? If you are asking me whether I will go out with a girly guy, the answer is no. I can look at a profile on PR [*PlanetRomeo*] and say if he is manly or not. I also always ask for a phone number so that I can chat to the person and gauge for myself if he is masculine or not. You can *look* masculine through photoshopping your display pic but you can't hide your voice. To *act* *masculine*, you have to actually *be masculine* (emphasis mine).
>
> (14 December 2012)

Eguchi (2009: 194) argues that the 'the rhetoric of "straight-acting" may play a dual role in both producing and reproducing homophobic and anti-feminine communication among gay men'. Raj's comments regarding looking, acting and being masculine also need further consideration. The selection of information, user name and display picture made by the user aids in the digital representation of his subjectivity which in turn aids people like Raj to make 'informed decisions' about the masculinity of the user. Kimmel (2003: 70) has argued that 'where masculinity is undermined by racism, heterosexism or classism [it] seeks the vigorous reassertion of traditionally patriarchal ideals of masculinity [as] a compensation, a restoration'. This is most clear in the hypermasculine posturing in certain 'straight-acting' gay men. As Mowlabocus (2010a: 92) asserts, at the heart of every profile is the question 'How do I want to be seen'. This is crucial in understanding both the user whose masculinity Raj wants to probe and users like HotTop, rahulversatile and Raj himself.

I agree with Mowlabocus (2010a) and Payne (2007) that creating an online profile can be understood as a form of performing and embodying a role from an existing sociocultural milieu informed by the user's own subjectivity. But I would like to extend this further, in order to consider the ways in which the user's profile in itself then comes to embody the user's offline existence and the ways in which the profile influences his physical embodiment offline.

Nitin (22) from New Delhi met me in the summer of 2013 at a mutual friend's flat where I was staying. One of the first things he told me was, 'You dont look like what I expected'. This statement was very surprising and I tried to remember if I had recruited him through *PlanetRomeo* (where he might have seen my 'gay' pictures) or through *Facebook* where he would have seen more personal and professional pictures. To unpack this a little, profile pictures are a very important part of the online profile. They tell people who you are and what you want to convey (am I fun, sexy or serious). Most gay websites would have pictures that attract desirability (through shots of the torso, strategically photographed body parts and a face). In either case, my photographs must have created a sense of 'me' for him, which my physical embodiment somewhat did not live up to. When I laughingly asked him what he meant, he explained that he knew that I was an academic living in the United Kingdom and so he was expecting someone 'slightly less flamboyant'. He had, in fact, looked up my profile on *PlanetRomeo* and found my name Astraeus17 very revealing. When pressed further, he explained that he was a student of literature and he knew that Astraeus was a Greek god; therefore, my choice in using this as my profile name indicated my love for 'high art and literature', which, to his way of thinking, my long hair, jeans and earrings failed to convey. This was an interesting moment for me as a researcher. Putting together my *PlanetRomeo* profile took a lot of thinking. I had carefully chosen my profile picture. I had wanted to come across as someone who was a young researcher. I did not want to give out too much information about myself, but did include my occupation, my relationship status and what I was looking for (research participants). Nitin's comment reminded me how I viewed the cyberspace – a space that is speculative, where 'I wonder' marks the ephemera of wandering through this space.

One major aspect of sites such as *PlanetRomeo* and *Gaydar* is their ability to normalise and homogenise identities by constructing profiles from an available template (Mowlabocus, 2010a; Payne, 2007). This includes categorisations such as body hair, body shape and sexual role to tastes in music and interests. *PlanetRomeo* allows a significant range of options within which the user can craft his profile, and make data easily searchable as commodities for the other (gay/queer) consumers in mind.[11] It, however, also allows certain forms of reading to take place by other users (such as Nitin's perception of me). In this case, I was being expected to fulfil the ideals that

I had invested in the profile by declaring my academic and 'love for classical music' credentials. In this case, according to Nitin, my offline existence was not reflective enough of the online existence I had created for my user account. As Nitin explained further, this disappointment was not new. He had encountered it numerous times. He explains:

> You see, I deduced you would be . . . I don't know quite serious because of the way your profile is written . . . I mean come on . . . you used the word solipsist to describe yourself. I think at times it becomes really important that we act like what we say on our profile. I remember I once met this boy with whom I had been chatting to for a while. I had told him I was 'straight-acting'. I mean I am not a flaming queen as you can see (hand gesture) but then I am not like some beer drinking engineering student; however I remember when I went to meet him the first thing he told me was he was expecting something else . . . I mean . . . For the rest of the evening I tried to overdo my manliness, and asking him questions about cricket. I did not want to come across as some faker.
>
> (5 July 2013)

This recognition, as Nitin's and my own example show, is that bodily performance in the offline space embodies the discursive details of the online personality. Nitin was aware that neither of us wanted to come across as a 'false advertiser'. In my case, I was unaware of the ways in which the discursive elements of my profile were creating a false ideal (or at least one I could not and did not want to live up to), whereas for Nitin it meant making an additional effort to embody and affirm his 'straight-acting' characteristic.

## Global gazing and homonormativity

Altman (1997: 419) has argued that a system of global queering is taking place across the world, where gay men are claiming a form of universality with their queer counterparts in the West. Through a process of globalisation, homogeneous Western identities such as gay have gained currency, perpetuating normative masculine 'gay identities' over other forms of queer identification. While Altman's thesis has some merits, it does not recognise the multiplicity of localised/regionalised identificatory categories that exist within Asian contexts (e.g. *metis* in Nepal or *kothis* and *hijras* in India). In this context, I would like to think of a transnational framework, as Pullen (2012) has outlined, where queer identities are explored as multiple and different but connected through a common sense of identity. Pullen explains (2012: 7), 'LGBT transnational identity is a theoretical idea . . . [which] offers a multifaceted scope, which is as much about individuals and personal agency, as collective groups and sustained coalescent action.'

While the notion of a global gay identity is not without its merits (Binnie, 2004), there have been examples of transnational queer movements, where queer activists from Europe supported the campaign against Section 28 in the United Kingdom, and, more recently, Indian activists signed a petition against the anti-gay law passed by President Musaveni in Uganda, among others. However, it is important to consider the Eurocentrism displayed by such movements that frequently tends to lead global actions which might be unsustainable in the home country or even obfuscate some of the ground realities. This was a point of criticism when several Western countries decided to introduce 'aid conditionality' attached to queer rights.[12] Several queer organisations in Africa rejected this measure arguing that it would lead to further discrimination and violent actions against the queer community.[13] However, as Binnie (2004) has noted, it is important to question the notion of the global gay identity in terms of who is included and who becomes othered, and more sinisterly, the ways in which Anglo-American queer sexual norms and identities are imposed.

As Rishik (20), a *kothi*-identified *launda* dancer from Kolkata, argued:

> We have been marginalised by the gays. Earlier when we marched during the Kolkata Pride Marches, you only saw us walking. No one else wanted to be seen with us. It was just us and the organisations. But now look what has happened. You see more gay men on tv, in the streets and then 377, but how has it helped any of us, we are still in the same place. I am still stared at and still can't go inside a restaurant dressed up. People are celebrating 377, but I dont understand.[14]
>
> (19 July 2013)

Rishik's narrative is significant in two ways. First, he clearly makes a distinction between his queerness and the queerness embodied by gay-identified men, and second, he is also aware of his non-normatively gendered and classed body which even after the decriminalisation of Section 377 in 2009 remains controlled and barred from several spaces. In this regard, I would like to echo Binnie's (2004: 39) concern of whether the developments of movement for gay liberation in many developing countries, such as India, is a form of false consciousness and class distinction, whereby the upper classes aspire to Anglo-American identities.

As I mentioned earlier, one of the most visible sites for global queering are social networking and dating sites such as *Gaydar*, *PlanetRomeo* and *Grindr*, which despite purporting to be social spaces for the gay, bisexual and trans\* communities rarely advertise their trans\*credentials. Take, for example, *PlanetRomeo*, which states clearly 'We're different, just like you. We like men', and then goes on to assert 'Right from the start *PlanetRomeo* has been a platform for the gay and bisexual male and transgender community.' They have never had a trans\* person or a non-masculine man on their home page which randomly changes every time a person visits their welcome page. I have reproduced (Figure 5.2) the five display images that have appeared on my visits to the website, which revert back to the first.[15]

The common factor between all five images is the masculine gay man, suggesting the ideal gay masculinity represented by the website. All the shots are cropped and change randomly with each new visit to the website. The images also embed the different 'types' of gay men that the website offers – from leather fetish, bears, otters to twinks.[16] The website has also tried to balance the representation in terms of race, having three white men and two black men (interesting that at no point have they ever had a South Asian man on the cover, despite *PlanetRomeo* being the single most popular gay social networking/dating site in the Indian subcontinent).

It is likely that the user is expected to identify with one of the models or that the models will be seen as objects of desire by the user. I am in agreement with Mowlabocus (2010a) and Payne (2007) that these images in a way serve to illustrate the consumerised nature of queer male sexuality, one where the potential of queer eroticism is directed at the normative masculine-identified queer male. As these images, as well as the images one can find on other

*Figure 5.2* Randomly generated display images on *PlanetRomeo* Homepage. Accessed on 15 December 2013. Screen grab and then assembled. Available on www.PlanetRomeo.com.

websites such as *Gaydar* and *Grindr*, demonstrate, the male body on display becomes a hypermasculine representation which projects and positions the 'global' gay male as masculine, muscular and normative. Visual representations of oneself on *PlanetRomeo* commodify the sexuality of the user embedded within specific meanings of attractiveness (masculine well-defined body) and affluence (speaking in English, visual signifiers of class). Light, Fletcher and Adam (2008: 306), writing about *Gaydar*, note that it 'draws out a type of gay masculinity that provokes direct and personal comparison . . . who fulfil this acceptable model of commodified identity'. *PlanetRomeo* functions in a similar way, creating a model of acceptable gayness and desirability.

## Desiring masculinity

> Its PlanetRomeo .what do you expect. people are on there to look for sex, not to be intellectually stimulating. and if they dont wanna have sex with someone feminine then they have the right to mention that on thier (sic) profile. 'girlish guys fuck off'' is kind of harsh, but even my profile on pr says very clearly. -unfit, uneducated and feminine guys please dont bother.and i dont think there is anything wrong with that?
>
> (Jash Khanna, 2 February 2012)

The above quote is from a thread that was started on PPK. I have already introduced this group and Jash in my previous chapter. Jash's comments are indicative of the unproblematic nature through which effeminophobia is prevalent on spaces such as *PlanetRomeo* and other gay/queer sites. Jash does not find the fact that he has asked 'unfit, uneducated and feminine guys' to stay away problematic. Rather, as another user defending Jash's position explains, 'This is about sexual chemistry.' Comments such as those made by Jash, and the numerous other profile texts mentioned earlier, evidence the hierarchisation of desire, where overt displays of gayness that are 'too transgressive' and lack 'heteronormative' masculinity are derided.

McGlotten (2013) argues that profile creation on digital spaces is a process laden with affective demands and effects. It also requires an amount of brevity to use few words to describe oneself and one's desires. Take, for example, Smartchap15's profile (Figure 5.3). He has a picture of himself in his underwear displaying his masculine (hairy) body. His profile text reads:

> A perfect blend of good looks, personality and humour is what I would call myself, Basically from delhi , shifted here recently, looking for some mature and manly guy like me. Fems, pansies, pure botts and trans, never ever visit this profile. Man looking for a Man :-)))

| SmartChap15<br>29, 184 cm, 78 kg<br>Pune India, Maharashtra |
| --- |
| Manly, Perfectly straightlooking and hairy guy looking for someone similar. Pls be manly. With place near Chandni Chowk |
| Language: English<br>Body and Ethnicity: Athletic and Asian<br>Hair: Short<br>Body hair: Very Hairy<br>Eyes: Other<br>Sex: Bisexual<br>Relationship: I am single<br>Looking for: sexdate, friends, relationship (Users between 28 and 45)<br>Dicksize: XL, Uncut<br>Position: Versatile<br>Safe Sex: Always |
| A perfect blend of good looks, personality and humour is what I would call myself, Basically from delhi , shifted here recently, looking for some mature and manly guy like me. Fems, pansies, pure botts and trans, never ever visit this profile. Man looking for a Man :-))) |

*Figure 5.3* Smartchap15's profile on *PlanetRomeo.* Accessed on 13 December 2013. Screen grab with identifying details removed. Available on www.PlanetRomeo.com.

Smartchap15's profile is relatively brief in relation to many other profiles on *PlanetRomeo*, where users choose to complete many more interest boxes. It is clear from SmartChap15's profile that he is probably not out (the headless torso), he is looking primarily for sex (place near Chandni Chowk) and he is quite confident about his 'manly, perfectly straightlooking and hairy' appearance. He displays a similar sense of misogyny to that displayed by Jash, indicating that he does not want 'fems, pansies and trans' men to visit his profile. He is, after all, a 'man looking for a man'. Structured through global queering and homonormativity, this also signals the undesirability of non-normative gender subjectivities within *PlanetRomeo*.

Interestingly, websites such as *Douchebags of Grindr* (DoG) have evolved in the last few years to combat the insensitivity, misogyny and politically incorrect profile texts that exist within the anonymous world of *Grindr*. DoG makes these insensitive comments public, tagged with words such as 'ageism', 'racism' and 'femmephobia', among others. While no such name and shame tactics have been used within PPK, the thread itself is revealing of the majoritarian effeminophobic views of the group members.

The *kothi* community has been a central part of this growing discourse on femmephobia. Rishik explained to me that not only did he enjoy being a part of the '*kothi* sisterhood', but much more importantly, one of the reasons for making the decision to enter the *launda* dance profession was to find a *parikh* (husband in this context). When asked if he found other *kothi* men attractive, he looked at me quite shocked and asked, 'What can two sisters do, knead bread together?' This exclamation itself is quite common and well known within *kothi* circles. It is used to make a point that the partner can never be another 'effeminate' *kothi*, he has to be a masculine *parikh*. According to Rishik, it was taboo to have feminine-feminine coupling amongst queer men (also see Dutta, 2013b; Dutta and Roy, 2014). Here, too, Rishik was valourising masculinity as an object of desire. Raj also presented a similar view about gay-identified men. He presents himself as a gender conforming masculine gay man, although he does not use the tag 'straight-acting' on his online persona. He did not like effeminate men and his own *PlanetRomeo* profile reflected this ('with no disrespect, but I dont like effeminate men'). He explained that he lived in a conservative locality in Kolkata and was not 'exactly out' about his sexuality, and thus he found it much more difficult if he brought back a 'loud gay queen' to his flat. Not only would it be likely to arouse suspicion, but it might also lose him his tenancy. Raj's argument is well placed, as this is an argument that other interviewees also made. However, what Raj did not mention was the lower class/working class origins of the *kothi* identity. The policing of class and gender conformity, both within the precincts of the cyberspace (only 'English speakers please' – which I have discussed in Chapter 5) and the physical space, shows how marked and policed the queer community in India is. Bersani (1988) is most critical of the ways in which gay sex operates through a hierarchised structure. Invoking the example of gay bathhouses in the United States, he critiques Altman's notion of gay sex being a form 'of Whitmanesque democracy'. Instead, he explains that bathhouses provide a glimpse into the ruthless ways in which male beauty is objectified, hierarchised and rejected:

> On the whole, gay men are no less socially ambitious, and, more often than we like to think, no less reactionary and racist than heterosexuals. To want sex with another man is not exactly a political radicalism.

(205)

Anyone who has ever spent one night in a gay bathhouse knows that it is (or was) one of the most ruthlessly ranked, hierarchized and competitive environments imaginable. Your looks, muscle, hair distribution, size of cock and shape of ass determined exactly how happy you were going to be during those few hours, and rejection, generally accompanied by two or three words at most, could be swift and brutal.

(206)

*PlanetRomeo* and other queer male dating sites are similar to the bathhouse that Bersani describes. There is an array of profiles that the user can search, and a detailed search can be used to enable specificity. For example, the user can even decide whether he wants to connect with someone with brown or black eyes. From a consumerist perspective, every profile on *PlanetRomeo* is vying for the same attention from other users. Users such as HotTop, Smartchap15 and str8_ladind are a part of this 'ruthlessly ranked space', where their masculine attributes are being advertised and the expected outcome is hoped to lead to sex, a date or, in some cases, a relationship. Within this space, rejection is probably even more brutal. Unlike the bathhouse, where Bersani suggests that rejection comes accompanied by a few words, on *PlanetRomeo* and *Grindr*, there are no words. One is just left to ponder whether the other person was too busy to reply or whether the message had slipped off their radar, and many unsuccessfully try to message again. However, the fact that one *Grindr* user (Figure 5.4) clearly indicated 'If I don't respond its not because I haven't got your message, its because I'm not interested' shows just how much more ruthless the new cyber-bathhouses are.

Within this context, hierarchy is based largely on a gay (hegemonic) masculinity. Not only is it something to be desired, but also something to aspire to (nice body, as the profile clearly explains). Bersani explains further that gay masculinity is not subversive, it is neither critiquing nor transforming hegemonic (heterosexual) masculinity; rather it is making it a part of the assimilative strategy for the queer male community.

Labels such as 'top', 'bottom', 'versatile', 'more top' and 'more bottom' circulate freely on PlanetRomeo. These sexual roles/sexual identities are examples of subjectivation (Payne, 2007: 536), where in an attempt to replicate the heterosexual male/female and active/passive role, the site is complicit in creating the authorial top/masculine/'straight-acting' man as the desired role to aspire to, or the object of desire. The masculine queer man is then purposely introduced as the authority to whom the effeminate queer man has to render himself and accept the authority of the heteronormative figure.

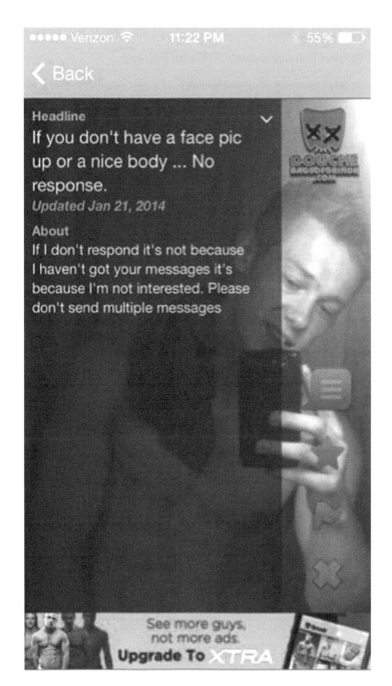

*Figure 5.4* Example of a profile named and shamed on *Douchebags of Grindr*. Accessed on 13 December 2013. Screengrab. Available on www. douchebagsofGrindr.com.

## Being 'too transgressive': effeminophobia

The concept of being 'too transgressive' is a growing issue within queer representations in India. During the course of my fieldwork, I was able to participate in two Pride marches that took place in Kolkata in 2012 and 2013. There was a fairly large number of trans* and femme men who had dressed up in female attire on the marches. Unsurprisingly, the reporters who came to cover the marches wanted to take pictures of these marchers. The reporters were not interested in the rest of the community, who, as one of the reporters told me (urging me to put on the feather mask), was dressed 'normally'. In the informal party that followed (which was held at a mutual friend's house) after the march in 2012, I met some of the marchers and became involved in a conversation with one of them named Neel (15 July 2012). He was from Barasat, a suburban city on the outskirts of Kolkata. This was his first Pride march and he was exceptionally happy to be a part of it. I asked him if he had dressed up for the march. He nodded, saying that he had met at a friend's house before the march and dressed in her clothes. He explained that he did not have much opportunity to express his gender subjectivity because he still lived at home, and his father had beaten him on several occasions when he caught him using his mother's cosmetics.

I later spoke to another queer/trans* activist about the shelter home he was opening for trans* and *kothi* men, and he agreed that for many *kothi* men there was an urgent need for a space where they could change. According to this activist, many *kothi* men would change in taxis which was both 'demeaning and risky' for them. For several of these men, effeminophobia was a daily occurrence – something they had to live with, which has seen little attitudinal transformation even after the landmark decision of 2009 which read down Section 377. In fact, there had been a whole debate previously within the Kolkata queer community where many participants found that the gendered assertion of people like Neel and Rishik who dressed up was both indecent and lowered the objective of the movement. Things came to a head when I last visited India in 2013 when the Pride march in Kolkata split in to two marches with one march being primarily for trans*/*kothi* and *hijras*. When I asked Nitin, one of my research participants, what he thought about *kothi* men and their presence within the queer space, he was slightly ambivalent and then replied:

> I personally don't have anything against them but to be honest, I think they are a little *too transgressive* (emphasis mine) for society. I mean people are just coming to terms with gayness and gay people and then you suddenly see these men dressed up in women's clothes. It is

slightly distressing for many who have just come to terms with the very idea of homosexuality.

(5 July 2013)

What is this 'too transgressive' that Nitin points to and how does one even start to understand this? Zizek (1998) explains that the emergence of a certain value that serves as a point of ideological identification relies on its transgression to make sense of it. By that logic, effeminate *kothi* men are systematically othered for the (masculine) gay identity to emerge. Effeminate men, both on cyberspace and in physical space, threaten to unmask the normativity that many gay men build around themselves. The transgressive body and identity disrupts the normative environment, within which gay privilege thrives in contemporary times. The neocolonial discourse of identity, which is built around an assimiliationist tendency, represses any form of transgression against this discourse of commonality. What I would like to suggest is that 'too transgressive' works within the concept of homonormativity, aligning itself with the same political criticality, however 'too transgressive', also seeks to unsettle that which is 'acceptable' and 'respectable'. In a way, 'too transgressive' stands against the homogeneity of global queering, critiquing and even challenging it.

The popular Bollywood film *Dostana* (*Friendship*, 2008) depicts the ways in which gay men in postcolonial India are constructed through a normative global queering. The hypermasculine images of Kunal and the hairy figure of Sam in the film give further justification to the ways in which masculinity is epitomised at the very centre of the queer male figure (Dudrah, 2012). In fact, in a telling scene from the film, where the two characters are arguing how to 'play it gay', one is reminded that gay men 'feel and look like a man but think like a woman'. My reason for invoking *Dostana* is because of its strong presence within the queer imagination in India and the way in which the figures have been appropriated within the digital spaces of *PlanetRomeo* and beyond (see Figure 5.5). Such films appropriate masculinity as a gay ideal. Through disseminating the masculine body as the desired queer body, the film takes part in the global queering process. As one of my interview participants, Neel directly referencing this film explained to me:

> There is a very deep-rooted transphobia within the community. People just dont want to meet you if they think you are girlish. Some of this has to do with many people fetishizing hypermasculinity. They are accustomed to seeing bare bodied white men in porn films and even within Bollywood you now see hypermasculine actors like John Abraham in Dostana and Ranveer Kapoor. I think these people need to understand

*Figure 5.5 PlanetRomeo* profile using John Abraham's picture as a profile
    image. Screengrabs with identifying information removed. Accessed
    on 13 December 2013.

the difference between reality and being made accustomed to a media
created beauty. Even three years ago, you never saw these 'gay men' out
in Kolkata but now suddenly they are and are pushing us out.

(5 July 2012)

Neel's consciousness about global queering (although he does not specifically reference it) is telling about the ways in which masculinity within
the queer community in India has been appropriated. While films such as
*Dostana* are commended (Dudrah, 2012) for opening up a dialogue on
queerness in mainstream India, it has also led to what Neel calls 'a media
created beauty'. For many of the men who I talked to, both during and
after the Pride march, effeminacy threatened to disturb the normalcy and

gave the community a skewed (and negative) image. As Tarun, one of my research participants, explained to me:

> I would not go out with an effeminate man. I think it would draw too much attention to myself. I am out about my sexuality so it is not about hiding that, however I am also not defined by my sexuality, but if it is very apparent that the man beside me is gay through his feminine behaviour then by rolling down this would affect me as well.
>
> (8 July 2012)

Clearly, here, being effeminate means being identified as gay and in the process being rejected for being a little 'too transgressive' – bringing one's sexuality into the public sphere and making people conscious of it. Here, claiming gayness in the public sphere through an overt display of one's effeminacy is controlled. For Tarun and others like Raj and Nitin, sexuality was not something to be displayed in a public space because of the ways in which their lives might be affected by being 'out'. Following this, Tarun, Raj and Nitin made a point of distancing themselves from effeminate queer men who they perceived as disturbing the normativity of the physical world.

Nitin is very particular when it comes to cruising online. He has used *Grindr* and he is very particular about how he would like his profile to be read. Nitin explained to me that within the *Grindr* 'scene' in New Delhi, it is important to come across as masculine.

> There are just far too many fems out there. I don't think I am like totally manly, though I do like doing masculine stuff. I have a shirtless pic of me on *Grindr*. I think it accentuates my muscles and chest and people know I go to the gym. I am not sure how to spot fems – I think on *Grindr* they usually never have a bare bodied picture and when they do you can say they are slim but not muscular. I guess I want people to know I am manly so I have my bare pictures and my interest in sports.
>
> (5 July 2013)

Nitin's statement exemplifies the difficulties of constructing the 'masculine' gay man – one who is not excessively transgressive. His inability to reflect on what makes the effeminate man on *Grindr* different from himself reveals that defining and reflecting on what gay male masculinity actually is, is not always straightforward. A number of my research participants denigrated effeminacy for being 'too loud' and expressed concern that such representations of gay men would lead to furthering of stereotypes. I found it very interesting that many of the users I spoke with viewed the film

*Dostana* as a 'progressive' movie for portraying gay men as 'manly'. Nitin mentioned that it was a film that he would gladly see with his mother and emphasised the normalcy of gay relationships. This perspective is important as it reiterates the desired homonormativity, within which gay relationships and by extension queer gender identities are inscribed to gain legitimacy from non-gay others (the mother in Nitin's case).

One of the crucial issues that I have tried to explore in this chapter is the source of effeminophobia and the ways in which this is manifested within the rhetoric of *PlanetRomeo* users. Raj mentioned that growing up as a gay man he was constantly confronted by images of gay men as 'effeminate, girlish and slightly abnormal'. The lack of any other representation within popular culture in India was seen as a deterrent for many of my participants. Interestingly, Raj also mentioned that having access to foreign television programmes such as *Queer as Folk* (which he viewed on *YouTube*), and hearing about international gay figures such as Rock Hudson, changed his views about homosexual men and the ways in which they should behave. The lack of queer representation within Indian popular culture (which has only seen a rise in the last decade) was the main reason given by the majority of the middle class gay and queer men I spoke with for turning to the West for affirming their sense of what gayness was and could be about. In this regard, my research participants were turning towards a 'global gay identity'. Altman (1997: 151) further argues that 'for many people, sexual desire coexists with a desire for modernity', by which he means a desire to be a 'part of the affluence and freedom associated with images of the rich world'. I am in agreement with Altman in this context, as Raj, Tarun and Nitin all at various points in their interviews asserted their desire to be similar to the characters portrayed in *Queer as Folk* – masculine, homonormative, rich and white!

Annes and Redlin (2012: 281) stress that effeminophobia does not originate through popular cultural representation alone, but that it is also embedded within our social interactions and practices. Connell (1996) suggests that masculinity is constructed from a very early age within the aegis of the education establishment, where practices such as curriculum division, sports and disciplining systems create gender binaries. Annes and Redlin (2012) argue along similar lines as Connell, asserting that the figure of the effeminate boy is a source of anxiety for other boys, and effeminophobia is possibly most prevalent amongst teenagers in schools. The effeminate boy poses a threat to masculinity. Raj himself described being bullied when he was in school; but when I confronted Raj with the misogyny he was himself displaying on his *PlanetRomeo* profile, he was quick to admonish me. He argued:

> I can understand what you are saying but I disagree. I dont think there is a problem if I say I want masculine guys. Thats what I am and

thats why I am gay. I like boys who are boys not girls. I really dont understand what the hulabaloo is all about. Its like if I say girly guys stay away people think I am being transphobic. That is not true at all. What has desire got to do with race or whether someone is girly or not. There are many profiles on *PlanetRomeo* where they clearly say, I want shemales only. How come no one protests that? That is hypocritical.

(17 December 2012)

This gesture by Raj is an effort to distance himself from the various 'negative others' within the queer male community (no fats, fems etc.), the effeminate man being one of them. While spaces such as *PlanetRomeo* offer an avenue to violate norms by being vocal about one's transgressive sexual/physical desires, it also creates boundaries amongst the users, where traditional gendered performances are safeguarded and the very heterosexual matrix which one set about to dislodge becomes reinscribed. Annes and Redlin's (2012: 283) study shows that the definition of normality (men are masculine, women are feminine), given under the regime of heterosexual hegemony, matches the definition of normality, given by their gay research participants where masculine gay men keep the trappings of masculinity and social norms.

Interestingly, however, there are users who have set about to challenge the rampant effeminophobia found on cyberspace. For example, one user, backroom_boy from India, used his online profile to critique these misogynist practices and used his profile text to celebrate his non-normativity/effeminacy (P.S: I am not 'straight-acting'). He writes:

Having an irrational fear of effeminacy in guys. It's basically misplaced misogyny. I know we all have things we are attracted to but there's a big difference being attracted to a masculine guy and being disgusted by so called 'queens', so take note all you people who write, 'No queens/fems/fashion divas in your profiles. Why without queens this world would be an undecorated deeply boring and highly uninspired place.

(Backroom_boy)

Backroom_boy's profile is relevant because it critiques the 'self-stabilisation' that a term such as 'straight-acting' attempts to achieve (Payne, 2007: 535). The profile itself is not explicitly sexually charged (although the user does have a few bare bodied images). When I looked through his guestbook entries, it was clear that he was quite popular on *PlanetRomeo*. The *PlanetRomeo* forums also display a very strong effeminophobia, where threads such as 'behaviour patterns of kothis' have a range of users arguing that the *kothis* are 'bringing the name of the community down' (Rusty83).

Undeniably, socio-economic factors play an intrinsic role in identification, and especially within urban India where gay specifically signifies urban, English speaking, educated and middle class. The term *kothi*, in this case, is generally used to identify working class and lower middle class queer men who do not necessarily have access to the dominant gay culture. Therefore, when users such as Rusty 83 and charismatic11 single out *kothi* men for being effeminate and at the same time identify *kothis* as money grabbers and prostitutes, it signals the classed nature that goes hand in hand with gender non-normativity within this discourse. Shahani (2008: 248) narrates that even within the site of a sexualities conference in 2008, there was a visible divide between the *kothis* and the gay men who attended. According to Shahani, the event was polarised and there was an unspoken understanding that they belonged to two different classes with two different agendas. Effeminophobia alongside language (which I discussed in the previous chapter) is merely another way in which this hierarchy is maintained and disciplined along class lines.

## Conclusion

In this chapter, I have specifically explored the way in which a form of gay typology, that is, overtly masculine, is being propounded through queer male social networking sites such as *PlanetRomeo*, *Grindr* and *Gaydar*. I have also looked at the ways in which the effeminate male is systematically being suppressed, as the gay male identity through a process of global queering and homonormativising is gaining currency as the only normative option. This chapter has evidenced the ways in which *PlanetRomeo* itself plays a very active role (beyond just being a conduit) in influencing some of these behaviours. The resignification of the 'global gay category' as the desired and acceptable form of queer sexual identity is catalysed through new media technologies, where valourisation of the gender normative continues to be the only viable and desired queer male typology, and is one that needs to be challenged.

## Notes

1 In this chapter, I have made a contrast between queer and gay. I have referred to some of my participants as gay men, because that is the way they introduced themselves to me. Also within the course of this chapter, I explain how this terminology is in itself not entirely straightforward. I thus only use the term 'gay' when it has been imposed as a separate identity by some of the research participants.
2 For example, see Figure 5.1 from the Kolkata Queer Pride, where almost all the images used by the print and digital media were of gender variant participants.

3 Davey Wavey has three channels on *YouTube* and is by far the most popular gay vlogger. His videos have had over a million hits. One of his channels can be found here: http://www.youtube.com/user/wickydkewl. Accessed on 5 July 2015.
4 Available at: < https://www.youtube.com/watch?v=TVY8OL0xeFY&list= PL18A73F1B5B5F00C3>. Accessed on 5 July 2015.
5 J. W. Harvey. 'The Obligatory Shirtless Gay Vlogger Video'. Available at: <http://www.youtube.com/watch?v=MBRdBMg9TFk&list=LLOUN62 dG2WmTJXQkQBArsTg>. Accessed on 5 July 2015.
6 J. Merridew. 'Feminine Gay Guys Ruin the Community'. Available at: <http://www.youtube.com/watch?v=T8XegaOZiSs>. Accessed on 5 July 2015.
7 All usernames used here are pseudonyms assigned by me. At the time of writing this chapter, these usernames were not in existence.
8 Trans* in this context refers to *Hijras, Kothis* and other non-gender normative categories.
9 Available at: http://www.douchebagsofGrindr.com/tag/femmephobia/. Accessed on 5 July 2015.
10 It is also important that the research documented that these men felt it was easier to manipulate how masculine one looks than how masculine one acts.
11 In fact, the demands of the market place are such that categories like 'more top' or 'more bottom' options (clearly based on practical considerations) add another level of understanding of the consumer culture that dictates queer spaces such as *PlanetRomeo, Gaydar* or *Grindr.*
12 Western governments would cut development assistance to governments in countries that committed violations based on sexual orientation and gender identity.
13 The statement on aid conditionality and a list of 53 organisations and 86 individuals from Africa who signed this is available here: <http://www. awid.org/Library/Statement-of-African-Social-Justice-Activists-on-the-Threats-of-the-British-Government-to-Cut-Aid-to-African-Countries-that-Violate-the-Rights-of-LGBTI-People-in-Africa>. Accessed on 5 July 2015.
14 This interview was conducted as part of a research project I undertook on *Launda* dancers, who primarily identify as *Kothi*. This was conducted in December 2013 through the Sir Peter Holmes Memorial Grant from the Royal Society for Asian Affairs. A short article emerging from this research (Dasgupta, 2013) explains more about the *launda* community.
15 These visits were made between 2011 and 2013.
16 These are the different 'types' of gay men that exist on the cyberspace. These are all quite flexible and adaptive terms.

# 6  Dissident citizenship

## Introduction

I started writing this chapter at a critical time during the history of the queer movement in India. The Supreme Court ruling on Section 377 had just come in on 11 December 2013 striking off the Delhi High court's earlier ruling, which decriminalised homosexuality in 2009, thereby reinstating this Victorian law back into the culture and social fabric of the country. While the law does not criminalise the identity itself, it does criminalise the sexual act (non-procreative, non-peno-vaginal sex), thus effectively criminalising most (if not all) queer-identified individuals in the country.[1]

Discussions of sexual culture in India always have a ritualistic and somewhat abject invocation of either the Kamasutra or the Gandhian discourse on the erasure of desire, as I have discussed in Chapter 1. This anxiety and concern over sexuality stretches back to colonial times both at the level of the state, which went out of its way to regulate practices, and at the level of the postcolonial Indian society was anxious to be seen as a virile heterosexual race against the effeminate discourse of colonialism (as discussed in the earlier chapter). The Indian state's adoption of the Sodomy Law of 1860, with its homophobic/masculinist and heteronormative bias, is in many ways an endorsement of the colonial control of sexuality – the fact that it has continued to hold on to this law demonstrates that postcolonial ideology similarly seeks to control sexuality.

In this final analysis chapter, I examine collective and individual acts of resistance and simultaneous efforts by dissident citizens to articulate strategies of critiquing civil society's role in the Supreme Court decision.[2] I examine the ways in which these strategies are deployed through digital media. In this chapter, I am particularly interested in seeing the role of digital media in creating a pluralistic dialogue to an evolving Internet-based public sphere.

The citizen has existed as a key component of the nation-building exercise, which is built on the notion of commonality (Castillo and Panjabi,

2011). Citizenship has increasingly becoming a contested term with critiques based on race, disability and sexuality. These differences impact the ways in which people experience citizenship (Bachcheta, 1999: 141). Bachcheta uses the term 'xenophobic queerphobia', which implies a particular form of queerphobia that is justified by constructing the queer individual as operating outside of the nation. By this logic, she claims that Indian nationalists see queer subjects as 'non-Indian', as I mentioned earlier in Chapter 1. By placing queerness as a foreign object, Bachcheta argues, Hindu nationalism dissociates itself from the queer figures, which according to these nationalists embody the anti-nationalist, sexually promiscuous, materialistic West – a West that colonised India and which India shook off in order to become a nation in charge of its own destiny. Meanwhile, Ahmed (2004: 132) has argued that the queer figure exists within a heterosexual, patriarchal monoculture where it confronts and unsettles the normative, 'looking strange and out of place'. This confrontation between the dissenting queer citizen and the state has given rise to queer activism in India.

In order to study queer activism, it is necessary to study the relationship between the virtual and the physical. As Dave (2012: 10) notes in her introduction to *Queer Activism in India*, 'activism begins, then, precisely as the virtual in the actual world, the previously unthinkable that is now a flickering possibility, just on the verge of entering upon the world of norms'. In this chapter, I extend Dave's study of activism by drawing upon a range of ethnographic experiences of activists and civilians 'within the field' alongside the digital articulation and assimilation of these movements on cyberspace. In the following sections, I turn to some of these practices that can be characterised as representations of dissident citizenship.

At the heart of queer politics is the dissident citizen and the notion of dissident citizenship. Sparks (1997: 75) characterises this as 'the practices of marginalized citizens who publicly contest prevailing arrangements of power by means of oppositional democratic practices that augment or replace institutionalized channels of democratic opposition when those channels are inadequate or unavailable'. Building on Sparks' definition, I extend this definition to the dissident queer citizen of India as one who continually challenges the law through their very public existence, imagining and critiquing new queer political practices and confronting public perceptions of queerness. This chapter will use two case studies to look at the ways in which queer dissidence manifests on digital spaces in India, and the ways in which the digital space supports and aids ongoing queer activism in India. In order to do so, this chapter explores the changing nature of protest cultures and their transactions within the complicated circuits of communication media.

## The news has just arrived

*Snapshot 1*

On 2 July 2009, the Delhi High Court decriminalised homosexuality with its judgement on *Naz Foundation v. government of NCT of Delhi and Others*. The PIL (Public Interest Litigation) filed by Naz, in 2001, sought to read down Section 377 (which I have discussed in Chapter 1), so that adult consensual same-sex sexual activity in private would no longer be criminal.[3] The judgement rendered an iconic victory for queer people in India. Puri (2013: 141–142), citing Shohini Ghosh's blog, identifies this irony as 'a momentous judgement as sexual rights were being used in the discourse of citizenship'. The euphoric response to the judgement in 2009 was a watershed moment for queer activism in India, which brought to a zenith over a decade of legal and social battles fought out in courts, other public institutions and the media.

As Puri (2013: 142), in reference to the 2009 judgement, notes, 'The Naz judgement sets the stage for more expansive understandings of discrimination and dignity for the marginalised that extend well beyond the scope of LGBT persons.' Puri's statement symbolises the intersectional victory that the Delhi High Court had afforded to the citizens of India.

*Snapshot 2*

It was 11 December 2013. The queer community in India and the rest of the world was looking at the Supreme Court to give its verdict on the pending challenges to the Delhi High Court's reading down of Section 377. There were celebrations planned all across the country, and in London (where I am based), we had just organised an impromptu meet up at Trafalgar Square.[4] The message on our *Facebook* event page remained slightly ambiguous, as we were not sure which way the decision will swing, though the public opinion seemed to suggest a victory for the 50 million queer men and women in the country:

> The Supreme Court of India is expected to give its verdict on Section 377 (which was read down by the High Court in 2009, effectively decriminalising homosexuality) tomorrow. We should have a clear picture by 11:30 of what is happening. We are hoping to meet around 4 in Trafalgar Square either to 1. celebrate 2. to march down to the High Commission on Strand to shout. Either ways we would love all you lovely people and supporters to join us. Please do message your friends/acquaintances/colleagues. We hope to see you all tomorrow.
>
> (*Facebook*, 10 December 2013)

*Figure 6.1* Popular meme circulating on the eve of Supreme Court ruling.
Courtesy of Manjul.

The image in Figure 6.1 also started trending across *Facebook*, as a friend
wrote:
    Final judgement on Section 377 to be pronounced tomorrow. GULP![5]

### Snapshot 3

The news arrived in the early morning of 11 December 2013 that the
Supreme Court had struck off the earlier decision of the Delhi High Court
and referred the case to Parliament. Overnight, the queer populace in India
had, once again, become criminalised. There was outcry from all over India
and across the world condemning this. *Twitter* and *Facebook* witnessed
a frenzy of activity, as people publicly shared their anger and feelings of
betrayal by the Supreme Court. The *Facebook* statuses of friends and colleagues from the community are filled with anger and disappointment:

    What a regressive move for India. Shame on you SC (Supreme Court)
        With one stroke of the pen I have been made a criminal again!
    After four years of being out of the closet, we are being asked to
    enter it again. Really how does one do that? What happens to everyone
    who is vulnerable to police blackmail now.[6]

While the anger and disappointment was palpable, it also provided a space for critical thinking as activists and academics began to come together to reflect on the movement so far and the ways forward from here.

## Dissident citizenship and the digital public sphere

The concept of sexual citizenship, first employed by Evans in 1993, is a way of focussing attention on the rights of a range of sexual identities and practices linked to the state. By recognizing the sexual nature of citizenship, Evans argued that existing models of citizenship are based on a heteropatriarchal principle that does not embrace the diversity of sexual (practices) and identities of the people under its umbrella. This is useful in theoretically framing narratives of rights discourse within the queer movement in India and elsewhere. Weeks (1998) has argued that all new sexual social movements are characterised by two moments – citizenship and transgression. In articulating a form of sexual citizenship, it is also imperative to recognise that on principle, the state is supposed to serve the rights and choices of its citizens. Thus, any fight for recognition, respect and rights is also an indictment against the functional failure of the state. Spivak and Butler (2007: 3–4) have, in a recent conversation, pointed out that:

> The state is supposed to service the matrix for the obligations and prerogatives of citizenship. It is that which forms the conditions under which we are juridically bound. We might expect that the state presupposes modes of juridical belonging, at least minimally, but since the state can be precisely what expels and suspends modes of legal protection and obligation, the state can put us, some of us, in quite a state. It can signify the source of non-belonging, even produce that non-belonging as a quasi-permanent state.

I would argue that Spivak and Butler are correct about the limitations that the state imposes on citizenship. The crucial role of the state in creating a dialectic demarcates and reflects the complexity between the transgression of (sexual) norms by citizens and the legal and moral standpoint of the state. Spivak and Butler draw upon Hannah Arendt's theories of statelessness to argue that the nation state produces the stateless and confers non-belonging on national minorities. By placing the minority outside the polity, Spivak and Butler claim that this deprivation of citizenship empowers the citizen, offering a form of political resistance to the production of state subjects without legal rights. This argument can be applied to the queer citizen in India.

Weeks (1998: 48) has identified three themes that contribute to the making of the sexual citizen: democratisation of relationships, new subjectivities and the development of new (sexual) stories. The sexual citizen, according to Weeks, is 'simply an index of the political space that needs to be developed rather than a conclusive answer to it'. The transformation of politics, especially in the Western world, has accordingly brought about new problems, agendas and possibilities. According to Weeks, the sexual citizen is at the heart of this new contemporary politics, 'because they are centrally concerned with the quality of life' (49). This concern with the quality of life goes against the Indian nationalist tenet of 'good sexuality' being concerned with family and reproductive rights and 'bad sexuality' pertaining to sexual enjoyment (Shrivastava, 2013: 5). Sexuality within the familial structure of India is of a particular concern to the state (Menon, 2007) because both family and sexuality exist within public and private lives. Fear of non-normative sexualities and queerness within both Hindu and Islamic Indian nationalism is well documented (Bachcheta, 2007). According to Bachcheta (2007), queerness circulates alongside a number of contexts of hate, fear and desire within the discourse of the Hindu Right. However, as the aftermath of the recent Supreme Court decision has shown, it is often quite difficult to posit simple differences between the Left and the Right, as there were several commentators from both sides supporting the recriminalisation and celebrating the Supreme Court's decision.

Much of the criticism against the decriminalisation of Section 377 is with respect to the decline in the moral and social fabric of the country that might follow. In the context of India, drawing on Shrivastava's (2013: 11) recent work in Indian sexuality, it can be argued that sexuality and the family are of particular concern to the state as these two contexts affect the 'foundations of society'. The fraught status of homosexuality and queerness in the Indian society, especially within social movements that aspire to state power, which was granted momentarily in 2009 and the subsequent recriminalisation in 2013, also points to the ways in which sexual (minority) citizens exist within a temporal space in the nation. Ram Murti, one of the petitioners to the High Court judgement, has argued, 'The population of these people (queer citizens) is 0.2% and 99.8%, the entire Nation gets affected . . . this is a serious problem for our culture and core values' (quoted in Kaushal, 2013: 124). Murti claims that the population of the queer community in India is 0.2 per cent, but more insidiously refers to the 99.8 per cent of the remaining as the 'entire Nation', thus failing to recognise the queer citizen as a part of the Nation.

What does it then mean for the queer citizen to be at once contained by the nation state, which binds it through its legal mechanism, and on the other hand to be (forcibly) dispossessed for their sexual choices? The queer citizen has to not only abide by the juridicial obligations of the state, but also deny himself or herself a life of 'dignity'. Justice Mukhopadhyay, one of the presiding judges of the Supreme Court proceedings, claimed that dignity is defined as 'quality of living, worthy of honour'.[7]

The importance of dignity is at the core of the NAZ writ. It draws on aspects of privacy to restore dignity and autonomy of consensual same-sex relations among adults (Puri, 2013: 146). Section 377 is a symbol for legalised homophobia in the country. While it has been used to prosecute around 200 cases since its inception in 1860, as the Supreme Court judgement has pointed out, its insidious nature lies in the ways in which it can be misused for harassment and stands as a legal protection for homophobia. It is important to note that this highlights and repeats many of the arguments that have been made in the name of law reform in other parts of the world, for example in the 1950s' Britain. Films such as *Victim* (1961), for instance, are understood as a mediated call for an end to what was dubbed 'the Blackmailer's charter', and highlighted the ways in which the criminalisation of homosexuality created means and methods for the extra-judicial harassment and exploitation of queer people. This chimes very well with the Indian situation. Gupta's (2011) work on the ways in which sexual blackmail operates as a parallel order of morality demonstrates that blackmail is a common experience for queer men in India, across an intersectional range (age, class, religion or caste) with little legal recourse. The moral standpoint of the society takes precedence here, which shields, defends and gives credence to the blackmailer.

At this point, I would like to introduce another theoretical concept that will provide a framework for my case studies in this chapter. I refer to Habermas's (1989) concept of the public sphere and apply it to the digital space, as a way to think about the ways in which media and more specifically digital media impacts upon civil society. Borrowing Fraser's (2008: 76) concerns that one should not simply employ the concept to develop an understanding of communication, but also consider the ways in which it helps us to understand critical democratic processes, it is useful to also scrutinise who participates and on what terms. This stream of problematising the public sphere theory has been grounded within a feminist, anti-racist and transnational ethos. In attempting to reconstruct the theory from its Westphalian underpinnings, Fraser (2008: 88) explains that 'public spheres today are not coextensive with political membership', but rather it empowers transnational elites possessing the material power for their opinions to generate interest, thus disempowering the non-elite from participating. Fraser's critique of Habermas remains important because what she demonstrates is that inequalities continue to operate within the cultural hierarchies of everyday life. In this regard, Fraser (2008: 83) offers the concept of 'alternative publics' and 'subaltern counterpublics' as ways to resist the cultural and political hegemony of the mainstream. Finally, Fraser also critiques Habermas's assumption that the public sphere advances a common good. Taking an intersectional position (though Fraser does not actually use that term), she contends that because of the stratified society we live in, there are limited shared interests. Therefore, according to Fraser, deliberation, which Habermas explained as a way to advancing common good, is not necessarily a productive exercise, as what is good for one group might actually be bad for another. The formation of multiple public spheres is an interesting phenomenon, and even if we were to talk of a queer public sphere, where specific identity-based claims can be engaged with, it would also not be wrong to claim that different people relate to their identities and experiences in multivalent ways which are classed and gendered (as I have shown in Chapters 4, 5 and 6). Thus, Fraser's concept of alternative publics can be useful even in this context.

Media theorists such as Butsch (2007) argue that mass media can be productively seen as creating a new form of public sphere. Butsch (2007: 6) explains that 'media is cast as allies of citizens in their role of supervising democratic government through public opinion'. It would not be unfair to problematise this a little more. While media and public service media are theoretically created to serve the public and give voice to mass opinions, in contemporary practice vast swathes of the media industry are controlled by elite conglomerates such as Rupert Murdoch and Star TV in India, which serve their own corporate interest (profit and political/social). This fact, together with media that is state controlled, raises the question if media can truly serve the public. I am in agreement with recent scholarship by Gerbaudo (2012) and Gournelos and Gunkel (2012), who emphasise the Internet's ability to contribute to a stronger public sphere. Digital media through its dialogic, reciprocative and participatory nature is creating a more vibrant public sphere which one-way mass media such as televisions and newspapers were unable to do.

However, theorists such as Papacharissi (2009) are critical of thinking about the digital as a public sphere. For example, Papacharissi argues that while the digital sphere offers many benefits for citizens to come together in a mutual fashion and take part in debates of subversive nature, they are not necessarily reviving the public sphere but rather 'inject[ing] a healthy dose of plurality to a maturing model of representative democracy' (Papacharissi, 2009: 241). Pariser (2012), on the other hand, invokes the concept of a 'filter bubble'. He argues that the Internet allows like-minded individuals and activists to cluster together in smaller circles. He further points out that through living within personalised media environments where people have control of the type of media they want to engage with, we are essentially only talking to other like-minded individuals. It thus becomes difficult for online activists to reach out to a wider public beyond their close circles. This viewpoint is reflected in Dean's (2005) argument that while the Internet and other related technologies allow abundant amount of information to circulate, in actuality they foreclose real-time activism. Dean makes two important contributions to this debate. First, Dean argues that the sheer amount of 'undigestible' information that we are inundated with is offered as a form of democratic engagement, but that rather than adding any meaningful participation, it ends up adding to the information overflow:

> The fantasy of abundance covers over the way facts and opinions, images and reactions circulate in a massive stream of content, losing their specificity and merging with and into the data flow.
>
> (Dean, 2005: 58)

The second point Dean makes is that the clusters within which we move around digitally and the conversations there 'contribute to the segmentation and isolation of users within bubbles of opinions with which they already agree' (Dean, 2005: 69).

I, however, disagree with these positions and find Fraser's (2008) argument about smaller counterpublics which are parallel spaces for subordinated people to formulate oppositional dialogues much more useful for this book. As my case studies on *YouTube* and *Facebook* will demonstrate, online media lends itself to create these counterpublics. In these terms, an opinion or comment posted on *YouTube* or *Facebook* presents 'an attempt to populate the public agenda' (Papacharissi, 2009: 231). The TV9 and Global Day of Rage case studies will demonstrate that in addition to enabling access to information, these digital platforms are also allowing politically motivated individuals to challenge homophobic public agenda of the state and other institutions in India. These go beyond the 'filter bubble' (Dean, 2005; Pariser, 2012), and are actually involved in direct action and change.

Gournelos and Gunkel (2012) argue about the importance of digital media in transforming and intervening in the politics of everyday life. A world led by participatory media made possible through platforms such as social networking sites, blogs and vlogs has significantly altered the geography of protest culture. Castells (2009) in his work on the network society argues that power relations in the networked society are increasingly shaped and decided in the communications field. In such a networked digital society, old and new media converge in enacting and diffusing mediated protests, often leading protests to take on a transnational perspective, as the following case studies will demonstrate.

# TV9

On 22 February 2011, almost one and half years since the historic Delhi High Court judgement which read down Section 377, a television channel in Hyderabad called TV9 ran a sinister story about 'Gay Culture Rampant in Hyderabad'. The story, based on a series of covert operations on the popular gay social networking/dating website *PlanetRomeo*, showed a reporter logging into the website and 'chatting' with gay men. The respondents were asked leading questions about their sexual lives on the telephone and all of this unbeknownst to them was broadcast on television without blocking out the faces or names of the individuals concerned. I have reproduced below one of the conversations that took place:

INVESTIGATOR: Hello
X: Who is this?
INVESTIGATOR: Is X there?
X: Tell me I am X speaking
INVESTIGATOR: You gave me this number on PlanetRomeo
X: Ya, tell me who is this where r u from?
INVESTIGATOR: I live in Banjara Hills Hyderabad where are u?
X: I am currently out of station but I am coming back soon
INVESTIGATOR: When exactly are you coming back?
X: I am coming back on Monday or Tuesday. Tuesday morning hopefully
INVESTIGATOR: What are your stats?
X: 5.6 ht and 68 wt
INVESTIGATOR: is it 5.8
X: 5.6 your height?
INVESTIGATOR: I am 5.9, 5 feet 9 inches What are you? Are you a top or a Bottom?
X: I am a top
INVESTIGATOR: So you are a top, what do you like?
X: Foreplay and getting sucked. Where do u stay?
INVESTIGATOR: I currently live in Banjara Hills
X: Would you have place?
INVESTIGATOR: ahhhhh
X: Would you have place?
INVESTIGATOR: I will call you when I have the place, Monday or Tuesday. I will only call you when I have a place. What do you do?
X: I go to JNTu
INVESTIGATOR: Jntu? What do you do in JNTu?
X: I study Mtech

The programme ended with the reporter concluding that 'A lot of employees in higher positions, white collared workers, highly qualified students are becoming slaves to lifestyle which is against nature.'[8] This was rebroadcast the next day, despite protests from the queer community in India.

*Gaysi Family* is a website run for South Asian queer people around the world, 'providing a safe and intimate space' for sharing opinions, reviews, coming out stories and event information.[9] It first ran the story of the TV9 exposé on the 23 February demanding that TV9 take down the video from their *YouTube* channel and release a statement promising better understanding and sensitivity towards queer issues. Protests were planned and carried out in Mumbai, Hyderabad and New Delhi. The email addresses of the channel were also released and readers were urged to write to them complaining about the television show.

I was in the middle of an interview with a participant when this news reached me and I was interested to see in what ways my participant addressed this. I was at that time in conversation with Sumit on *PlanetRomeo*. His first response was to ask if TV9 had only targeted Hyderabad, in other words making sure that he (based in Kolkata) would not be directly affected by this covert operation.

> This is quite shocking. You would have thought that PR [*Planet-Romeo*] would be a safe place. I am here 24x7 and even have my picture on display. Imagine what would happen if this got leaked to the papers or television. My parents would be shocked. I would probably be too ashamed to go back home. I thought now that 377 is gone, things will get better. Can you imagine this still happening. Did you say they called us against Nature? What a fucking homophobe. Thank god this is not on National or Bengali channels. I mean this is quite bad isn't it!
>
> (23 February 2011)

Sumit's reaction was one of anger and fear, clearly worried that this might happen to him. It was interesting that Sumit connected this incident to Section 377. As Puri (2013: 156), in response to the judgement by the High Court, notes, 'The judgment offers a modern democratic vision in which sexual minorities are located within the national imaginary. That the status of sexual minorities is a measure of national modernity is the unstated assumption in the judgement.' Sumit's response to *PlanetRomeo* as a 'safe space' is also an important point to consider. After all, queer social networking sites are built upon the premise that they offer a space (see Chapter 5) beyond the purview of society or the state. However, the very fact that a safe space such as this was being breached by an external body (TV9 in this case) was a matter of concern for Sumit.

Sumit's final point about 'things getting better' with the reading down of Section 377 is slightly more complicated. For one, Section 377 was seldom used in the courts to prosecute same-sex activity. It was rather a weapon that was wielded in daily life by law enforcement. There are countless reports of extortion and violence at the hands of police and blackmailers by the MSM and queer population (Seabrook, 1999), and the removal of Section 377 in 2009, while lessening this, still had a long way to go before it truly brought about a societal change, as many of my respondents pointed out in the interviews. This can be seen in the context of several countries around the world, and more recently another South Asian state, Nepal, where queer rights have been enshrined in law, but homophobia still remains rife. Boyce and Coyle (2013: 19), for instance, found that despite the progress made by Nepal in the context of legal reforms for queer people, especially with their Supreme Court ruling in 2007 which decided to develop legislation that would remove discrimination and provide gender-variant people full recognition as citizens, stigmatisation and social marginalisation were still experienced by sexual and gender minorities in the country.

The queer community, however, did not take the TV9 covert operation lightly. The Naz petition for the removal of Section377 had created a vocal queer community, and this did not dissipate following the High Court judgement. As Mayank, a 23-year-old student from Delhi I interviewed last year, pointed out after the Supreme Court judgement:

> We are not the same community that was ten years ago, when people shied away from the camera and less visible. We have grown since then and have got a voice, which we are no longer scared to use. The Delhi High Court empowered us and we are not going back. We have fought and marched and will continue doing so until justice is served.
> (28 December 2013)

On behalf of Adhikaar, a LGBT human rights organisation based in New Delhi, Aditya Bandyopadhyay sent a notice to TV9 under the National Broadcasters Association Guidelines giving an ultimatum to the channel to either redress the situation or risk the threat of following this through to the News Broadcasters Association (NBA) complaints redressal procedure. Bandyopadhyay primarily raised nine points of contention that were based on the infringement of privacy through entrapment, but in the final point, Bandyopadhyay invoked Section 377 and pointed out that:

> After the Delhi High Court judgment reading down Section 377 of the Indian Penal Code, private consensual adult homosexuality is no

more a criminal activity in India. Therefore, you have by this telephonic sting violated the NBA mandated ground rule that a news channel will ensure that a sting operation is carried out only as a tool for getting conclusive evidence of wrong doing or criminality.[10]

Bandyopadhyay's swift reaction to the TV9 episode was widely acknowledged, and *Facebook* petitions were set up and the notice shared by several individuals and activists. It also sparked a discussion on the TV9 episode, forcing several people to rethink their visibility in public and especially cyberspaces:

> Very well said. Will they ever pay for the unrepairable damage done to the LGBT community as many people will be forced back into the closet as a result of this stupid news?
>
> (Hrishi, 24 February 2011)

Another individual, Deep, also commented, 'Lets fight for the rights. . . . This is not done. It is not about sexuality. It is all about human dignity . . .' (23 February 2013). Deep's comment links back to the earlier point I made on dignity and citizenship. Both Hrishi and Deep's concerns are equally illuminating. While Hrishi is concerned about the infringement of privacy which would push several queer men back in to the closet, Deep is slightly more upbeat about the subsequent protest and fight. It is also interesting that Deep has decided to shift the argument stating that it is not about sexuality but about human rights. I would suggest that Deep wanted to say this was not *only* about sexuality. As TV9 demonstrated with an earlier report on sex workers, they have very little consideration for privacy or civil rights.[11] This particular report was also a 'name and shame' endeavour that led to violence and several threats against sex workers who were named.

One of the most interesting responses to the sting operation was by Sushil Tarun, who commented on the *Gaysi* webpage:

> To use the real names of people without their permission was most unethical and outrageous. Would such a channel dare do a sting on straight men who frequent brothels or dance bars? Imagine if all the guys who went to a disco hoping to find a date with the opposite sex were treated like this? Such behaviour has to be roundly condemned so that it never happens again. But there is an important lesson for the entire gay community. We must organize and act in ways so that our lives our accepted and respected in broad daylight. Whether we seek partners for sex or for love, we need to be treated with dignity and

equality. That means that we still have a huge task ahead of us in edu-
cating the Indian public so that people can learn to accept us without
being judgemental or unkind.

(February 24 2011)

Sushil's comment evokes the social and emotional complexity that the TV9
report brought forth. In envisioning and categorising the queer subject,
TV9 was using the discourse of sexual deviancy, individuals who needed
to be named and shamed for their sexual practices which went 'against
nature'. They were also targeting *PlanetRomeo*, and the two profiles they
targeted were individuals who were not publicly out about their orientation. What Sushil's comment brings to light is the need for education and
advocacy within the general populace to lessen the stigma around being
queer, which would in turn encourage new understandings of the experiences of queer people and to understand the queer subject in India better.
Sushil's comment also indicates that queer lives need to be respected in
'broad daylight', again an indictment of the simple reading down of Section 377.

Bandyopadhyay and Adhikaar's notice made its way to the News Broadcasting Standards Authority (NBSA) in India in New Delhi, which issued
a show cause notice to the channel on the 24 February 2011 asking the
channel to respond within the stipulated 14 days.[12] TV9 defended their
investigative journalism for bringing to public knowledge activities that
were enticing people to 'illegal and unlawful activities' ('Gaysi'). They
further defended their position by arguing that because the website was
public there was no privacy violation (forgetting to mention that they had
to make an account as a queer man to join the website in the first place).
The NBSA and Justice (Retd.) S. Verma, who presided over the case, dismissed TV9's justification, censuring the channel for creating a sensation-
alised report about gay culture in Hyderabad. They also took notice of the
reading down of Section 377 by the Delhi High Court and pointed out
that same-sex activity/queer sexual orientation was no longer a criminal
act in India.

> The Programme needlessly violated the right to privacy of individuals
> with possible alternate sexual orientation, no longer considered taboo
> or a criminal act; and the Programme misused the special tool of a
> 'sting-operation' available only to subserve the larger public interest.[13]

NBSA also pointed out that TV9's claim that photographs, personal information and telephone numbers of the people targeted in the sting operation
as 'being public' was invalid, as they were operating in a membership-only

area. The NBSA finally imposed a fine of INR 100,000 on 21 March 2011, and ordered TV9 to telecast an apology for three consecutive days expressing their regret over the incident, with the following text:

> TV9 apologizes for the story 'Gay Culture Rampant In Hyderabad' telecast on this channel on 22nd February, 2011 from I5:11 hrs. to 15:17 hrs. particularly since the story invaded the privacy of certain persons and was in violation of the Code of Ethics & Broadcasting Standards of the News Broadcasters Association. Any hurt or harm caused to any person thereby is sincerely regretted.[14]

This was one of the first major victories made by the queer movement in India since the Delhi High Court decriminalisation in 2009. The short six-minute report by TV9 is one instance of the ways in which queer cultures and identities are conceived by some sections of the media and public as a site of criminality where illegal sexualities are practiced and performed, with the queer individual being cast as a criminal and anti-national. As dissident citizens, the queer community (now emboldened after the Delhi High Court decision) decided to fight back against this homophobic story. The desire for being recognised as equal citizens was at the heart of this fight, as was the desire to reclaim the imagined safety of spaces such as *PlanetRomeo*.

Digital media, in this case, allowed the homophobic reporting of TV9 to go viral on a transnational scale. The viral nature of it brought this issue to the forefront of a pan-Indian queer community (and a global queer community), thus bringing a local event in Hyderabad to national attention and instigating queer Indian people to speak out against the report. At the same time, the affective afterlife of the apology also exists on *You Tube*, where the TV9 apology is still in existence, thus creating an archive of queer dissidence. Reflecting on the role of the Internet in civic culture, I would like to draw two main conclusions from this case study. One, the Internet is an important resource when it comes to knowledge creation and knowledge dissemination (Castells, 2009), and this case study is a primary example of the ways in which digital media was used to disseminate a homophobic story leading to public opinions and finally a legal challenge. The very fact that TV9's story and apology is still available digitally is an example of the digital afterlife of queer activism. Second, in a mediatised world, the complex (and symbolic) process of uniting spatially dispersed people with similar interests and convictions is made possible through new media and cyberculture. The transnational potential of online media and the ways in which this enables conversation to transcend cartographic boundaries is demonstrated very well in this case study, and can also be seen in the next case. The symbolic assemblages of acts such as Bandyo-padhyay's against TV9 materialises into bodily assemblies unifying and creating a dissident queer politic through civil participation and facilitating the formation of counterpublic (Fraser, 2008). As Fraser articulates in her thesis on counterpublics, the dual aims of recognition and redistribution are central. In this episode, the subordinated sexual identities of the pro-testers are being recognised, and through an agitation movement, it shifts and redistributes the power balance. The need for creating a strong queer public sphere has grown stronger since the recent Supreme Court ruling on the 11 December 2013, thus making it imperative once more for the queer movement to build alliances with other oppressed dissident citizens to fight for their rights.

## Global day of rage: @IPC377 #377gdr

While the earlier case study of TV9 showed the ways in which a queer counterpublic could work on a local level, this case study will show how digital media responds to transnational politics. Fraser's (2008) notion of the subaltern counterpublic will again be a productive framework to anal-yse the ways in which communication networks and social media operates in transnational advocacy.

The date 11 December 2013 shall remain an important day for the queer movement in India. The Supreme Court delivered its infamous decision putting aside the Delhi High Court judgement and reinstating Section 377, thus effectively criminalising queer people once again. It would be wrong to argue that the Delhi High Court decision changed everything within the social and cultural fabric of India. Even as recently as 4 July 2011, a mere two years since the reading down of Section 377, Ghulam Nabi Azad, the Health Minister of India, gave a live broadcast on television denouncing homosexuality.

It would be useful to point out here that online queer networks in India made this video available to viewers, both through its dissemination on online listservs and forums. This video also developed a critical response from the community towards the minister and his comments.[15] Through new media, the queer public was informed about the ideological policies of the minister of health, and by extension critiquing institutions of gov-ernance and the very legitimacy of having a homophobic health minister. First-hand accounts and incriminating statements such as those made by Azad can now be captured and communicated almost instantly via digital technologies and thereby contributing to 'processes of protest diffusion and the mass mobilisation of civil societies' (Cottle and Lester, 2011: 8). Cottle and Lester further argue that in such ways 'local and global communications can impenetrate, conditioning each other and intensifying political pressures for change' (Cottle and Lester, 2011: 8).

The government in India has been divided over the issue of decriminalising homosexuality in India. When Voices Against 377, a Delhi-based coalition of human rights groups, filed an intervention in support of the original petition by Naz in 2001, the Home Ministry submitted a defence of Section 377 while the Health ministry supported a 'reading down' in the later stages of the proceedings. Following the historic judgement by the Delhi High Court which decriminalised homosexuality, various private individual (mostly from faith-based religious organisations) as well as a government panel was set up to review the judgement.

> We declare that Section 377 IPC, insofar it criminalises consensual sexual acts of adults in private, is violative of Articles 21, 14 and 15 of the Constitution.[16]

The government panel was composed of the Home Minister Palaniappan Chidambaram, and the Health Minister Ghulam Nabi Azad, amongst others. The panel decided not to participate in an appeal and let the Supreme Court determine the 'correctness' of the High Court ruling, prompting many to see this as tacit governmental approval[17] (Waites, 2010: 977). However, the International Gay and Lesbian Human Rights Commission (IGLHRC) cautioned that leaving the decision to the Supreme Court was unpredictable as it might be 'unwilling to intervene in moral issues'.

The IGLHRC caution came true when the Supreme Court decided to reinstate Section 377. In fact, during the proceedings, Justice Mukhopadhyay, in response to one of the petitioners Mr. Grover, who pointed out the societal repercussions that Section 377 has in it leading homosexuals to be seen as degraded and perverse by the society, argued that it was the social reformer's job to change society and not the Court's.[18]

The judgement by the Supreme Court sent shockwaves across the country and the wider world. There was surprise that the Supreme Court of a democratic (perceivably liberal) country such as India would have such a blatant disregard for the dignity and rights of sexual minorities in the country. The retrogressive nature of the judgement did not just impede the progress of sexual minority rights in India alone, but also across the world. Activists were very quick to respond, and within hours of the judgement, my *Twitter* and *Facebook* feed was filled by the outrage expressed by scores of people. In an attempt to organise a collective global action, a Global Day of Rage was announced for 15 December 2013 which would take place all around the world (Figure 6.2).[19]

*Figure 6.2* Global Day of Rage Poster, 2013. Downloaded from Global Day of Rage Facebook Page. December 2013. Courtesy of Charan Singh.

The official press release condemning the judgement articulated the following points:

> We are outraged. . . .
>
> - That the Supreme Court of India on 11 December 2013 set aside the July 2009 Delhi High Court judgement which decriminalised consensual sex between adults in private, effectively recriminalising all lesbian, gay, bisexual, transgender and queer Indians and reduced them to the status of 'unapprehended felons'.
> - That the Supreme Court has betrayed its own progressive history of extending rights for all by taking away rights from Indian citizens with this judgment.
> - That the Supreme Court has failed to live up to its role as the protector of rights for all citizens without discrimination, as guaranteed by one of the world's most progressive texts – the Indian Constitution.
> - That the Supreme Court has thus betrayed the fundamental constitutional promise that the dignity of all citizens would be recognised and that equal treatment is a non-negotiable element of the world's largest democracy, thereby shredding the very principles it has sworn itself to uphold.
> - That the Supreme Court has criminalised all consensual sexual acts that do not involve penile-vaginal penetration. This applies to all people, irrespective of their gender identity or sexual orientation, including heterosexual people and not just LGBT Indians.
> - That the Supreme Court has empowered blackmailers, bullies and homophobes who will now find easy victims in LGBT people whose rights have been denied.
> - That the Supreme Court has encouraged corporations and companies to discriminate against their LGBT staff and discouraged those few companies which moved after the Delhi High Court judgment to ensure non-discrimination against LGBT staff within their organisations.
> - That the Supreme Court can use the phrase 'miniscule minorities' to dismiss the rights of LGBT people, thus ignoring the spirit of inclusiveness which is at the heart of the Indian Constitution. The size of a minority is irrelevant, what matters is that every member of it, every Indian citizen, has an equal right to protection granted by our Fundamental Rights and it is the SC's duty to enforce this, not throw it away.

This Global Day of Rage is being organised by queer Indians, the queer India diaspora, queer people of all countries, our supporters, relatives and friends. All are coming out on the streets of cities across the world on Sunday 15 December, to together raise our voices against this travesty of justice.

The press release is illuminating in many ways. It was a collective effort drawn together by activists all over India (as well as the world) done mostly online. I was part of the email list that was started by queer activist Lesley Esteves on 12 December 2013 at 16:25 hours. The email called 'Next Steps' first mooted the idea of holding a Global Day of Rage. An initial email was sent out to a select group of people, who then further disseminated this within their personal networks, and each person was asked to comment and provide ideas on the ways in which the press release could be structured and the content within it. This is an example of what Brinkerhoff (2009) calls the 'digital diaspora'. She argues that diasporic communities across the world are taking up the social affordances of the Internet to enable expression and negotiate cultural identities. Taking this idea forward, what we see here is an example of a digital 'queer' diaspora. The press release and the ways in which communication technologies were used to engage with the queer Indian diaspora provides evidence of what Brinkerhoff has called the 'liberal' uses of the Internet in promoting 'pluralism, democracy and human rights' (Brinkerhoff, 2009).

The press release statement makes it clear that the Supreme Court's decision to take away rights from a community and make them 'unapprehended felons' was directed at queer citizens who are also Indian citizens. The statement unambiguously makes it clear that queer citizens were no longer to be construed as the 'other', but were very much a part of the Nation. Turning back to Weeks (1998), where he posits that queer activism (he uses the term 'gay and lesbian movement') has two elements – a moment of transgression where a new self is created and moment of citizenship where equal rights and laws are demanded and claimed – we can say that this statement heralds that moment. The fact that queer citizens have a history of alliances and have been a part of the larger women's and human rights movements is part of the larger narrative (Dave, 2012; Dhall, 2005). Sparks (1997: 83), writing about the dissident citizen, contends that dissident democratic citizenship can be conceptualised as the public contestation of prevailing arrangements of power. By this logic, the term can be applied to all citizens of India fighting for human rights and resisting hegemonic laws and norms. Dave (2012: 140), in her study of the Indian lesbian movement, notes that the emergence of the nation within queer politics in India occurred with the release of the film *Fire* and a single protest placard which boldly spelt out 'Indian and Lesbian'. The Global Rage statement makes it even clearer by addressing all the points at 'the citizens of India' rather than merely queer citizens.

Queer people occupy a particularly complex place when attempting to demarcate their claim for citizenship. They are a part of multiple communities based on their gender, sexuality, class, ethnicity and so on. This has always posed a certain degree of problem when trying to theorise 'the' Indian citizen. While privilege is accessed through one aspect of the identity (social class, caste etc.), it is simultaneously denied by another (gender or sexuality).

One of the other complications is discerning queer as an identity (which the law does not criminalise) and queer as sexual practice (which the law vociferously puts down). This rupture in the link between the sexual/ gender identity and sexual practice, however, cannot and should not be seen separately. Sexual activity may emerge or indeed lead on from one's sexual identity; however, at the heart of the judgement, lies the regulation and moral/religious and state interference. Citizenship cannot be downplayed or forgotten within sexual identity politics. Plummer (2003: 59) states:

> To speak of citizenship usually also implies an identity – a person, a voice, a recognised type, a locus, a position, a subjectivity – from which the claim of citizenship can be made. And such identities bring with them . . . a defining 'other' different from us, and hints for future conduct based in part on this otherness.

Looking only at the documented evidence where Section 377 has been invoked, the Supreme Court declared the following: 'While reading down section 377 IPC, the Division Bench of the High Court overlooked that a miniscule fraction of the country's population constitute lesbians, gays, bisexuals or trans* and in last more than 150 years less than 200 persons have been prosecuted' (Kaushal, 2013: 83). However, what the Supreme Court overlooks is the linkage between harassment, the law and the enforcement of that law. The People's Union for Civil Liberties in Karnataka produced two reports in 2001 and 2003, where they documented the various forms of harassment and discrimination sexual and gender minorities face within institutions and society, where in many cases Section 377 might not have been employed directly; however, the resonance of that law played an important part. Second, the remit of the law goes beyond the public sector. As the statement also points out, it could lead to discriminatory practices within the corporate sector against their queer employees.

The final point that the statement raises is the Supreme Court's reference to the queer population as a miniscule minority. The Constitution of India guarantees the same freedom to all its citizens regardless of their numbers. The state of India set up the National Commission for Religious Minorities in 1992 and Scheduled Castes and Tribes in 2004. Thus, in these earlier instances, the state affirmed that the number of a minority group was irrelevant to its protection under the law. The minority in question now, the queer populace, are also citizens of India and should be afforded the freedom and guarantee of equal rights and protection.

The Global Day of Rage was entirely planned and executed remotely using social networking sites such as *Facebook* and *Twitter*. Within hours, the statement was written and commented upon by a global Indian queer network. This was happening across geographically specific locations from New Delhi to London aided through network technology. Initially, the idea was to hold a protest across several cities in India and around the world, wherever five people were available to come together and protest. By the end of the day, volunteers from almost 32 cities across the world had signed up to take part in the protest. Within a single day, a logo, a press release and *Twitter* hashtags had been developed to document the event and maintain pressure on the Indian government.

Cultural activist Sunil Gupta proposed the London leg of the global protest, and later I joined in as one of the team of co-organisers. It was fitting and ironic that the colonial centre (London, England) that had created the law in the first place was now joining in to condemn its continued existence. A significant justification for colonial rule lay in the notion of 'reform' that was provided by the colonisers with respect to the colonised nations (Shrivastava, 2013: 6). As I have already argued in previous chapters, the colonies were also a place favoured by many Europeans to travel for its relative lack of proscription against 'queer sexual practices' that provided many possibilities where dissident sexualities could be performed (Aldrich, 2003; Ballhatchet, 1980). Mclintock (1995) also argues that colonialism was driven by the gendered process of subordination, where social differences are both invented and performed leading to a sanctioned institutionalisation of gender and sexual differences. Shrivastava (2013: 6) extends this by arguing that native sexual mores were regarded as the key object of such reform and held up as proof of the 'moral inferiority of colonised populations . . . characterised by passionate unreason and unruliness'.

Weeks argues that one of the central issues as a sexual citizen is being able to 'balance the claims of different communities . . . affirming the importance of collective endeavours' (49). Similarly, the Global Day of Rage movement in London targeted not just queer organisations for support, but also women's rights and South Asia specific organisations. It was much to our surprise that diverse organisations such as Southall Black Sisters, SARBAT (the Sikh LGBT support group) as well as allies from trade unions provided us with overwhelming support. Collectivism is after all at the heart of the civic society where groups work together to mobilise subversive movements promoting a plural democratic model of society. The recent film

*Pride* (2014) is a good example of the ways in which disparate groups such as the lesbian and gay community in London joined hands with the Welsh coal miners to protest against the government closure of mines in 1984. These forms of new publics and collective groups offer greater scope for the identification and introduction of local and personal issues into national and transnational social movements.

The Global Day of Rage protest received widespread coverage from the global media, with UK-based celebrities and activists such as Peter Tatchell and Stephen Fry supporting it on *Twitter* and media outlets such as the BBC and Pink News reporting on the event. The protest also provided a platform for people to speak up about the ways in which they have been affected emotionally as well as socially (the social ramifications on their lives) by the decision and the argument for continuing the fight. UK-based organisations were especially encouraged to speak up, and it was interesting to hear the ways in which the resonance of Section 377 was felt within the South Asian community in Britain.

Mohit (35), one of the protesters I met during the London leg of the Global Day of Rage, later told me:

> I was born in the midlands. My parents migrated to Britain in the early 70's from an Indian village. When they moved here they had a hard time integrating to the culture and they always impose (sic) on the fact that we must always uphold and celebrate our own Indian culture. The fact that this Indian culture was homophobic, casteist and misogynist is not a concern for them.
>
> (15 December 2013)

The figure of the 'home', left behind as one that is pure and unsullied, is a central trope of articulating the nation. Gopinath (2005: 15) uses the notion of 'impossibility' as a way of signalling the fraught and unthinkable position of a queer subject 'within the various mappings of nation and diaspora'. While men like Mohit are considered marginalised in the nation of their origin because of their 'deviant sexuality', they are also largely marginalised within their host country (Britain, in this case), where they are marginalised in the context of the predominant white gay scene as well as the heterosexual community.

Dave (2012: 21) argues that queerness has a way of moving about – be it queer people escaping oppressive regimes or running away from small towns and families. The movement of queer people is part of a larger continuing historical pattern where queer people leave home for places where they feel safer 'precisely because they are foreigners there' (Vanita, 2013: 139). Mohit's motivation to come for the protests was inspired by joining

*Facebook* groups for queer South Asians in London, where he felt he was part of the global discourse on queer rights. Scholars such as Cottle and Lester (2011), Gerbaudo (2012) and Papacharissi (2009) argue that new media technologies make loosely structured social networks crucial for activism and coordination. In this case, Mohit demonstrates how social media such as *Facebook* facilitates and provides local activists and those from India opportunities to frame their claims in global terms to connect with like-minded individuals elsewhere. In fact, when Sunil Gupta and I organised this event, we were trying to do the same – mobilise other like-minded individuals who may not be directly affected by the Supreme Court decision to still identify with the collective action and unify for this protest.

Another battle that broke out almost immediately after the Global Day of Rage campaign pitted these very conceptions of nation, belonging and the queerness over a *Facebook* picture of a Sikh man kissing another man which led to a *Facebook* censure followed by intense online campaign to have the picture reinstated and an apology. Saini wrote:

> Last night my uncle told me if they knew i was gay before 20 they would have killed me. He also said im gay cause i was molested as a kid and im on 'the wrong path' . . . and when was i getting married? . . . i laughed and hung up. He comes from the same backwards place a whole minority were just recriminalized . . . Fuck my uncle. Fuck section 377. Im very proud to be illegal in any context. I owe that to my sikhi heritage and my mom. Also, for all the ranting about genocide i hear . . . i rarely see solidarity. So . . . fuck em all. #sikhknowledge #baagi #377 #section377 xoxox

Kanwar Saini (known as Sikh Knowledge on his *Facebook* page), is a 32-year-old Sikh man who posted a picture of himself kissing another man on the Global Day of Rage in Toronto on his *Facebook* page (Figure 6.3). The picture elicited a lot of discussion, with many commentators unhappy that a Sikh man was more concerned with 'his own selfish lust' when there were '*real* Sikhs doing hunger strike for political prisoners' (available on Sikh Knowledge's *Facebook* page).

It is interesting that this commentator along with a few others found it objectionable that a Sikh man should be campaigning for queer rights, asserting that there are other more important issues to be dealing with. This argument about hierarchy within issues is not new. Karim (2012: 214), in her study on the reception of the dissident Bangladeshi writer in exile Taslima Nasrin, comments that within conservative societies like Bangladesh, feminist groups have to be strategic about their advocacy of women's rights. Thus, issues such as rural poverty and economic and legal

*Figure 6.3* Sikh Knowledge photo of two South Asian men kissing taken down by *Facebook*. Accessed on 15 March 2014. Available at: http://www. huffingtonpost.ca/2013/12/17/sikh-knowledge_n_4461735. html. Courtesy of Kanwar Saini.

safeguards for women gain ascendancy at the cost of silencing discussions around sexuality. This commentator seemed to be working within a similar space, where they found it impossible that Saini should be focussing his attention on his own sexuality instead of campaigning for the release of Sikh prisoners like a 'real' Sikh man. This obliteration of alternative sexuality from within the pure discourse of nationalism is a compliance mechanism to view the state as singular and homogenous. As Spivak and Butler (2007: 30) argue:

> The nation-state assumes that the nation expresses a certain national identity, is founded through the concerted consensus of a nation, and that a certain correspondence exists between the state and the nation. The nation, in this view, is singular and homogeneous, or, at least, it becomes so in order to comply with the requirements of the state.

Saini's representation of gay male sexuality and what could be construed as his dissent against his Indian and Sikhness calls to mind the relation of diasporic subjects and the complex relationship between the 'home' identity and the foreign body. As one of the commentators critical of the photograph pointed out, his queerness was a 'greed for lust', and as a true Sikh his religious and national identity should be at the centre of his subjectivity. The resonance of Section 377, when carried over to the diaspora, causes a disruption. The nation and the national identity gets deeply implicated within 'foreign space' with the dissenting actor, for example, Saini or Mohit revealing the challenges posed to queer male desire through the dominant dialogue imposed by the nation.

These two connected incidents – The Global Day of Rage and the furore over Saini's picture – are further examples of queer dissidence being played out on offline and online spaces. The role of cyberspace in these events makes visible the ways in which sites such *Facebook* facilitates collective action and what Gerbaudo (2012: 12) terms as 'choreography of assembly', by which he means the process through which a public space is symbolically constructed. I am in agreement with Gerbaudo's view of cyberspace as complementing existing forms of face-to-face gathering rather than an alternative space for gathering. The Global Day of Rage hashtag on *Twitter* and *Facebook* triggered a response from a worldwide queer community of activists, across 32 cities around the world. Similarly, in the case of Saini, a picture that was intended to show his solidarity for the Global Day of Rage movement went viral and the ensuing debate surrounding it developed new kinship structures of support for Saini and the anti-Section 377 movement in India. These social movements have developed in the absence of any formal organisational structures, aided by new media technologies.

One of the criticisms against social media activism has been to see it as 'armchair revolution' that overlooks physical participation. While several studies, including Gerbaudo's (2012) work on the role of *Twitter* in the Arab Spring revolution, are already out there to dismantle this notion, the two examples I provide in this section demonstrate the corporeal nature of online activism. Dissidence on cyberspace here was followed by 'bodily' collective global action. For social movements that are led by actors scattered across the globe, the availability of technological devices and spaces facilitates rapid assembly and deliver action. However, as Gournelos and Gunkel (2012: 2) argue in their book *Transgression 2.0*, one ought not to think of digital media as merely making it easier to organise but rather view it as a double-edged sword, one that is used to organise and circulate discussions and protest outside the immediate city (or place) involved in it, but at the same time it also signals the new era of surveillance and censorship and the foreclosure of discourse.

## Conclusion

The year 2014 is a defining moment for queer politics in India. The judgement followed the earlier High Court judgement which through 'reading down' of Section 377 also made queer people the subject of rights. The positive recognition of queer people by the law has also been accompanied by broader acceptance of queer people in public culture, as numerous media stories testify. As this chapter has evidenced, it also marks a significant emphasis on the role of new media in structuring and critiquing the nature of queer politics in India. As Narrain and Gupta (2011: xi) eloquently note, 'even though the Naz decision effectively only decriminalise[d] sodomy, at its heart it is about positive recognition of the right to love'.

Dave (2012: 161) has argued that within a democratic system certain forms of political speech are rendered intelligible while other forms are rendered silent. In this chapter, I have discussed a range of dissident actors who offer a discursive voice to the public emergence of the queer citizen in India, ranging from political articulations of Indianness to dissident activism. Narrain and Bhan (2005: 2) question how a queer language can describe India, given that the idea of an inclusive and tolerant nation continues to be challenged by brutalities in maintaining a 'pure' caste, class, religion and so on. In fact, recent events such as the rape of Jyoti Singh in Delhi (Sen, 2013), atrocities against the African population in India (Buncombe, 2014) and the swing to the right in the political polls signal this rupture.

As I have explained in this chapter, the real danger of Section 377 lies in the fact that it exists beyond the pages of the law, permeating social lives, media representations and popular discourse. Incidents such as TV9 become a rallying point for the queer community to act. The emergence of a vocal queer voice is also present in the widened nature of the movement, as evidenced by the Global Day of Rage across the world. New media and the Internet offer queer people the opportunity to construct a public identity and to speak to a public, offering a sense of democracy. Queer people in India are engaged in creating a citizenry that challenges the power of heteronormativity. I have also argued about the ways in which dissident citizenship takes the form of counterpublic (Fraser, 2008), allowing subordinate social groups such as the queer community to regroup and circulate counter-discourses. The lives of queer people in India as dissident citizens lie at the core of this chapter. As this chapter has argued, dissenting practices take many forms and shape – from discursive and performative to organisational and everyday dissent. Identity politics gets convoluted when dissident sexualities are placed within the discourse of the nation state. The emergence and validation of queer identities encourage us to examine the impact of class, gender and sexuality on democratic participation in India. In the era of new media, the proliferation of dissent on the Internet, as my two case studies have demonstrated, becomes iconic emblems of oppositional politics. This marks a shift in democratic politics and social movements, where Web 2.0 technologies are being harnessed to increase the visibility of such movements and choreograph oppositional politics.

In conclusion, I would like to signpost the most important contributions that this chapter makes towards extending the discourse on the public sphere and dissident citizenship. First, both case studies can be thought of as collective action that takes the form of a counterpublic. While Fraser (2008) theorises it as primarily political, my case studies have demonstrated that it is both political and inclusive of the cultural. Second, this chapter has challenged the outsider status that is afforded to queer people in India in relation to nation building and democracy, and finally by stepping beyond geographical borders, it has also demonstrated the transnational nature of queer activism and politics in India. Third, both case studies demonstrate that the online element of queer activism needs to be seen in the context of other offline activities that is being carried out. As Banaji and Buckingham (2013: 118) explain, the online and offline elements of politics and activism need to be seen not as separate or opposed but 'rather as parts of a symbiotic whole'. Both case studies, I have discussed in this chapter, demonstrate the ways in which queer citizens in India are dissenting through creative practices aided through digital technology and social media and creating new public spheres for collective action and debates. It represents an important advance for queer groups to use digital media technologies to build counter-hegemonic political projects and demonstrates the agency of queer publics in India to control the terms of their political and social representation.

## Notes

1 This act includes queer women and heterosexuals who are engaged in non-reproductive forms of sex, but as scholars such as Dave (2012) have articulated and a point I myself advance in this book, this has been used to generate a powerful structure where it is used to blackmail and terrorise all queer-identified individuals.

2 Partha Chatterjee defines civil society as elite construct, which includes all social institutions outside the strict domain of the State and considers the political society as a more appropriate way of reflecting on the politics and engagement of the modern world (2004: 39). Democratic politics involves this constant shift between compromising values of modernity and the moral assertions of popular demands. The civil society is restricted to only a few, and, according to Chatterjee, it needs to work alongside the political society for any legitimate change to take place.

3 The movement to repeal Section 377 was started by Naz Foundation India, a non-governmental organisation that works on programmes related to HIV/AIDS advocacy, sexual health, sexuality and related areas.

4 Since its construction in the early 1800s, Trafalgar Square has been an important landmark within British sociocultural history. Rallies and demonstrations are frequently organised at the Square, including the annual Pride Parade March which significantly culminates into a day of celebration at the Square. The Mayor supports this democratic tradition and allows the square to be used for these purposes. See the official London government website for more details: http://www.london.gov.uk/priorities/arts-culture/trafalgar-square/history. Accessed on 5 July 2015.

5 These two status messages are from 10 December 2013. The image/meme has been around since 2009.

6 All three comments are from *Facebook* status messages on 11 December 2013.

7 Ibid.; p. 77.

8 All Telegu translations of the show are available from Gasysi. Available at: http://gaysifamily.com/wp-content/uploads/2011/02/TV9_Gay_Cul ture_Hyd_nonames.pdf. Accessed on 24 December 2013.

9 Gaysi is a short form of Gay Desi.

10 Bandyopadhyay posted a copy of the notice on his *Facebook* page (23 February 2011) that was widely distributed.

11 This was broadcast in May 2011. A video can be viewed here: <https://www.youtube.com/watch?v=q_8JSQkQksQ>. Accessed on 2 February 2015.

12 Show cause notice or show cause order requires a party/individual to appear before the court to explain why a certain course of action should not be taken against it.

13 This is available on the order issued by NBSA to TV9 Hyderabad. A copy of this was asked to be made available to all viewers who had complained and

the Minister of Information and Broadcasting. A copy can be viewed here: http://www.nbanewdelhi.com/images/Upload/tv9.pdf.

14 A video of the apology can be viewed here: <http://www.youtube.com/watch?v=nC6Sf9X4-uI>.

15 It is beyond the scope of this book to look at these critical responses in detail. A useful resource would be http://www.gaysifamily.com.

16 *Naz Foundation v. Government of NCT of Delhi and Others*, 2 July 2009, WP(C)7455/2001, p. 105, Section 132.

17 The IGLHRC reported that 'Indian activists are praising this decision as a symbol of tacit support for decriminalization in this landmark case'.

18 This is available from *Notes of Proceedings in Suresh Kumar Kaushal v. Naz Foundation* 23 February to 27 March 2012; Supreme Court of India; p. 76.

19 The worldwide page can be accessed here: https://www.facebook.com/events/1374294672825321/.

# Conclusion
## Pleasures and politics of researching new queer media

This book makes a number of significant interventions within queer and digital media scholarship on India. In Chapters 1 and 2, I set out to sketch a social and media history of queer expressions in India. As I argued in Chapter 1, the queer history of India that can be traced far back to the pre-medieval period and colonialism (more specifically, during the Victorian period) can be seen as a starting point for homophobia in the subcontinent. This dismantles the colonial view of homosexuality as an 'oriental vice' and the postcolonial view of homosexuality being a 'Western import'. In Chapter 2, I discussed the evolution of Indian media. The liberalisation period can be traced to 1991, which marked a transition from a state monopoly to an era of cosmopolitan internationalism, when queer-related media started to be circulated, but it is in the last decade that media and especially new media have firmly pushed the figure of the queer person into public consciousness.

In Chapter 3, which is the first analysis chapter of the book, I have explored the concept of virtual intimacies on digital space and the various ways in which queer men in India articulate this. This chapter also introduced the concept of phatic forms of communication that are ephemeral in nature but have deeply embedded forms of meaning. It demonstrates the importance of ambivalent gestures and the promise of digital technology in mediating queer intimacies in India. This chapter also argued that intimacy is another way to explore queer male subjectivity in India beyond the legal and national framework where queer politics is currently situated.

Chapter 4 took an intersectional lens to interrogate and critique online queer 'communities'. As I argued in this chapter, the community discourse is extremely limiting when studying Indian queer communities. Class, which is an intrinsic part of South Asian communities, also plays an important role in the segregationary politics of these groups. The chapter further challenged the primacy of a singular queer subjectivity by linking issues of class difference with language. On a theoretical level, this chapter engaged with and extended the scope of subaltern theory. The subaltern school in India has left out sexual minorities from its discourse. By bringing them in, I am also offering a lens by which subaltern studies might be used within queer scholarship.

Chapter 5 extended the critique of 'community' that I began in Chapter 4, by shifting the focus to effeminacy and homonormativity. As I argued in this chapter, contemporary queer politics in India is aligning itself with global queer homonormativity. In doing so, it systematically discriminates against gender non-conforming bodies and the ways in which sites such as *PlanetRomeo* contribute towards perpetuating this behaviour. The masculine gay man as the accepted and desired form of queer male sexuality is catalysed through platforms such as *PlanetRomeo* and *Grindr*.

Finally, in Chapter 6, I interrogated the concept of dissident citizenship and what that means for queer citizens in India. Through two case studies, I have shown the ways in which new media technologies mediate and choreograph new forms of dissent. By creating and sustaining a public space, the Internet allows diverse forms of debates and dissent to take place.

The Internet, as this book has explored, is used in various ways by queer males in India – for purposes of intimacy, support and social networking as well as offering new opportunities for political and social actions, thus forming a new kind of digital public sphere. The Indian queer male community has only recently started to mediate their lives through the digital medium, unlike the West. However, the history of digital networking and development in India almost parallels the growth of new queer media. The use of the early listservs to the proliferation of mobile apps such as *Grindr* tells a story about the 'virtual' lives of queer men in India. While contemporary Indian society continues to normalise and privilege heteronormativity/heteropatriarchy, there have been subtle changes both on the social and political level which has led to improvements in civil rights of queer people. The historic judgement of 2 July 2009, when the Delhi High Court proudly struck off the antiquated Section 377, thus decriminalising homosexuality, remains a milestone in the narrative of queer India. While legal and social recognition are entirely different, it cannot be discounted that the 2009 judgement had an impact on the ways in which gay/queer men in India have renegotiated their lifestyles. The growth of queer parties and social spaces, as I argued in Chapter 5 on PKP, and the burgeoning of queer representation in Indian cinema and television (Datta, Bakshi and Dasgupta, 2015; Dudrah, 2012) are cases in point.

A simplistic linear explanation of the birth of the cyberqueer in India would be to attribute it to globalisation and economic liberalisation in the 1990s, followed by media representations of queer men leading to queer consciousness and backlash, then queer activism and finally the move to the digital sphere. While this might seem the most logical explanation, it does not succinctly capture the nuances and circumstances, which led to its mass proliferation.

The virtual lives of Indian queer men, as this book has outlined, are not so much to do with their negotiation with digital technologies; rather it is more productive to see the ways in which digital technologies have been used to navigate a mainstream heterosexual/patriarchal society. As Ahmed (2004) writes, inhabiting and leading queer lives is a matter of everyday negotiation:

> This is not about the romance of being off line or the joy of radical politics (though it can be), but rather the everyday work of dealing with the perception of others, with the 'straightening devices' and the violence that might follow when such perceptions congeal into social forms.
>
> (2004: 107)

The public visibility of the queer community in India has indeed grown exponentially in the last decade, with queer pride marches in almost all the major metros (Bangalore, New Delhi, Mumbai and Kolkata) and smaller cities such as Bhubaneshwar and Madurai. This, however, should not be seen as some form of tacit endorsement/acceptance. It is important to also remember that queer struggles in India are far from being intersectional. Issues such as class and caste are especially compelling within the 'Indian context'. As Narrain and Bhan (2005: 15) remark in their landmark anthology *Because I Have a Voice*:

> Perhaps the most relentless construct which assaults queer people is the conceptualisation of their lives as the preoccupations of a small, Western educated, and elite minority, whose understanding of sexuality is thus aped from the West.

While the West certainly informs certain aspects of the discourses on sexuality, being queer in India is also constituted within local discourses that go beyond the Western framework of identity – *kothi, hijra, laundas* and others. During the course of this fieldwork, I was also introduced to several other examples that have gained currency within digital and local contexts (terms such as 'gayboy', *meyelichele* and *rituparno*).

When I started this book, I was extremely optimistic about the non-exclusionary politics that queer spaces online would afford its users, but was far from surprised to see the same hierarchies and exclusionary mechanisms had been carried over from their physical counterpart. Queer spaces in India suffer from several biases and segregation politics that reflect the gendered and classed nature of Indian society. *Kothis* are largely missing from the Internet discourse, both because of language constraints and the urban and class bias that these spaces underscore.

The various examples of queer digital culture that this book has explored are the various responses from the community to the societal and cultural reactions. Whether they are queering mainstream spaces like *Facebook*, establishing user profiles on *PlanetRomeo*, accessing *Grindr* from their family room or using these spaces to mobilise people into going on protests, the users of digital culture are taking part in the process of visibility and representational politics. The issue that undergirds all of this is kinship. As I have explained in Chapter 3, kinship refers to a form of lived relationality. As Freeman (2007) argues, kinship matters to non-heterosexual people who might not fit the dyadic model of family structures so prevalent within heteronormative societies, whose emotional, financial and domestic patterns exceed the patterns dictated by marriage and reproduction. In a gay/queer digital culture that is so preoccupied with sex, kinship might seem rather out of place, especially following Bersani's (1988) line of argument that sex defamiliarises and estranges ultimately and does not lead to any form of meaningful exchange between the two subjects. I have suggested that this line of argument – that sex negates any social value and does not provide a form of community and kinship – is unfounded. This was something that the majority of my research participants critiqued. They were very positive about ways in which intimate encounters (of sexual and non-sexual nature) opened up a larger kinship and friendship network.

It would also not be wrong to acknowledge that my own class position as well as the marker of having an English education and studying abroad may have facilitated my entry into the lives of some of my research participants. Through a form of queer Indian male kinship, I was recognised as 'one of them'. Indeed, by connecting into these social networks by virtue of a shared kinship, I was able to gain insights and develop the research in ways that I had not envisioned.

In one sense, these kinds of kinship networks not only challenge the hierarchies of heterosexual kinships, but they are also entrenched in a very segregated and exclusionary politics. In fact, I had to constantly move between the different registers of kinship recognition, when I worked with participants I had recruited through NGO contacts and those I had met through friends and digital sites. I was aware of my metropolitan location in terms of class, linguistic and economic privilege, and I cannot discount that this might have also been a deterrent to other potential research participants from taking part in this project.

The virtual queer populace, as this book has gone on to demonstrate, is quite homogeneous in terms of class, economic background, gendered identity and politics, but there is also a growing number of spaces that have opened up to those in the 'margins of the margin'. My institutional location and academic privilege opened up several doors for me, and I was able to seamlessly chat online and interview people from most backgrounds.

As a politically engaged and activist/community-centred academic, I believe that it is imperative I should be engaged with 'participatory research' and collaborative community-based knowledge. One of my prime goals is also communicating this knowledge back to the community and participants I have worked with in ways they can understand. I would not wish to be accused of creating the same hierarchical structures with my own knowledge dissemination that I have been critiquing throughout this book. In fact, during the course of my research, the two publications that arose directly from it was circulated amongst my kinship/friendship networks, discussed at meetings and on Skype and led to engaged critique between the community/NGO members and myself.

In this conclusion, I wish to register some of these issues that have been at the core of my thinking process during my ethnography and questions that were posed to me by my research participants. Rik, for example, questioned me:

> What good will this research do for the community? Are you going to come up with a set of recommendations or toolkit?

Unlike other social science projects that develop a tool kit and a set of recommendations for users (I was a part of one such project very recently; Mowlabocus et al., 2014), this book can make no such legitimate claims. Through engaging with issues of social significance and within the academic production of knowledge as capital, I have tried to provide a narrative of a community and space that I have been a part of, which has been an integral part of my life and informed my subjectivity. I would also like to take this opportunity to not self-aggrandise community-based research as the only legitimate form of ethical research. In fact, as Spivak (1999) has pointed out, this sense of continuity is often dangerous from the position of the postcolonial academic as the native informant. However, community-based research is the approach that has worked for me in the context of this project.

I have attempted in this book to avoid a totalising narrative. This approach has been critiqued in the past and has the potential for creating problematic divisions. Using words like 'queer'/'gay community' has also been a problem from the very start. As I explain in Chapters 4 and 5, the political, gendered, classed and cultural tensions that exist and operate within the gay/queer male categories is an important area of concern, as any homogenising project would run the risk of being exclusionary.

The locations of the majority of my research participants have been the urban metropolitan cities of New Delhi and Kolkata. I am conscious that a similar project carried out with a range of queer identities and in other peri-urban locations would reveal different findings. While this book did not have the scope for this, this is an area that I will be looking to develop in the coming years. The focus on the urban groupings, as I mentioned before, has to do with my own social positioning as well as the recruitment of participants through the snowballing technique during this project. Queer digital culture is located within the urban space with peripheral influence in the suburban locations. While there has been some work done on the use of mobile telephones for health advocacy amongst trans* communities (Ganesh, 2010), this is not an area I have explored in this book. Framing the discourse of queer identities in India through health and sexual health narrative is an institutional necessity at times, constrained by funding politics (Boyce, 2014). I hoped to move beyond that with this book.

Since I began writing the book, there have been some significant changes in queer politics in India. I began my research in 2011, two years since the decriminalisation of homosexuality in India. This has now been reinstated by a Supreme Court decision and the country elected a new (right-wing) government in 2014. The ruling party has at the very outset made it clear that they would not support the decriminalisation of homosexuality and their major win signals a shift toward the right, practicing what Baccheta (1999: 144) calls 'the dual operations of xenophobic queerphobia and queerphobic xenophobia'. Within xenophobic queerphobia, being gay or queer is positioned as being non-Indian – it is a marked as a Western import and something against Indian culture. Within queerphobic xenophobia – 'queerdom is assigned (often metaphorically) to all designated others of the nation, regardless of their sexual identity' (1999: 144).

It is indeed a complicated time for queer male citizens in India. After seven years since decriminalisation, they have been criminalised again and many have been pushed back into their closets. Victories such as the TV9 sting operation, which I discussed in Chapter 6 and which paved the way for similar confrontations, are now likely to cease. The potential for digital sites to enable and support a global/transnational movement of activism can be seen in the recent Syrian conflict, the images that came from Egypt during the Tahrir Square demonstrations (Gerbaudo, 2012) and closer to home, the planning and execution of the Global Day of Rage against the Supreme Court's decision, which I discussed in Chapter 6. The role of the digital in dissident politics has shown a remarkable growth and it is an area that will benefit from further research in the future. Protests have been integral to the recognition of queer people as legitimate citizens and equal human beings. The resonances of the Stonewall protest on 29 June 1969 found its presence in India on 29 June 2003, when Kolkata organised one of the first Pride marches in India (Narrain and Gupta, 2011: xxvii). Significantly, the first queer pride in Mumbai (called Queer *Azaadi* March) took place on 16 August 2008, a day after the Independence Day of India, to specifically highlight how the queer communities still lacked complete freedom. Protests have been a part of the social fabric in India with its colonial past and postcolonial legacy. The frequency of violence against the queer communities have relied not only on the legal structures that criminalise queerness through antiquated laws such as Section 377, but also those that invisibilise queer people through social and cultural strictures that does not allow access to civil rights. Queer individuals are after all absent from the rights and benefits bestowed upon a citizen by the state.

In addition to the political and activist potential of online spaces, the possibilities of intimacies cannot be discounted. McGlotten (2013) argues about the 'Janus faced' effect of digital culture in intimate encounters. While on one level it has expanded areas of sexual encounters, it has also foreclosed the possibility of unpredictable desire. Practices such as cruising and anonymous sex still exist, but erotic intimacies facilitated by digital spaces have grown in urban and some suburban locations such as Barrackpore, Barasat and Chandannagore, Malda in West Bengal alone (if the statistics of users available from these locations on *PlanetRomeo* are taken into account). Of course, particularities such as class, language and gender identification have an impact on the possibilities that digital space offers, as I have discussed in Chapters 4 and 5 in particular. As Mowlabocus (2010a: 211) contends, 'digital media provides the means for the marginalised to form new, meaningful discourses of the self and forge alternative queer experiences'. By locating my research within the ostensible spaces of queer male digital culture, I have been able to explore and critique a space that has been under-represented within the growing literature on queer identities in India. I am also aware that by focussing my research on digital culture alone, there is bound to be criticism on the narrow focus of my exploratory field. However, as discussed in my introduction as well as in Chapters 1 and 2, queer male digital culture is not limited to the online experience alone, but rather it is a negotiation and flow of information from online/offline spaces. In fact, not all the spaces I have looked at can also be termed as urban specific, with many spaces being accessed and used by users from a range of urban and peri-urban locations. In the course of looking at some of these spaces, I have also engaged with peri-urban and transnational spaces in Chapters 3, 5 and 6.

While I do not accept the 'Internet as a queer utopia' argument, the sense of freedom that it has afforded some people – to live a life unconstrained – is worthy of exploration. The freedom to script one's desires and put these into practice is widely accepted in these spaces. Freedom for one does not necessarily mean freedom for another, as my chapters on imagined queer communities (Chapter 4) and effeminophobia (Chapter 5) have demonstrated. The queer utopia can only exist when freedom for one spells freedom for everyone. While this is an idealistic argument, it also has the potential for changing attitudes and positions. Citing Narrain and Gupta (2011: xxv) again, I would like to point out that focussing on the rights of *hijras*, *kothis* and other trans* and lower class/lower middle class people also 'opens up queer politics to the issues of class and economic disparities that form a central division in Indian society'.

The book's aim was to articulate a contemporary moment in India's queer history by researching digital culture, and examining issues of class, gender, dissidence, activism and community. I hope that the book has successfully managed to go beyond the online/offline binary and encompass the online aspect as a central part of the queer male experience in India. Additionally, I hope that my work on this project will not just feed into the growing academic literature on queer identities, digital culture and South Asian studies, but will also be rendered intelligible to realms beyond academia.

# Appendix 1
## Research participants

List of research participants cited in this book and dates of interviews are as follows. Interviews were conducted both online and offline. Even though 25 face-to-face interviews were conducted, not all have been used in this book.

| Name of research participant | Date | Place |
| --- | --- | --- |
| a-kshays | 23 October 2013 | Location Unknown (online) |
| Amit | 22 December 2012 | Kolkata (offline) |
| | 30 July 2013 | Kolkata (offline) |
| Haider | 6 July 2013 | New Delhi (offline) |
| | 7 July 2013 | New Delhi (offline) |
| Jasjit | 13 August 2013 | Kolkata (offline) |
| Johhnyred | 27 December 2011 | Location Unknown (online) |
| Mayank | 28 December 2013 | New Delhi (offline) |
| Mohit | 15 December 2013 | London (offline) |
| | 18 December 2013 | London (offline) |
| Muscle_ind | 15 November 2012 | Location Unknown (online) |
| Neel | 15 July 2013 | Barasat (offline) |
| Nitin | 5 July 2013 | New Delhi (offline) |
| Pawan | 11 July 2013 | Kolkata (offline) |
| | 23 August 2013 | Kolkata (offline) |
| Rahul | 09 December 2012 | Kolkata (offline) |
| | 03 January 2013 | Kolkata (offline) |
| | 20 July 2013 | Kolkata (offline) |
| Raj | 14 December 2012 | Kolkata (offline) |
| | 17 December 2012 | Kolkata (offline) |
| Rajeev | 12 August 2013 | Kolkata (offline) |
| Rishabh | 3 August 2013 | Kolkata (offline) |
| Rishik | 21 July 2013 | Barasat (offline) |

(*Continued*)

(Continued)

| Name of research participant | Date | Place |
|---|---|---|
| Rik | 22 July 2013 | New Delhi (online) |
| Rudranil | 23 July 2013 | Kolkata (offline) |
| Ruhin | 15 December 2012 | Kolkata (offline) |
| Sumit | 23 February 2013 | Kolkata (offline) |
| | 22 June 2013 | Kolkata (offline) |
| Tarun | 3 January 2012 | New Delhi (online) |
| | 8 July 2012 | New Delhi (offline) |
| | 5 June 2013 | New Delhi (online) |

# Appendix 2
## Research methods

In this appendix, I have elaborated on my research methods and the ethical framework that structured my research process. It is hoped that this framework will be found useful for other researchers who are attempting similar research projects.

## Introduction

Digital culture and queer studies are situated at the crossroads of several disciplines, and there is no single research method or schema to study these research areas. The broad aim of this research was to generate in-depth qualitative insights into the role of digital culture in queer men's lives in India. In trying to understand the ways in which queer men in India negotiate their identities in digital spaces and the ways in which such spaces challenge the status quo of Indian nationalism, I needed to gather data which would allow me to analyse a wide range of issues such as virtual intimacies (Chapter 3), community and class (Chapter 4), masculinity and effeminophobia (Chapter 5) and dissident citizenship (Chapter 6).

The three key digital sites *Facebook, PlanetRomeo* and *Grindr* were identified in the initial planning stage of this research project. I concur with Edwards (2010: 161) when she notes that 'online conversations are an important source of knowledge, given the frequency with which individuals participate and given the direction these conversations take'. The sites chosen for this study developed out of my own background of being a user and the pilot study where my research participants discussed some of these sites, together with information gathered through observing community groups and informal conversations with friends and research participants in New Delhi and Kolkata. One of the primary reasons amongst many for choosing these is the frequency of their use by Indian queer men, although no substantial data exists on the exact number of Indian users.

It should be noted that my methodological approaches were motivated by very practical concerns over the safety and comfort of my research participants.

## Sampling: stigma, safety and difference

As it is difficult to reach queer men across a range of social classes in India, I had to use a variety of approaches to recruit participants for this research. One of the main methods I used was 'snowball sampling'. This technique uses a chain referral system, whereby after identifying an initial subject, the researcher asks him/her to help identify other participants and disseminate information about the research. This method has been used successfully in the past by researchers working with queer communities (Atkinson and Flint, 2001; Rumens, 2011). I also 'lurked' (Mowlabocus, 2010a: 121) on these sites, observing conversations and debates without actually taking part. As a member of these communities, the participants were aware of my presence on the site.

Initially, I set up a *Facebook* page advertising my interest in recruiting queer men from India to participate in a study on the role of digital culture in the lives of queer Indian men. I sent out invitations to my friends, and then requested them to send the information out to their friends and acquaintances on *Facebook*. Hine (2000: 20) has pointed out that 'establishing oneself as a bona fide researcher is not automatic'. Thus, a key part of establishing myself was making my institutional affiliation public. At the same time, I also asked my friends to 'validate' my intentions by sharing my profile with their friends and network, and in turn asking them to invite others who would be interested to take part in this project. While *Facebook* proved immensely helpful with many participants expressing a desire to be interviewed, it also posed certain problems. At the very outset, I decided to eliminate participants with whom I have a personal connection, fearing personal biases. However, as some of my participants over the course of research became part of my friendship and kinship network, I realised that this would not necessarily be possible. Instead, borrowing the concept of bracketing (Campbell, 2004) through which a researcher's knowledge about an experience is set aside, I continued to work with these research participants. Bracketing also required me to be open about my role as a researcher (or if I was talking only as a friend or community member). It was important to make this distinction, so that my data was not skewed and to ensure that I was not using data that was revealed to me in the confidentiality bestowed upon friends. In situations where a bond of friendship developed, I avoided using revelations that were made during our conversations outside more formal interviews.

My personal connections also catered to a certain urban demographic, which was not fully encompassing of the diversity of participants that I hoped to reach. In addition to using *Facebook*, I also got in touch with several personal contacts in different community organisations that serve the queer community in India (PKP, *People Like Us* and *SAATHII*) with whom I had already established a working relationship (Dasgupta, 2012). These organisations were helpful in disseminating information about this study to their members and partner organisations in the suburbs. Some potential participants appear to have subsequently found this form of recruitment safe, as it allayed their fears about safety knowing that I was connected to a community organisation. A third group of people I recruited was through *PlanetRomeo*. I created a profile on the website, clearly stating my intention of wanting to recruit participants for my study and to follow the discussion forums. Many of these participants found it easier to share intimate details with me without fear of subsequent public revelation of their identities. As one participant during the interview process pointed out:

> Physical proximity to someone I don't know, especially when it involves, giving them personal details about myself, is very uncomfortable for me. I don't know you and why should I even trust you. There have been many recent cases where men have been trapped by journalists, police and other miscreants and then blackmailed. I think I will be more comfortable talking to you online than in person. I am sorry but I am just very careful about these things, especially since my parents don't know and I am not in any position to support myself if thrown out.
>
> (Tarun, 3 January 2012)

Participants were recruited from a range of ages between 18 and 40, with most men falling between the age range 22 and 28. Jones and Pugh (2005: 257) argue that 'research on gay sexuality in general, ignores older people, and research on older people largely ignores sexuality'. This was apparent in the age range of my participants. However, there are several reasons for this. Few middle-aged Indian men use the Internet. Sixty per cent of the users in the BRICI countries (Brazil, Russia, India, China, Indonesia) are below 35. The Internet and Mobile Association of India have reported that in India 75 per cent of the users are between the ages of 15 and 34 (see Figure A1.1). Thus, there is an age bias amongst Indians using the Internet and this had an effect on the participant age group for this research.

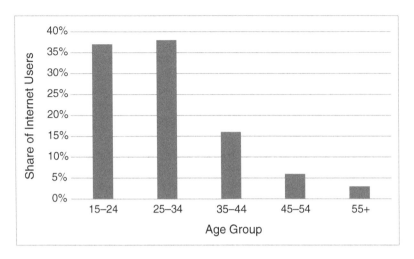

*Figure A1.1* Age groups of Internet users in India

Another factor in my recruitment process was to make sure that participants were actively recruited from all social classes. This decision was based on the premise that sexual and gender identities cannot be studied without addressing the issues of religion, class and caste, especially in the context of India. Borrowing from Crenshaw (1989), who first put forward the notion of intersectionality, I have actively taken an intersectional position in both my recruitment process and in addressing the various issues that this research examines. I was also actively recruiting people with help from the community organisations who work with the queer community in peri-urban and rural areas.

The first round of interviews, which formed a pilot study, was conducted between December 2012 and January 2013, with five participants in Kolkata, India. A second round of interviews followed in 2013, with 20 participants from New Delhi and Barasat. To make sure that there was a well-represented balance of participants, recruitment was carried out in West Bengal (Kolkata and Barasat) and New Delhi. I consciously decided not to include Mumbai in this study, despite a well-documented queer history of the city, as there is already a significant study conducted on the digital lives of Mumbai's queer community (Shahani, 2008). These locations were also chosen in an attempt to be as rich and diverse as possible in terms of recruiting participants of different backgrounds with respect to age, class and linguistic difference.

## Interviewing process: online/offline

In order to find out about queer men's interactions with digital media technologies in India, I conducted semi-structured interviews because these would allow for the exploration of a topic in flexible and adaptive ways. Participants were briefed about the interview and the project prior to carrying out the interview, so they were aware of the basic themes on which questions would be asked. However, because of the structure of this form of interview, it allowed participants to steer the conversation to topics that they wanted to discuss.

The semi-structured interview format allowed my participants to talk broadly about their experiences of using digital media as queer men living in India. The interview questions were open ended and focussed on a number of themes relevant to this research. The themes varied broadly, including (1) being queer in India, (2) the role of family and friends in shaping queer identities, (3) participation in digital queer spaces, (4) expressing queer identities both online and offline and (5) balancing queer identities with other aspects of one's identity (ethnicity, nationality, class).

Prior to each interview, participants received an information sheet that explained the aims and purposes of the research as well as the research procedure, including their involvement. It also covered the ways in which their identity and the information they provide would be protected through standard procedures with regard to confidentiality and anonymity. Participants were also given information on the data protection and storage protocols, and the proposed strategies for dissemination and representation. They were given time to consider their participation and to ask questions or express concerns before completing the informed consent form and taking part in the research (if they chose to do so). Participants were made aware that they could withdraw from the study at any time without consequence. Some participants were anxious that people might be able to identify them through their online 'profile names'. They were assured that all profile names would be changed and that participants would be anonymised by assigning new profile names for the purposes of this research. Additionally, participants were informed that photographs or textual material that directly identified the participants would only be used with their consent, and only those parts of the profile (text and visual) would be used for which permission had been explicitly given. All interviews were recorded and transcribed for qualitative analysis by myself for the purposes of this project.

Some participants indicated that they would prefer to be interviewed online. The interviews conducted online took place through email, Instant Messaging and video/voice conferencing (Skype). In all instances, the participants were made aware that their conversations were being recorded (electronically and textually) and retained as data for the purposes of this project, and any texts that revealed the participant's identity were removed prior to being used.

As I have mentioned in this book, language is intrinsically linked to the class identities of many participants. Thus, language was also a crucial aspect of this research, as some of the participants were not very conversant in English. The interviews in Kolkata were conducted in English and Bengali, while those in Barasat were conducted primarily in Bengali. The interviews conducted in New Delhi were in English and Hindi. In terms of economic and linguistic ability, Internet usage in India correlates strongly with the ability to speak English (Haseloff, 2005). Where the participant had chosen to speak in Hindi or Bengali, I made translations of the interview from which excerpts were then selected for analysis.

Using online methods of data collection, interviews were also conducted through electronic media (emails, Instant Messaging, group chat, listservs and telephone). These online methods have in no way been detrimental to my research, but rather they complemented it. In doing this, I am in agreement with Shahani (2008: 138), who has remarked, 'I am merely collecting data from the group using the same device they use in their regular interaction.' Hine (2000: 14) points out that early researchers held the belief that 'computers could not support the same richness of communication offered by face to face to face situations'. She further argues:

When we move from face to face interaction to electronically mediated contact, the possibilities for informants to fool the ethnographer seems to multiply. Identity play is acknowledged almost as a norm in online settings.

(2000: 22)

Hine's comment made in 2000 would seem out of date today, considering the long way that we have come in terms of both hardware and software. In fact, I found the online interviews as rich as the offline interviews. Ethnographers such as Barton (2011) demonstrate the strength of total immersion in the culture being studied. Since the field of this research is online cultures, it made complete sense to conduct my ethnography online. Hine (2000) has questioned whether interactions in electronic space can be viewed as authentic, since the ethnographer cannot readily confirm the details face to face. I argue that the identity performance seen in cyberspace might be vastly different from those in offline settings, and this 'online role playing' is crucial for marginalised queer youth (Driver, 2005). Driver asserts in her research on representations in queer youth home pages that online representations of queer youth provide crucial insights into the variety of ways in which they assert their identity. She argues that online spaces inhabited by queer youth:

> provide insight into new forms of representing the self that exceed institutional categorizations. It is because these homepages actively reach beyond the controlling gaze of parental, psychiatric, and educational authorities as well as the ridicule of peer scrutiny and shame, that queer youth risk taboo subjects and build their own queer cultural spaces and identifications.
>
> (2005: 113)

I, therefore, consider online ethnography as strength rather than a limitation of this research. A number of researchers have also questioned the appropriateness of the Internet for asking personal questions about intimate sexual activities or sexual behaviour. Sanders (2005), for example, details that in her research on female sex workers, she found that the Internet did not foster sufficient rapport for her to start asking her participants about their sexual activity. I recognised this limitation; however, my interviews, despite having sexuality as an overarching theme, had very little engagement with the participant's actual sexual life (unless the participant wanted to talk about it, without any prompts from myself). In fact, I found my online/offline interviews offered the same level of richness in detail that I was seeking for this study.

### Ethical concerns

The ethics of online ethnography is problematic and there has been considerable amount of debate around it. I would like to particularly point to the work by scholars such as Bassett and O'Riordan (2002) and Zimmer's (2010) on the ethics of online research that I used in developing my own research methodology.

Bassett and O'Riordan (2002) and Zimmer (2010) acknowledge that evidence of harm to individuals resulting from virtual research necessitates the need for a code of ethics similar to that used for human subjects in the offline world. They also caution that such ethical considerations should not be used uncritically. Bassett and O'Riordan further state:

> The Internet user is also entitled to a degree of representation and publication in the public domain. If an individual or group has chosen to use Internet media to publish their opinions, the researcher needs to consider their decision to the same degree that they would to a similar publication in a traditional print media.
>
> (2002: 244)

In agreement with Bassett and O'Riordan, I believe that researchers need to create ethical frameworks in relation to specific communities and groups. While journalists use social media updates freely available on the Internet for their research, I agree that the identities of research participants needed to be protected, and because something is online does not mean it should be used indiscriminately. I encoded all data collected immediately to protect the privacy of my participants. Whereas in a space like *PlanetRomeo* the overwhelming majority of users use 'self-created' usernames that make their 'real' identities unidentifiable, people tend to use their 'real' names on *Facebook*. Zimmer discusses a study that was conducted at Harvard on *Facebook*, which brought up several ethical issues on carrying out research on *Facebook*. The data collected by the researchers was used without consent from the individuals whose profiles provided the data. The researchers did not find this unproblematic, since the 'information was already on *Facebook*' (2010: 323). However, Zimmer notes that as researchers we need to 'recognis[e] that just because personal information is made available in some fashion on a social network, [it] does not mean it is fair game for capture and release to all' (2010: 323).

### Researcher's position

Disclosing my own position as an Indian queer man was an important way in which I was able to mobilise confidence amongst the research participants, allowing them to share their stories with me. Many participants said that they felt more comfortable talking to another queer man about sex and sexuality issues, an observation also made by other researchers (Weeks, Heaphy and Donovan, 2001). However, Rumens also notes that 'disclosing sexual identity is not a license to accessing deeper insights into others experiences' (2011: 169). Being an 'insider' and doing research on my own community has its advantages. Jones (1995: 60) observes that such a researcher knows the language, has grown up in the culture and has little difficulty in becoming involved with the people. He also states that 'the native anthropologist should be one who looks at social phenomena from a point of view different from that of the traditional anthropologist'.

The fact that I had declared my intentions and interests at the outset of each interview means that I cannot claim or pretend a distance from the topic in question. My insider/outsider status meant that while I might not be aware of everything that was taking place within the community, my presence within it would not be problematic for my research participants. I was interwoven into the research process from the beginning, in terms of my broad South Asian and queer identity. When I began this research, I was also concerned about my personal attachment to the subject. As a queer man growing up in India, I was already aware of the ways in which digital culture was being used by queer men for meeting up or for soliciting sex. Thus, it could be argued that there was an emotional aspect to my research. Dudrah, writing about his own position as a researcher, says:

> Researchers many times may find themselves struggling to maintain emotional neutrality. Neutrality is important but difficult when the research is intimate. However, emotion was part of doing research but also the issue of my research.

> (cited in Acciari, 2011: 37)

This statement by Dudrah also captures my emotional engagement with this project. I was aware that researching on such an intimate subject would have an effect on my research neutrality. However, I would like to point out that I do not see the insider/outsider dichotomy to be a clash between subjectivity and objectivity; rather this research project attempts to reconcile subjectivity and objectivity through a process of reflexivity (Ruby, 1980). I am implicated within this research process and my understanding of my participant's experiences reflects my own experience of these sites. While this research project was not conceived as an auto-ethnographic project, the reflexive nature of my participant's stories, their thoughts, feelings and observations intersect with my own. Ruby, writing about reflexivity, explains:

> It is necessary to recognize that our knowledge of ourselves and of the universe within which we live comes not from a single source but, instead from two sources-from our capacity to explore human resources to events in which we and others participate through introspection and empathy, as well as from our capacity to make objective observations on physical and animate nature.

> (1980: 164)

This element of reflexivity provides a rich depth and understanding to my analyses. Being introspective, I was able to compare these experiences against my own and make better judgements and conclusions.

# Appendix 3
## Participant handout

## Participant information sheet

**Project Title:** How do digital queer spaces interrogate identity politics and challenge nationalist ideologies in India?

*Researcher: Rohit K Dasgupta*

You are being invited to take part in a research project. Before you decide to take part it is important for you to understand why the research is being done and what it will involve. Please take time to read the attached information sheet carefully and discuss it with others if you wish. Ask if anything is unclear or if you would like more information.

### Purpose of the project

This project aims to look at the use of social networking sites by Indian gay/queer/MSM men. It will study how Indian gay/queer/MSM men relate their online and offline identities and how such sites challenge nationalist ideologies of Indianness. This project will look at both the urban and suburban experience of gay/queer/MSM men using these sites. This is an important research at this point of time, as online queer communities in India have seldom been studied and this could benefit further strands of research within this field.

### Who we are looking for

As users of queer social networking sites you are being encouraged to take part in this research. Participation in this project is entirely voluntary and the participant may discontinue participation at any time. This project offers you a chance to reflect upon your experience as a gay/queer/MSM Indian man using these sites.

I hope to hear from older and younger men. I would like to hear from men of any ethnicity, sexuality, religion, socio-economic or cultural background, or location in India. To participate, you must be male, at least 18 years old, and currently reside in India. Your participation is completely voluntary and you are free to withdraw from the study at any time, without giving a reason, and this will not affect you in any way. Please let me know if there is anything we can do to make it easier for you to take part.

## The role of the participants

Participation includes online interviews through email, instant messaging through this site (www.planetromeo.com) and filling out brief questionnaires. This will be followed up by a second round of face to face interviews in some cases.

All data collected will be analysed using a variety of research methods to cover the aims of this project.

## Confidentiality

All information about you will be kept confidential at the researcher's current institute on a password-protected computer network and in security protected hard disk for the duration of the study. The primary researcher will have access to this data and it may be shared with supervisors and other colleagues, but only in anonymised form. No information that could identify any individual will be disclosed in reports on the project or shared with third parties. If you have any specific concerns, the researcher will work with you to come to an arrangement in which you feel respected and comfortable.

## What will I be asked?

In the broadest sense you will be asked to talk about your life and your experience of using PlanetRomeo and other queer social networking sites from your personal perspective queer man living in India. You will be asked to reflect on the following topics:

- Family heritage, birth, your childhood and adolescence
- Awareness of sexual orientation and early experiences and the role of queer social networking sites, if any
- Adulthood – education, work, leisure, past relationships

- Use of queer social networking sites
- Reasons for using a social networking site
- Current relationship – how it began and developed and if the social networking site had any role to play in it

## Results of the research

Online interviews will be transcribed and questionnaires and emails securely saved. Face to face Interviews will be digitally recorded and transcribed by the researcher into text for analysis. The results of the research will take the form of a thesis, but will also be shared with wider audiences through, for example, publications in academic journals and gay media, or presentations at conferences. In each case, your identity will be protected by using a pseudonym (a false name which you can choose), and changing or removing any other references that could reveal your identity or that of other individuals that you mention. You will also receive a copy of the overall research findings if you would like to. Any unused data will be destroyed.

## Funding

Funding for this research has been provided variously by various sources including UAL and the Royal Society for Asian Affairs.

## Contact

The researcher can be contacted at xxx@xxx.ac.uk (redact email address)

I would like to thank you for taking your time to read this and agreeing to be a part of this project.

Rohit K Dasgupta

# Glossary

The following is a glossary of terms used in this book:

**bear**  This term is used to describe large hirsute gay men.

**blog**  A blog is a regularly updated website or webpage which could work like a journal.

*burkha*  *Burkha* is a form of covering used by Muslim women.

**chat/online chat**  Chat or Online Chat refers to communication on the Internet that offers real-time transmission of text (and media such as images and videos) from sender to receiver.

**cruising**  Trying to find a casual sex partner in a public place.

*dosti/dostana*  This is a Hindi term for friendship.

**handle**  A person's online alias or shortened name. Also called a 'nick' (short for nickname; also see username).

*hijra*  A term used to refer to trans* or intersex individuals. In 2014, hijras were legally recognised as a 'third gender' in India. A definition of trans* is given later in this glossary.

**hook up/hooking up**  'Hook up' or 'hooking up' is a colloquial term referring mostly to casual sex, but could also refer to a causal relationship.

**instant messaging/chat**  A type of online chat offering real-time text transmission.

*kothi*  Feminised male identity characterised by gender non-conformity. Also known by other terms such as *dhurani* (Kolkata), *metis* (Nepal).

*launda*  Young male/*kothi* performers.

**Leathers**  This term refers to gay men who fetshise leather as a sartorial choice organised around sexual practices.

**LGBT**  Acronym for lesbian, gay, bisexual and trans*. Some literature in India also use LGBTQKHIA (lesbian, gay, bisexual, trans*, queer, *kothi, hijra*, intersex, asexual).

**Listserv**  Listserv is an application that distributes messages to subscribers on an email list.

**lurking** A methodological framework borrowed from Mowlabocus (2010a). It is a form of participant observation carried out on social networking platforms.

**MSM** This is an acronym for men who have sex with men. MSM includes all biological males who have sex with other men regardless of their gender or sexual identity.

**NGO** Non-governmental organisation that is not 'for profit'. Also called development sector, third sector, charity and voluntary sector.

*sati* *Sati* is a funeral practice in India, in which a widowed woman immolated herself, typically on the husband's funeral pyre. It was outlawed in India in 1829.

**stud** Stud usually refers to heterosexual men who are popular amongst women. In the queer context, it can also mean a butch woman or a gay man who is masculine.

**trans\*** Includes all transgender, non-binary and gender non-conforming identities, including but not limited to transgender, transsexual, transvestite, third gender.

**twink** A young boyish-looking gay man, usually between the ages of 18 and 22.

**username** A name that uniquely identifies an individual on a computer system. Also see handle.

*yaarana* This is a Hindi word for friendship.

# Bibliography

Acciari, M. (2011) *Indo Italian Screens and the Aesthetic of Emotions*. Unpublished PhD Thesis. Manchester: University of Manchester.

Ahmed, S. (2004) *The Cultural Politics of Emotion*. Durham: Duke University Press.

Aldrich, R. (2003) *Colonialism and Homosexuality*. London: Routledge.

Alexander, J. (2002) 'Homo Pages and Queer Sites: Studying the Construction and Representation of Queer Identities on the World Wide Web.' *International Journal of Sexuality and Gender Studies*. 7 (2–3), pp. 85–106.

Alexander, J. and Losh, E. (2010) 'A Youtube of One's Own: Coming out Videos as Rhetorical Action', in Pullen, C. and Cooper, M. (eds.) *LGBT Identity and Online New Media*. Oxon: Routledge, pp. 37–50.

Altman, D. (1997) 'Global Gaze/Global Gays.' *GLQ: A Journal of Lesbian and Gay Studies*. 4 (3), pp. 417–436.

Anderson, B. (1991) *Imagined Communities: Reflections on the Origin and Spread of Nationalism*. London: Verso.

Annes, A. and Redlin, M. (2012) 'The Careful Balance of Gender and Sexuality: Rural Gay Men, the Heterosexual Matrix, and "Effeminophobia".' *Journal of Homosexuality*. 59 (2), pp. 256–288.

Appadurai, A. (1996) *Modernity at Large: Cultural Dimensions of Globalisation*. Minneapolis: University of Minnesota Press.

Appadurai, A. and Breckenridge, C. (1988) 'Why Public Culture.' *Public Culture*. 1 (1), pp. 5–10.

Arondekar, A. (2009) *For the Record: On Sexuality and the Colonial Archive in India*. Durham: Duke University Press.

Athique, A. (2012) *Indian Media*. London: Polity Press.

Atkinson, R. and Flint, J. (2001) 'Accessing Hidden and Hard-to-Reach Populations: Snowball Research Strategies.' *Social Research Update*. 28 (1), pp. 93–108.

'AWID' (n.d.) Available at: <http://www.awid.org/Library/Statement-of-African-Social-Justice-Activists-on-the-Threats-of-the-British-Government-to-Cut-Aid-to-African-Countries-that-Violate-the-Rights-of-LGBTI-People-in-Africa>. Accessed on 5 July 2015.

Bachcheta, P. (1999) 'When the (Hindu) Nation Exiles Its Queers.' *Social Text.* 61, pp. 141–166.

Bachcheta, P. (2007) 'Rescaling Transnational Queerdom: Lesbian and Lesbian Identitary Positionalities in Delhi in the 1980's', in Menon, N. (ed.) *Sexualities.* New Delhi: Women Unlimited, pp. 103–127.

Ballhatchet, K. (1980) *Race, Sex and Class under the Raj.* London: Weidenfeld and Nicolson.

Banaji, Shakuntala and Buckingham, David (2013) *The Civic Web: Young People, the Internet and Civic Participation.* Cambridge, MA: MIT Press.

Banerjea, N. (2014) 'Critical Urban Collaborative Ethnographies: Articulating Community with Sappho for Equality in Kolkata, India.' *Gender, Place and Culture: A Journal of Feminist Geography.* 22 (8), pp. 1058–1072.

Barton, B. (2011) 'My Auto/Ethnographic Dilemma: Who Owns the Story?' *Qualitative Sociology.* 34 (3), pp. 431–445.

Basham, A.L. (1959) *The Wonder That Was India.* New York: Grove Press.

Bassett, E. and O'Riordan, K. (2002) 'Ethics of Internet Research: Contesting the Human Subjects Research Model.' *Ethics and Information Technology.* 4 (3), pp. 233–247.

Basu, A. (2008) 'Breaking Free: Indian Gays Are Getting Organised and Boldly Coming Out.' *The Telegraph* (India). August 31, 2008.

Beck, U. (2008) *Cosmopolitan Vision.* Cambridge: Polity Press.

Berlant, L. (2004) *Compassion: The Culture and Politics of an Emotion.* Abingdon: Routledge.

Bernstein, B. (1960) 'Language and Social Class.' *British Journal of Sociology.* 11 (3), pp. 271–276.

Berry, C., Martin, F. and Yue, A. (2003) 'Introduction', in Berry, C., Martin, F. and Yue, A. (eds.) *Mobile Cultures: New Media in Queer Asia.* Durham: Duke University Press, pp. 1–19.

Bersani, L. (1988) 'Is the Rectum a Grave?', in Crimp, D. (ed.) *Aids: Cultural Analysis, Cultural Activism.* Cambridge: MIT Press, pp. 197–222.

Bhaskaran, S. (2002) 'The Politics of Penetration: Section 377 and the Indian Penal Code', in Vanita, R. (ed.) *Queering India: Same Sex Love and Eroticism in Indian Culture and Society.* London: Routledge, pp. 15–29.

Bhaskaran, S. (2004) *Made in India.* New York: Palgrave Macmillan.

Bhowmick, S. (2013) 'Film Censorship in India: Deconstructing an Incongruity', in Gokulsing, K.M. and Dissanayake, W. (eds.) *Handbook of Indian Cinemas.* London: Routledge, pp. 297–310.

Billig, M. (1995) *Banal Nationalism.* London: Sage.

Binnie, J. (2004) *The Globalisation of Sexuality.* Thousand Oaks: Sage.

Bose, B. (2015) 'Notes on Queer Politics in South Asia and Its Diaspora', in McCallum, E. and Tuhkanen, M. (eds.) *The Cambridge History of Gay and Lesbian Literature.* Cambridge: Cambridge University Press, pp. 498–511.

Bose, B. and Bhattacharya, S. (2007) 'Introduction', in Bose, B. and Bhattacharya, S. (eds.) *The Phobic and the Erotic: The Politics of Sexualities in Contemporary India.* Kolkata: Seagull, pp. ix–xxxii.

Bourdieu, P. (1985) 'The Genesis of the Concepts of Habitus and Field.' *Sociocriticism.* 2 (2), pp. 11–24.

Boyce, P. (2006) 'Moral Ambivalence and Irregular Practices: Contextualizing Male-to-Male Sexualities in Calcutta/India.' *Feminist Review.* 83 (1), pp. 79–98.

Boyce, P. (2007) '(Dis)Locating Men Who Have Sex with Men in Calcutta: Subject, Space and Perception', in Bose, B. and Bhattacharyya, S. (eds.) *The Phobic and the Erotic: The Politics of Sexualities in Contemporary India.* Kolkata: Seagull, pp. 399–416.

Boyce, P. (2012) 'The Ambivalent Sexual Subject', in Aggleton, P., Boyce, P., Moore, H.L., and Parker, R. (eds.) *Understanding Global Sexualities.* London: Routledge, pp. 75–88.

Boyce, P. (2014) 'Desirable Rights: Same-Sex Sexual Subjectivities, Socio-Economic Transformations, Global Flows and Boundaries in India and Beyond.' *Culture, Health & Sexuality: An International Journal for Research, Intervention and Care.* 16 (10), pp. 1201–1215.

Boyce, P. and Coyle, D. (2013) *Development, Discourse and Law: Transgender and Same Sex Sexualities in Nepal.* Sussex: Institute of Development Studies.

Boyce, P. and Hajra, A. (2011) 'Do You Feel Somewhere in Light That Your Body Has No Existence? Photographic Research with Men Who Have Sex with Men and People of Transgender in West Bengal.' *Visual Communication.* 10 (1), pp. 3–24.

Boyd, D. (2008) 'Facebook's Privacy Trainwreck.' *Convergence: The International Journal of Research into New Media Technologies.* 14 (1), pp. 13–22.

Brinkerhoff, J. (2009) *Digital Diasporas: Identity and Transnational Engagement.* Cambridge: Cambridge University Press.

Buncombe, A. (2014) 'Racism in India Blamed for Unrest in the Streets.' *The Independent.* Available at: <http://www.independent.co.uk/news/world/asia/racism-in-india-blamed-for-unrest-in-the-streets-as-african-migrants-claim-they-are-victims-of-discrimination-9085426.html>. Accessed on 3 March 2014.

Burton, R. (1994) *The Kama Sutra.* London: Penguin.

Butler, J. (2002) 'Is Kinship Always Already Heterosexual?' *Differences.* 13 (1), pp. 14–44.

Butler, J. (2004a) *Undoing Gender.* London: Routledge.

Butler, J. (2004b) *Precarious Life: The Powers of Mourning and Violence.* London: Verso.

Butsch, R. (2007) 'Introduction: How Are Media Public Spheres?', in Butsch, R. (ed.) *Media and Public Spheres.* Basingstoke: Palgrave Macmillan, pp. 1–14.

Campbell, J.E. (2004) *Getting It on Online: Cyberspace: Gay Male Sexuality and Embodied Identity.* New York: Harrington Park Press.

Campbell, J.E. and Carlson, M. (2002) 'Panopticon.com: Online Surveillance and the Commodification of Privacy.' *Journal of Broadcasting and Electronic Media.* 46 (4), pp. 586–606.

Castells, M. (2009) *The Information Age: Economy: Society and Culture: Volume 1: The Rise of the Network Society.* Oxford: Blackwell.

Castillo, D. and Panjabi, K. (2011) 'Introduction', in Castillo, D. and Panjabi, K. (eds.) *Cartographies of Affect: Across Borders in South Asia and the Americas.* New Delhi: Worldview Publication, pp. 1–48.

Chakraborty, D. (1997) 'The Difference Deferral of a Colonial Modernity: Public Debates on Domesticity in British Bengal', in Cooper, F. and Stoler, A. (eds.) *Tensions of Empire: Colonial Cultures in a Bourgeois World.* Berkeley: University of California Press, pp. 373–405.

Chanana, K. (2012) *An Evening Rainbow: Queer Writings in Bhasha Literature.* New Delhi: Sanbun Publishers.

Chandra, S. (2008) 'The Construction of Queer Culture in India: Pioneers and Landmarks (Review).' *Intersections: Gender and Sexuality in Asia and the Pacific.* 16. Available at: <http://intersections.anu.edu.au/issue16/chandra_review.htm>. Accessed on 24 February 2011.

Chatterjee, P. (2004) *The Politics of the Governed: Reflection of Popular Politics in Most of the World.* New Delhi: Permanent Black.

Chowdhury, I. (1998) *The Frail Hero and Virile History.* New Delhi: Oxford University Press.

Connell, R.W. (1996) 'Teaching the Boys: New Research on Masculinity, and Gender Strategies for Schools.' Teachers College Record. 98 (2), pp. 206–235.

Connell, R.W. (2001) *The Men and the Boys.* Berkeley: University of California Press.

Cooper, M. (2010) 'Lesbians Who Are Married to Men: Identity Collective Stories and the Internet Online Community', in Pullen, C. and Cooper, M. (eds.) *LGBT Identity and Online New Media.* Oxon: Routledge, pp. 75–86.

Cooper, M. and Dzara, K. (2010) 'The Facebook Revolution: LGBT Identity and Activism', in Pullen, C. and Cooper, M (eds.) *LGBT Identity and Online New Media.* Oxon: Routledge, pp. 100–112.

'Cops Bust Gay Racket, Nab SAT Official, 3 Others.' (2006) *Hindustan Times.* January 5, 2006. Available at: <http://www.hindustantimes.com/News-Feed/NM4/Cops-bust-gay-racket-nab-SAT-official-3-others/Article1–38816.aspx>. Accessed on 4 November 2012.

Correia-Afonso, J. (1981) *Indo-Portuguese History: Sources and Problems.* Bombay: Oxford University Press.

Cottle, S. and Lester, L. (2011) 'Transnational Protests and the Media: An Introduction', in Cottle, S. and Lester, L. (eds.) *Transnational Protests and the Media.* Oxford: Peter Lang, pp. 3–16.

Crenshaw, K. (1989) 'Demarginalizing the Intersection of Race and Sex: A Black Feminist Critique of Antidiscrimination Doctrine, Feminist Theory and Antiracist Politics', in *University of Chicago Legal Forum* (1), pp. 139–167.

Crooks, R.N. (2013) 'The Rainbow Flag and the Green Carnation: Grindr in the Gay Village.' *First Monday.* 18 (11). Available at: <http://firstmonday.org/ojs/index.php/fm/article/view/4958/3790>. Accessed on 22 August 2014.

Cvetkovich, A. (2003) *An Archive of Feelings: Trauma, Sexuality and Lesbian Public Cultures.* Durham: Duke University Press.

Daley, B. (2014) 'India Print Media Alive.' Available at: <http://www.edelman.com/post/india-print-media-alive-well/>. Accessed on 6 July 2015.

Dasgupta, R.K. (2011) 'An Exodus Scripted in Blood: A Gendered Reading of the Partition', in Castillo, D. and Panjabi, K. (eds.) *Cartographies of Affect: Across Borders in South Asia and the Americas.* New Delhi: Worldview Publication, pp. 276–285.

Dasgupta, R.K. (2012) 'Digital Media and the Internet for HIV Prevention, Capacity Building and Advocacy among Gay, Other Men Who Have Sex with Men (MSM) and Transgenders: Perspectives from Kolkata, India.' *Digital Culture and Education.* 4 (1), pp. 88–109.

Dasgupta, R.K. (2013) 'Launda Dancers: The Dancing Boys of India.' *Asian Affairs: Journal of the Royal Society for Asian Affairs.* 44 (3), pp. 442–448.

Dasgupta, R.K. (2015) The Visual Representation of Queer Bollywood: Mistaken Identities and Misreadings in Dostana. *JAWS: Journal of Arts Writing.* 1 (1), 91–101.

Dasgupta, R.K. and Banerjee, T. (2016) 'Exploitation, Victimhood and Gendered Performance in Rituparno Ghosh's Bariwali.' *Film Quarterly.* 69 (4), pp. 35–46.

Datta, S., Bakshi, K. and Dasgupta, R.K. (2015) 'The World of Rituparno Ghosh: Texts, Contexts and Transgressions.' *South Asian History and Culture.* 6 (2), pp. 223–237.

Dave, N. (2012) *Queer Activism in India: An Anthropology in Ethics.* Durham: Duke University Press.

Dean, J. (2005) 'Communicative Capitalism: Circulation and Foreclosure of Politics.' *Cultural Politics.* 1 (1), pp. 51–74.

Demory, P. and Pullen, C. (eds.) (2013) *Queer Love in Film and Television.* Basingstoke: Palgrave Macmillan.

Desert, J.U. (1997) 'Queer Space', in Ingram, G.B., Bouthilette, A., and Retter, Y. (eds.) *Queers in Space.* Washington: Bay Press, pp. 17–26.

Dhall, P. (2005) 'Solitary Cruiser', in Narrain, N. and Bhan, G. (eds.) *Because I Have a Voice: Queer Politics in India.* New Delhi: Yoda Press, pp. 115–142.

Dhar, U. (2014) 'Queer Reactions to Celina Jaitley Musical.' Available at: <http://pink-pages.co.in/the-gay-agenda/queer-reactions-celina-jaitley-musical/>. Accessed on 1 February 2015.

Donner, H. and De Neve, G. (2011) 'Introduction', in Donner, H. (ed.) *Being Middle Class in India: A Way of Life.* London: Routledge, pp. 1–22.

'Douchebags of Grindr.' (n.d.) Available at: <http://www.douchebagsofGrindr.com/tag/femmephobia/>. Accessed on 5 July 2015.

Driver, S. (2005) 'Out, Creative and Questioning: Reflexive Self Representations in Queer Youth Home Pages.' *Canadian Woman Studies.* 24 (2–3), pp. 111–116.

Drushel, B. (2010) 'Virtually Supportive: Self Disclosure of Minority Sexualities through Online Social Networking Sites', in Pullen, C. and Cooper, M. (eds.) *LGBT Identity and Online New Media.* Oxon: Routledge, pp. 62–74.

Dudrah, R. (2012) *Bollywood Travels: Culture, Diaspora and Border Crossings in Popular Hindi Cinema.* London: Routledge.

Duggan, L. (2003) *The Twilight of Equality: Neoliberalism, Cultural Politics and the Attack on Democracy.* Boston: Beacon Press.

Dutt, B. (n.d.) 'We the People.' Available at: <http://www.youtube.com/watch?v=x5_1aXfyw74&feature=share&list=SPE77B5BBB6220A28F>. Accessed on 4 November 2012.

Dutta, A. (2012) 'An Epistemology of Collusion: Hijra, Kothi and the Historical (Dis)Continuity of Gender/Sexual Identities in Eastern India.' *Gender & History.* 24 (3), pp. 825–849.

Dutta, A. (2013a) *Globalising through the Vernacular: Gender/Sexual Transnationalism and the Making of Sexual Minorities in Eastern India.* Unpublished PhD Dissertation. Minnesota: University of Minnesota.

Dutta, A. (2013b) 'Legible Identities and Legitimate Citizens: The Globalisation of Transgender and Subjects of HIV/AIDS Prevention in Eastern India.' *International Feminist Journal of Politics.* 15 (4), pp. 494–514.

Dutta, A. and Roy, R. (2014) 'Decolonising Transgender in India.' *Transgender Studies Quarterly.* 1 (3), pp. 320–337.

Edelman, L. (1994) *Homographesis: Essays in Gay Literary and Cultural Theory.* New York: Routledge.

Edwards, M. (2010) 'Transconversations: New Media, Community and Identity', in Pullen, C. and Cooper, M. (eds.) *LGBT Identity and Online New Media.* London: Routledge, pp. 159–172.

Eguchi, S. (2009) 'Negotiating Hegemonic Masculinity: The Rhetorical Strategy of "Straight-Acting" among Gay Men.' *Journal of Intercultural Communication Research.* 38 (3), pp. 193–209.

Elder, G. (1998) 'The South-African Body Politic: Space, Race and Heterosexuality', in Nast, H.J. and Pile, S. (eds.) *Places through the Body.* London: Routledge, pp. 153–164.

Evans, D. (1993) *Sexual Citizenship: The Material Construction of Sexualities.* London: Routledge.

Farman, J. (2012) *Mobile Interface Theory: Embodied Space and Locative Media.* Abingdon: Routledge.

Farr, D. (2010) 'A Very Personal World: Advertisement and Identity of Trans-Persons on Craigslist', in Pullen, C. and Cooper, M. (eds.) *LGBT Identity and Online New Media.* London: Routledge, pp. 87–99.

Fernandes, L. (2006) *India's New Middle Class: Democratic Politics in an Era of Economic Reform.* Minneapolis: University of Minnesota Press.

Foucault, M. (1986) 'Of Other Spaces.' *Diacritics.* 16 (1), pp. 22–27.

Foucault, M. (2001) *The History of Sexuality: Volume 1: An Introduction.* London: Random House.

Foucault M (2004) *The Birth of Biopolitics: Lectures at the College de France 1978–1979.* New York: Picador.

Fraser, N. (2008) *Scales of Justice: Reimagining Political Space in a Globalising World.* London: Polity Press.

Freeman, E. (2007) 'Queer Belongings: Kinship Theory and Queer Theory', in Haggerty, G. and McGarry, M. (eds.) *A Companion to Lesbian, Gay, Bisexual, and Transgender Studies*. Malden: Blackwell, pp. 295–314.

Gajjala, R. and Gajjala, V. (2008) 'Introduction', in Gajjala, R. and Gajjala, V. (eds.) *South Asian Technospaces*. New York: Peter Lang, pp. 1–6.

Gajjala, R. and Mitra, R. (2008) 'Queer Blogging in Indian Digital Diasporas: A Dialogic Encounter.' *Journal of Communication Inquiry*. 32 (4), pp. 400–423.

Gajjala, R., Rybas, N. and Altman, M. (2008) 'Racing and Queering the Interface: Producing Global/Local Cyberselves.' *Qualitative Inquiry*. 14 (7), pp. 1110–1133.

Ganesh, M. (2010) 'Mobile Love Videos Make Me Feel Healthy: Rethinking ICTs for Development.' *IDS Working Paper*. 2010 (352), pp. 1–43.

Ganguly-Scrase, R. and Scrase, T. (2012) 'Cultural Politics in the New India: Social Class, Neoliberal Globalization and the Education Paradox', in Weis, L. and Dolby, Nadine (eds.) *Social Class and Education: Global Perspectives*. New York: Routledge, pp. 198–210.

Ganti, T. (2013) 'The Corporatisation of the Hindi Film Industry', in Gokulsing, K.M. and Dissanayake, W. (eds.) *Handbook of Indian Cinemas*. London: Routledge, pp. 337–350.

Garcia-Arroyo, A. (2006) *The Construction of Queer Culture in India: Pioneers and Landmarks*. Kolkata: Booksway.Gaysi (n.d.) Available at: <http://gaysifamily.com/wp-content/uploads/2011/02/TV9_Gay_Culture_Hyd_nonames.pdf>. Accessed on 24 December 2013.

Gaysi (2011) 'Gaysi: TV9's Homophobic Coverage.' Available at: <http://gaysifamily.com/2011/03/24/tv9-pays-the-price/>. Accessed on 15 September 2014.

Gerbaudo, P. (2012) *Tweets and the Streets: Social Media and Contemporary Activism*. London: Pluto Press.

Ghosh, S. (2007) 'False Appearances and Mistaken Identities: The Phobic and the Erotic in Bombay Cinema's Queer Vision', in Bose, B. and Bhattacharya, S. (eds.) *The Phobic and the Erotic: The Politics of Sexualities in Contemporary India*. Kolkata: Seagull, pp. 417–436.

Giddens, A. (1991) *Modernity and Self Identity: Self and Society in the Late Modern Age*. Cambridge: Polity Press.

Giddens, A. (1992) *The Transformation of Intimacy*. Cambridge: Polity Press.

Global Day of Rage (2013) [Facebook page]. Available at: <https://www.facebook.com/events/1374294672825321/>. Accessed on 28 December 2014.

Gokulsing, K.M. (2004) *Soft-Soaping India: The World of Indian Televised Soap Operas*. Staffordshire: Trentham Books.

Gokulsing, K.M. and Dissanayake, W. (2012) *From Aan to Lagaan and Beyond: A Guide to the Study of Indian Cinema*. Staffordshire: Trentham Books.

Gopinath, G. (2005) *Impossible Desires: Queer Diasporas and South Asian Public Cultures*. Durham: Duke University Press.

Gopinath, K. (2009) 'Internet in India', in Rajagopal, A. (ed.) *The Indian Public Spheres: Readings in Media History*. Oxford: Oxford University Press, pp. 291–311.

Gournelos, T. and Gunkel, D. (2012) 'Introduction: Transgression Today', in Gournelos, T. and Gunkel, D. (eds.) *Transgressions 2.0: Media, Culture and Politics of a Digital Age*. London: Continuum, pp. 1–24.

Gupta, A. (2005) 'English Pur ki Kothi: Class Dynamics in the Queer Movement in India', in Narrain, A. and Bhan, G. (eds.) *Because I Have a Voice: Queer Politics in India*. New Delhi: Yoda Press, pp. 123–142.

Gupta, A. (2011) 'The Moral Order of Blackmail', in Gupta, A. and Narrain, A. (eds.) *Law Like Love: Queer Perspectives on Law*. New Delhi: Yoda Press, pp. 483–509.

Gupta, P. (2011) 'Do Desi Parents Accept Their Gay Children.' *Times of India*. July 11, 2011.

Gupta, S. (2011) *Queer*. London: Prestel.

Habermas, J. (1989) *The Structural Transformation of the Public Sphere*. Cambridge: MIT Press.

Hajratwala, M. (ed.) (2012) *Out: Stories from the New Queer India*. Mumbai: Queer Ink.

Halberstam, J. (2008) 'The Anti-Social Turn in Queer Studies.' *Graduate Journal of Social Science*. 5 (2), pp. 140–156.

Halberstam, J. (2011) *The Queer Art of Failure*. Durham: Duke University Press.

Hall, S. (1995) 'New Cultures for Old', in Massey, D. and Jess, P. (eds.) *A Place in the World? Places, Cultures and Globalisation*. Oxford: Oxford University Press, pp. 175–213.

Hansen, K. (2002) 'A Different Desire, a Different Feminity: Theatrical Transvestism in the Parsi, Gujarati and Marathi Theaters', in Vanita, R. (ed.) *Queering India: Same Sex Love and Eroticism in Indian Culture and Society*. London: Routledge, pp. 163–180.

Harvey, J.W. (n.d.) 'The Obligatory Shirtless Gay Vlogger Video.' Available at: <http://www.youtube.com/watch?v=MBRdBMg9TFk&list=LLOUN62d G2WmTJXQkQBArsTg>. Accessed on 5 July 2015.

Haseloff, A. (2005) 'Cybercafés and Their Potential as Community Development Tools in India.' *The Journal of Community Informatics*. 1 (3), pp. 53–65.

Hawley, J. (2001) 'Introduction', in Hawley, J. (ed.) *Postcolonial Queer: Theoretical Intersections*. Albany: SUNY Press, pp. 1–18.

Henderson, L. (2013) *Love and Money: Queers, Class and Cultural Production*. New York: New York University Press.

Hine, C. (2000) *Virtual Ethnography*. London: Sage.

India Today (2014) (n.a.) '112 Million Facebook Users in India, Second Largest User after US.' Available at: <http://indiatoday.intoday.in/tech nology/story/112-milion-facebook-users-in-india-second-largest-userbase-after-us/1/407261.html>. Accessed on 3 February 2014.

Ingram, G.B., Bouthilette, A. and Retter, Y. (1997) 'Conclusion', in Ingram, G.B., Bouthilette, A., and Retter, Y. (eds.) *Queers in Space*. Washington: Bay Press, pp. 447–458.

Internet and Mobile Association of India (2014) 'Internet in India: 2014 Research Report.' Available at: <http://www.iamai.in/rsh_pay.aspx?rid=4hjkHu7GsUU=>. Accessed on 6 July 2015.

Jenkins, H. (2006) *Convergence Culture: Where Old and New Media Collide*. New York: New York University Press.

John, M.E. and Nair, J. (1998) 'Introduction', in John, M. and Nair, J. (eds.) *A Question of Silence: The Sexual Economies of Modern India*. New Delhi: Kali for Women, pp. 1–51.

Jones, D. (1995) 'Anthropology and the Oppressed: A Reflection on "Native" Anthropology.' *NAPA Bulletin*. 16 (1), pp. 58–70.

Jones, J. and Pugh, S. (2005) 'Aging Gay Men.' *Men and Masculinities*. 7, pp. 248–260.

Karim, L. (2012) 'Transnational Politics of Reading and the (Un)Making of Taslima Nasreen', in Loomba, A. and Lukose, R. (eds.) *South Asian Feminisms*. Durham: Duke University Press, pp. 205–223.

Katyal, A. (2011) *Playing a Double Game: Idioms of Same Sex Desire in India*. Unpublished PhD Thesis. London: School of Oriental and African Studies.

Kauffman, J.C. (2012) *Love Online*. Bristol: Polity Press.

Kaushal, S.K. (2013) 'Suresh Kumar Kaushal vs NAZ Foundation and Others, Supreme Court of India.' December 11, 2013. Available at: <http://Judis.nic.in>. Accessed on 5 January 2014.

Khanna, A. (2011) 'The Social Lives of 377', in Gupta, A. and Narrain, A. (eds.) *Love Like Law: Queer Perspectives on the Law*. New Delhi: Yoda Press, pp. 174–202.

Kimmel, M. (1994) 'Masculinity as Homophobia: Fear, Shame, and Silence in the Construction of Gender Identity', in Brod, H. and Kaufman, M. (eds.) *Theorizing Masculinities*. London: Sage, pp. 119–141.

Kimmel, M. (2003) 'Towards a Pedagogy of the Oppressor', in Mutua, A. (ed.) *Progressive Black Masculinities*. New York: Routledge, pp. 63–72.

Kugle, S. (2002) 'Sultan Mahmud's Makeover: Colonial Homophobia and the Persian-Urdu Literary Tradition', in Vanita, R. (ed.) *Queering India: Same Sex Love and Eroticism in Indian Culture and Society*. London: Routledge, pp. 30–46.

Kuntsman, A. (2012) 'Introduction: Affective Fabrics of Digital Culture', in Karatzogianni, A. and Kuntsman, A. (eds.) *Digital Cultures and the Politics of Emotions*. Basingstoke: Palgrave Macmillan, pp. 1–19.

Kuntsman, A. and Miyake, E. (2008) 'Introduction', in Kunstman, A. and Miyake, E. (eds.) *Out of Place: Interrogating Silences in Queerness/Raciality*. New York: Raw Nerve, pp. 7–11.

Leung, L. (2008) 'From "Victims of the Digital Divide" to "Techno-Elites": Gender, Class and Contested "Asianness" in Online and Offline Geographies', in Gajjala, R. and Gajjala, V. (eds.) *South Asian Technospaces*. New York: Peter Lang, pp. 7–24.

Light, B., Fletcher, G. and Adam, A. (2008) 'Gay Men, Gaydar and the Com-
  modification of Difference.' *Information Technology & People.* 21 (3), pp.
  300–314.
Llewyn Jones, R. (2015) 'The British Raj and the British Mandate in Iraq.'
  *Asian Affairs: Journal of the Royal Society for Asian Affairs.* 46 (2), pp.
  270–279.
Macaulay, T.B. [1835] (2004) 'Minute on Indian Education', in Keen, P. (ed.)
  *Revolutions in Romantic Literature: An Anthology of Print Culture, 1780–
  1832.* Peterborough: Broadview Press, pp. 313–315.
Mackley, L. and Karpovich, A. (2012) 'Touching Tales: Emotion in Digital
  Object Memories', in Karatzogianni, A. and Kuntsman, A. (eds.) *Digital
  Cultures and the Politics of Emotion.* Basingstoke: Palgrave Macmillan, pp.
  127–144.
Majumder, D. (2013) *Taar Cheye She Onek Aaro* (More Than a Friend). Film
  Trailer. Available at: <http://youtu.be/7CDoLRQ8vmk>. Accessed on
  2 March 2015.
Matarrita-Cascante, D. and Brennan, M.A. (2012) 'Conceptualizing Commu-
  nity Development in the 21st Century.' *Community Development: The Jour-
  nal of the Community Development Society.* 43 (3), pp. 293–305.
McDermott, E. (2011) 'The World Some Have Won: Sexuality, Class and
  Inequality.' *Sexualities.* 14 (1), pp. 63–78.
McGlotten, S. (2007) 'Virtual Intimacies: Love, Addiction, and Identity @ the
  Matrix', in O'Riordan, K. and Phillips, D.J. (eds.) *Queer Online: Media, Tech-
  nology and Society.* New York: Peter Lang, pp. 123–137.
McGlotten, S. (2013) *Virtual Intimacies: Media, Affect and Queer Sociality.*
  Albany: SUNY Press.
McIntosh, P. (1988) 'White Privilege and Male Privilege: A Personal Account
  of Coming to See Correspondence through Work in Women's Studies.'
  *Working Paper* (189). Wellesley, MA: Wellesley College Center for Research
  on Women.
Mclain, K. (2009) 'Gods, Kings and Local Telugu Guys: Competing Visions of
  the Heroic in Indian Comic Books', in Gokulsing, K.M. and Dissanayake, W.
  (eds.) *Popular Culture in a Globalised India.* London: Routledge, pp. 157–173.
Mclelland, M. (2002) 'Virtual Ethnography: Using the Internet to Study Gay
  Culture in Japan.' *Sexualities.* 5 (4), pp. 387–406.
Mclintock, A. (1995) *Imperial Leather: Race, Gender and Sexuality in the Colo-
  nial Contest.* London: Routledge.
Menon, N. (2005) 'How Natural Is Normal: Feminism and Compulsory Het-
  erosexuality', in Narrain, A. and Bhan, G. (eds.) *Because I Have a Voice:
  Queer Politics in India.* New Delhi: Yoda Press, pp. 33–39.
Menon, N. (2007) 'Outing Heteronormativity: Nation, Citizen, Feminist Dis-
  ruptions', in Menon, N. (ed.) *Sexualities.* New Delhi: Women Unlimited,
  pp. 3–51.
Merchant, H. (ed.) (1999) *Yaarana: Gay Writing from India.* New Delhi:
  Penguin.

Merridew, J. (n.d.) 'Feminine Gay Guys Ruin the Community.' Available at: <http://www.youtube.com/watch?v=T8XegaOZiSs>. Accessed on 5 July 2015.

Miller, V. (2008) 'New Media, Networking and Phatic Culture.' *Convergence: The International Journal of Research into New Media Technologies.* 14 (4), pp. 387–400.

Mitra, A. (2000) 'Virtual Commonality: Looking for India on the Internet', in Bell, D. and Kennedy, B. (eds.) *The Cybercultures Reader.* London: Routledge, pp. 676–694.

Mitra, R. (2010) 'Resisting the Spectacle of Pride: Queer Indian Bloggers as Interpretive Communities.' *Journal of Broadcasting and Electronic Media.* 54 (1), pp. 163–178.

Mowlabocus, S. (2010a) *Gaydar Culture: Gay Men, Technology and Embodiment in the Digital Age.* Farnham/Burlington: Ashgate.

Mowlabocus, S. (2010b) 'Look at Me! Images, Validation and Cultural Currency on Gaydar', in Pullen, C. and Cooper, M. (eds.) *LGBT Identity and Online New Media.* London: Routledge, pp. 201–214.

Mowlabocus, S., Harbottle, J., Dasgupta, R.K. and Haslop, C. (2014) 'Reaching out Online: Digital Literacy and the Uses of Social Media in Health Promotion.' *Working Papers of the Communities & Culture Network+.* 3 (April 2014).

Nandy, A. (1983) *The Intimate Enemy: Loss and Recovery of Self under Colonialism.* New Delhi: Oxford University Press.

Narrain, A. (2004) *Queer: Despised Sexuality, Law and Social Change.* Bangalore: Books for Change.

Narrain, A. and Bhan, G. (2005) 'Introduction', in Narrain, A. and Bhan, G. (eds.) *Because I Have a Voice: Queer Politics in India.* New Delhi: Yoda Press, pp. 1–30.

Narrain, A. and Eldridge, M. (2009) *The Right That Dares to Speak Its Name: Naz Foundation vs. Union of India and Others.* Bangalore: Alternative Law Forum.

Narrain, A. and Gupta, A. (2011) 'Introduction', in Narrain, A. and Gupta, A. (eds.) *Law Like Love: Queer Perspectives on Law.* New Delhi: Yoda Press, pp. xi–lvi.

'NBSA' (n.d.) Available at: <http://www.nbanewdelhi.com/images/Upload/tv9.pdf>. Accessed on 5 July 2015.

Nerurkar, S. (2013) 'Indians Hit Mobile Apps to Find Love.' Available at: <http://timesofindia.indiatimes.com/tech/apps/Indians-hit-mobile-apps-to-find-love/articleshow/22597148.cms>. Accessed on 5 July 2015.

Oswin, N. (2008) 'Critical Geographies and the Uses of Sexuality: Deconstructing Queer Space.' *Progressive Human Geography.* 32 (1), pp. 89–103.

Papacharissi, Z. (2009) 'The Virtual Sphere 2.0: The Internet, the Public Sphere, and Beyond', in Chadwick, A. and Howard, P. (eds.) *Routledge Handbook of Internet Politics.* London: Routledge, pp. 230–245.

Pariser, E. (2012) *The Filter Bubble: How the New Personalised Web Is Changing What We Read and How We Think.* New York: Penguin.

Payne, R. (2007) 'Str8Acting.' *Social Semiotics.* 17 (4), pp. 525–538.

Plummer, K. (2003) *Intimate Citizenship: Private Decisions and Public Dialogues.* Seattle: University of Washington Press.

Povinelli, E. (2006) *The Empire of Love: Toward a Theory of Intimacy, Genealogy and Carnality.* Durham: Duke University Press.

Pullen, C. (2010) 'Introduction', in Pullen, C. and Cooper, M. (eds.) *LGBT Identity and Online New Media.* London: Routledge, pp. 1–13.

Pullen, C. (2012) 'Introduction', in Pullen, C. (ed.) *LGBT Transnational Identity and the Media.* Basingstoke: Palgrave Macmillan, pp. 1–21.

Pullen, C. (2014) 'Media Responses to Queer Youth Suicide: Trauma, Therapeutic Discourse and Co-Presence', in Pullen, C. (ed.) *Queer Youth and Media Cultures.* Basingstoke: Palgrave Macmillan, pp. 63–85.

Pullen, C. and Cooper, M. (eds.) (2010) *LGBT Identity and Online New Media.* London: Routledge.

Puri, J. (1999) *Woman, Body, Desire in Postcolonial India: Narratives of Gender and Sexuality.* London: Routledge.

Puri, J. (2013) 'Decriminalization as Deregulation? Logics of Sodomy Law and the State', in Shrivastava, S. (ed.) *Sexuality Studies.* New Delhi: Oxford University Press, pp. 141–160.

Rangaswamy, N. (2007) 'Representing the Non Formal: The Business of Internet Cafes in India.' *Ethnographic Praxis.* (1), pp. 115–127.

Rao, R. (2014) 'Queer Questions.' *International Feminist Journal of Politics.* 16 (2), pp. 199–217.

Ratti, R. (1999) 'Beta', in Merchant, H. (ed.) *Yaarana: Gay Writing from India.* New Delhi: Penguin, pp. 103–105.

Raun, T. (2012) 'DIY Therapy: Exploring Affective Self Representations in Trans Video Blogs on Youtube', in Karatzogianni, A. and Kuntsman, A. (eds.) *Digital Culture and the Politics of Emotion.* Basingstoke: Palgrave Macmillan, pp. 165–180.

Ray, S. (2000) *Engendering India: Woman and Nation in Colonial and Postcolonial Narratives.* Durham: Duke University Press.

Reiman, J.H. (1995) 'Driving to the Panopticon: A Philosophical Exploration of the Risks to Privacy Posed by the Highway Technology of the Future.' *Santa Clara Computer & High Tech.* 11, pp. 27–45.

Rheingold, H. (1993) *The Virtual Community: Homesteading on the Electronic Frontier.* Cambridge: MIT Press.

Richardson, N. (2003) 'Effeminophobia, Misogyny and Queer Friendship: The Cultural Themes of Channel 4's "Playing It Straight".' *Sexualities.* 12 (4), pp. 525–544.

Richardson, N. (2009) 'Queer Masculinity: The Body of John Paul Pitoc's Body in "Trick".' *Paragraph.* 26 (1–2), pp. 232–244.

Robins, N. (2006) *The Corporation That Changed the World: How the East India Company Shaped the Modern Multinational.* London: Pluto Press.

Row-Kavi, A. (1999) 'The Contract of Silence', in Merchant, H. (ed.) *Yaarana: Gay Writing from India.* New Delhi: Penguin, pp. 12–15.

190   *Bibliography*

Roy, S. (2003) 'From Khush List to Gay Bombay: Virtual Webs of Real People', in Berry, C., Martin, F., and Yue, A. (eds.) *Mobile Cultures: New Media in Queer Asia*. Durham: Duke University Press, pp. 180–200.

Roy, S. (2015) 'What's It Like to Be Gay in Modern India.' *The Telegraph* (UK). Available at: <http://www.telegraph.co.uk/men/relationships/11365516/What-its-like-to-be-gay-in-modern-India.html>. Accessed on 2 March 2015.

Ruby, J. (1980) 'Exposing Yourself: Reflexivity, Anthropology and Film.' *Semiotica*. 30 (1–2), pp. 153–179.

Rumens, N. (2011) *Queer Company: The Role and Meaning of Friendship in Gay Men's Work Lives*. Farnham: Ashgate.

SAJA Forum (2008) 'Media Watch: Gay Rights and the Indian Press.' *SAJA Forum*. July 2008. Available at: <http://www.sajaforum.org/2008/07/media-watch-gay.html>. Accessed on 8 December 2012.

Sanchez, F.J. and Vilain, E. (2012) ' "Straight-Acting Gays": The Relationship between Masculine Consciousness, Anti-Effeminacy, and Negative Gay Identity.' *Archives of Sexual Behaviour*. 41 (1), pp. 111–119.

Sanders, T. (2005) *Sex Work: A Risky Business*. Devon: Willan.

Sarkar, T. (2003) 'Many Faces of Love: Country, Woman and God', in Datta, P.K. (ed.) *The Home and the World: A Critical Companion*. New Delhi: Permanent Black, pp. 27–44.

Seabrook, J. (1999) *Love in a Different Climate: Men Who Have Sex with Men in India*. London: Verso.

Sen, R. (2013) 'The Need for an Everyday Culture of Protest.' *Economic and Political Weekly*. Available at: <http://www.epw.in/web-exclusives/need-everyday-culture-protest.html>. Accessed on 25 March 2014.

Sethi, R. (2011) *The Politics of Postcolonialism: Empire, Nation and Resistance*. London: Polity Press.

Shahani, P. (2008) *GayBombay: Globalisation, Love and Belonging in Contemporary India*. New Delhi: Sage.

Shaw, D. (1997) 'Gay Men and Computer Communication', in Jones, S. (ed.) *Virtual Culture: Identity and Communication in Cybersociety*. New Delhi: Sage, pp. 133–145.

Shrivastava, S. (ed.) (2004) *Sexual Sites, Seminal Attitudes: Sexualities, Masculinites and Culture in South Asia*. London: Sage.

Shrivastava, S. (2013) 'Introduction', in Shrivastava, S. (ed.) *Sexuality Studies*. New Delhi: Oxford University Press, pp. 1–23.

Sinfield, A. (1994) *Cultural Politics: Queer Readings*. London: Routledge.

Sinha, M. (1995) *Colonial Masculinity: The Manly Englishman and the Effeminate Bengali*. Manchester: Manchester University Press.

Sirisena, M. (2012) 'Virtually Yours: Reflecting on the Place of Mobile Phones in Romantic Relationships', in Karatzogianni, A. and Kuntsman, A. (eds.) *Digital Culture and the Politics of Emotion*. Basingstoke: Palgrave Macmillan, pp. 181–195.

Sparks, H. (1997) 'Dissident Citizenship: Democratic Theory, Political Courage, and Activist Women.' *Hypatia*. 12 (4), pp. 74–110.

Spivak, G. (1988) 'Can the Subaltern Speak?', in Nelson, C. and Grossberg, L. (eds.) *Marxism and the Interpretation of Culture*. Urbana, IL: Illinois University Press, pp. 271–313.

Spivak, G. (1999) *A Critique of Postcolonial Reason*. Cambridge: Harvard University Press.

Spivak, G. and Butler, J. (2007) *Who Sings the Nation State*. Kolkata: Seagull.

Subhramanyam, K., Greenfield, P. and Tynes, B. (2004) 'Constructing Sexuality and Identity in an Online Teen Chat Room.' *Applied Developmental Psychology*. 25, pp. 651–666.

Sweet, M.J. (2002) 'Eunuchs, Lesbians, and Other Mythical Beasts: Queering and Dequeering the Kama Sutra', in Vanita, R. (ed.) *Queering India: Same Sex Love and Eroticism in Indian Culture and Society*. London: Routledge, pp. 77–84.

Swiss, T. and Hermann, A. (2000) 'The World Wide Web as Magic, Metaphor and Power', in Swiss, T. and Hermann, A. (eds.) *The World Wide Web and Contemporary Cultural Theory*. London: Routledge, pp. 1–4.

'Trafalgar Square: A Brief History' (n.d.) *London.Gov.Uk*. Available at: <http://www.london.gov.uk/priorities/arts-culture/trafalgar-square/history>. Accessed on 5 July 2015.

Tsang, D. (2000) 'Notes on Queer "n" Asian Virtual Sex', in Bell, D. and Kennedy, B. (eds.) *The Cybercultures Reader*. London: Routledge, pp. 432–438.

*TV9 Apology* (n.d.) Video, TV9. Available at: <http://www.youtube.com/watch?v=nC6Sf9X4-uI>. Accessed on 5 July 2015.

*TV9 Report on Sex Workers* (n.d.) Video, TV9. Available at: <https://www.youtube.com/watch?v=q_8JSQkQksQ>. Accessed on 2 February 2015.

Usher, N. and Morrison, E. (2010) 'The Demise of the Gay Enclave, Communication, Infrastructure Theory, and the Transformation of Gay Public Sphere', in Pullen, C. and Cooper, M. (eds.) *LGBT Identity and Online New Media*. London: Routledge, pp. 271–287.

Vanita, R. (2005) *Love's Rite: Same Sex Marriage in India and the West*. New Delhi: Penguin.

Vanita, R. (2006) *Gandhi's Tiger and Sita's Smile: Essays on Gender, Sexuality and Culture*. New Delhi: Yoda Press.

Vanita, R. (2009) *Chocolate and Other Writings on Male Homoeroticism*. Durham: Duke University Press.

Vanita, R. (2013) 'Sexual Exiles or Citizens of the World.' *Jindal Global Law Review*. 4 (2), pp. 131–150.

Vanita, R. and Kidwai, S. (2000) *Same Sex Love in India: Readings from Literature and History*. New Delhi: Palgrave Macmillan.

Varshney, A. (1993) 'Contested Meanings: India's National Identity, Hindu Nationalism and the Politics of Anxiety.' *Daedalus*. 122 (3), pp. 227–262.

Vertovec, S. (2010) *Transnationalism*. Abingdon: Routledge.

Wafer, J. (1997a) 'Muhammad and Male Homosexuality', in Murray, S. and Roscoe, W. (eds.) *Islamic Homosexualities*. New York: New York University Press, pp. 87–96.

Wafer, J. (1997b) 'Vision and Passion: The Symbolism of Male Love in Islamic Mystical Literature', in Murray, S. and Roscoe, W. (eds.) *Islamic Homosexualities*. New York: New York University Press, pp. 107–131.

Waites, M. (2010) 'Human Rights, Sexual Orientation and the Generation of Childhoods: Analysing the Partial Decriminalisation of "Unnatural Offences" in India.' *International Journal of Human Rights*. 14 (6), pp. 971–993.

Wakeford, N. (1997) 'Cyberqueer', in Munt, S. and Medhurst, A. (eds.) *Lesbian and Gay Studies: A Critical Introduction*. London: Cassell, pp. 20–38.

Wavey, Davey (n.d.a) Available at: <http://www.youtube.com/user/wickyd kewl>. Accessed on 5 July 2015.

Wavey, Davey (n.d.b) Available at: <https://www.youtube.com/watch?v=TVY 8OL0xeFY&list=PL18A73F1B5B5F00C3>. Accessed on 5 July 2015.

Weeks, J. (1995) *Invented Moralities*. Cambridge: Polity Press.

Weeks, J. (1998) 'The Sexual Citizen.' *Theory, Culture and Society*. 15 (3), pp. 35–52.

Weeks, J., Heaphy, B. and Donovan, C. (2001) *Same Sex Intimacies: Families of Choice and Other Life Experiments*. London: Routledge.

Weston, K. (1991) *Families We Choose: Lesbians, Gays, Kinship*. New York: Columbia University Press.

Woodland, R. (2000) 'Queer Spaces, Modem Boys and Pagan Statues: Gay/Lesbian Identity and the Construction of Cyberspace', in Bell, D. and Kennedy, D. (eds.) *The Cybercultures Reader*. London: Routledge, pp. 417–431.

Zimmer, M. (2010) 'But the Data Is Already Public: On the Ethics of Research in Facebook.' *Ethics and Information Technology*. 12 (4), pp. 313–325.

Zizek, S. (1998) 'The Inherent Transgression.' *Cultural Values*. 2 (1), pp. 1–17.

# Index